THE FIRST BRUSH

THE FIRST BRUSH

Paul Kane & Infrared Reflectography

General Editor

Kenneth R. Lister

With essays by

Ian Longo and George Bevan
Heidi Sobol

ROYAL ONTARIO MUSEUM

DEDICATED

To Our Parents

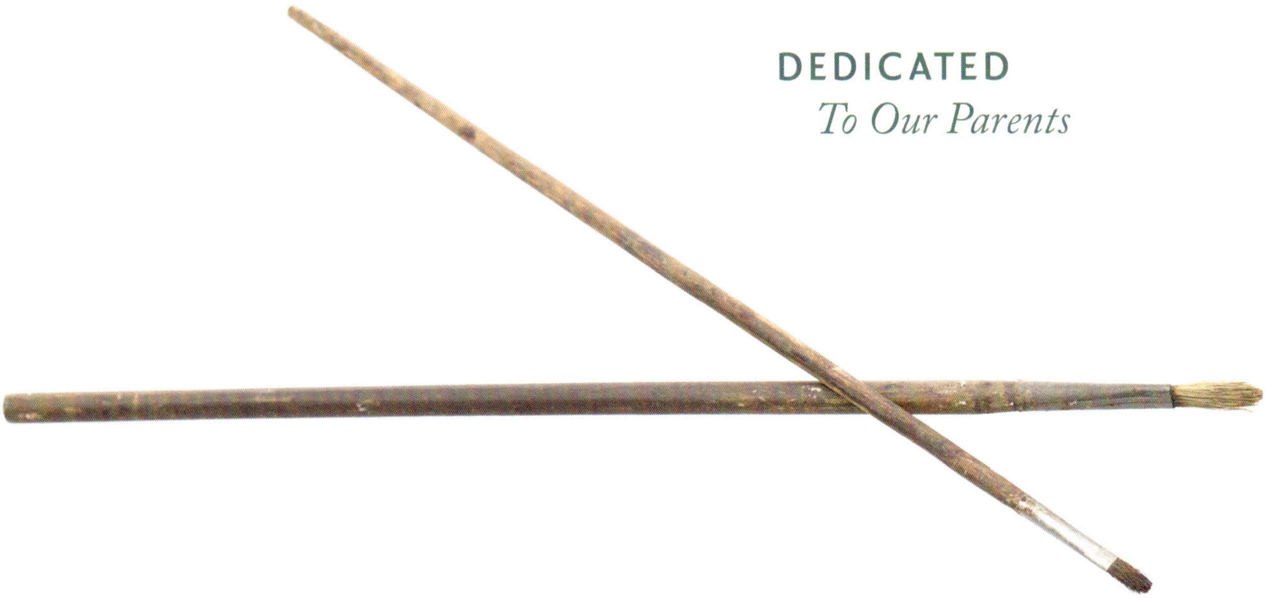

Published by the Royal Ontario Museum with the generous support of Gretchen and Donald Ross, the Elizabeth Walter Endowment Fund, and the Louise Hawley Stone Charitable Trust.

Royal Ontario Museum
100 Queen's Park
Toronto, Ontario
M5S 2C6
www.rom.on.ca

Distributed in Canada by
University of Toronto Press
5201 Dufferin Street
Toronto, Ontario
M3H 5T8
Toll-free tel. 1-800-565-9523

Library and Archives Canada Cataloguing in Publication

The First Brush : Paul Kane & Infrared Reflectography / general editor, Kenneth R. Lister ; with essays by Ian Longo and George Bevan, and Heidi Sobol.

Catalogue of an exhibition held at the Royal Ontario Museum, April 26, 2014 to April, 2015.
Includes bibliographical references and index.
ISBN 978-0-88854-498-8 (pbk.)

1. Kane, Paul, 1810-1871—Exhibitions. I. Royal Ontario Museum, host institution, issuing body II. Title: Paul Kane & Infrared Reflectography.

ND249.K3A4 2014 759.11 C2014-901605-0

Copy Editor: Dimitra Chronopoulos
Project Coordinator: Sheeza Sarfraz
Designer: Tara Winterhalt
ROM Press Assistant: Alice Tallman

Care has been taken to trace the ownership of any copyright material contained in this text. ROM Press welcomes any information that will enable it to rectify, in subsequent editions, any incorrect or omitted reference or credit.

Printed and bound in Canada.
The Royal Ontario Museum is an agency of the Government of Ontario.

Cover illustration: detail of Paul Kane's paintbrushes on loan to the exhibition from Paul James Kane. Photograph by Brian Boyle.

On Display

The Exhibition: *The First Brush: Paul Kane and Infrared Reflectography*

"to paint their likenesses:" Great Lakes to North Saskatchewan River
April–July 2014

"to paint their likenesses:" Columbia River to Vancouver Island
August–October 2014

"a most faithful representation"
November 2014–January 2015

"out of a series of Paintings"
February–April 2015

CONTENTS

ACKNOWLEDGEMENTS

The exceptional Paul Kane collection at the Royal Ontario Museum forms the nucleus and focus of this exhibition and catalogue, and the ROM is indebted to Sir Edmund Osler and Raymond A. Willis, who through their generosity and foresight secured this vital part of Kane's legacy in his hometown. At the ROM, we are grateful for the support of Janet Carding (Director and Chief Executive Officer), Mark Engstrom (Deputy Director, Collections and Research), Xerxes Mazda (Deputy Director, Engagement Dan Rahimi (Vice President, Programs), Cathy Stewart (Manager, Conservation), Chen Shen (Vice President, Department of World Cultures), Ulrica Jobe (Senior Director, Development, ROM Governors), and Scott Forfar (Vice President and Chief Operating Officer, ROM Governors).

Thanks to Mary Montgomery (Exhibit Planner) who took our early thoughts and developed the initial exhibition brief. Dave Garvin (Senior Preparator) and Tracey Forster (Technician, Anthropology) were instrumental in making the collections available for study; this included removing many paintings from exhibition. On a regular bi-weekly basis the core exhibition team met to discuss content and design and to review progress. We are grateful for the input and expertise of our team members: Steven Laurie (Associate Project Manager) who oversaw schedule, budget, and production; Barb Rice (Registration Coordinator) orchestrated loans; Susan Ventura (Senior Preparator) spearheaded the installations; Tom Henriksson (Exhibit Designer, Graphics) developed the design; Christine Caroppo (Gallery Text Editor) reviewed the exhibit text; and Dominique Picouet (Manager, French Language Services) oversaw the translation of the exhibition text into French. The exhibition was generously supported by Diane Blake and Stephen Smith.

The exhibition and catalogue have incorporated collections from a number of institutions and appreciation is extended to the Art Gallery of Ontario, the National Gallery of Canada, Library and Archives Canada, and the Stark Museum of Art for permission to access and include their Paul Kane holdings. We are deeply grateful to the staff at the Art Gallery of Ontario and the National Gallery of Canada who took the time and gave their resources to the temporary removal of their collections from their exhibition halls for our study. From the Art Gallery of Ontario we thank Matthew Teitelbaum (Michael and Sonja Koerner Director and CEO), Gregory Humeniuk (Curatorial Assistant, Canadian), Maria Sullivan (Manager, Conservation), Sandra Webster-Cook (Conservator of Paintings, Historical and Modern), The Thomson Collection, and Peter and Elizabeth Porebski of The Gilder Framemakers. From the National Gallery of Canada appreciation is expressed to Marc Mayer (Director and CEO), Charles Hill (Curator of Canadian Art), Susan Walker (Paintings Conservator), and Stephen Gritt (Director of Conservation and Collections).

The study of Paul Kane's art always benefits from the interest and support of his family. We would like to especially thank Paul James Kane who graciously loaned his great-great-grandfather's paintbrushes to the exhibition. The cover image, photographed by Brian Boyle, is a detail of Paul Kane's brushes.

This project has been a cooperative effort between the ROM and Queen's University and numerous Queen's University students have provided valuable support and insight. We single out Michael Fergusson with special thanks for his extensive and indispensible assistance with both still photography and video photography. Students from the Department of Classics and the Art Conservation Program helped out in numerous ways: Fiona Beckett, Ana Crisan, Tessa Thomas, Daniela Vogel, and Brittany Webster.

We extend appreciation to Chris Vogt at Channel Systems of Pinawa, Manitoba, for the loan of the Xenics Xeva InGaAs camera. Shane Elen of Beyondvisible.com provided invaluable technical advice on Infrared Reflectography and Ultra Violet photography and illumination.

The staff of ROM Press accepted this project with enthusiasm. Sheeza Sarfraz (Project Coordinator, ROM Press), with her usual humour and dedication, navigated the book through the publication process. Tara Winterhalt (Senior Designer, ROM Press), with creativity and a steady eye on detail, gave the book its artistry and design.

Brian Boyle (Senior Photographer, Registration) took the visible light images of the Kane collection and Alice Tallman (ROM Press Assistant) made the necessary arrangements for the use of images from external collections. We are grateful to Dimitra Chronopoulos for her attentive and assiduous edit of the text and for the valuable comments offered by two anonymous reviewers who gently nudged us toward greater consistency and clarity.

We are indebted to the Queen's University Senate Advisory Research Council, the Queen's University Alumni Association, and the Office of the Principal for funding. We are thankful for the funding support of the ROM's Department of World Cultures Field Research Fund and the Louise Hawley Stone Charitable Trust. This book has been generously supported by the Elizabeth Walter Endowment Fund. We also express sincere appreciation to Gretchen and Donald Ross who over the years have supported liberally the research and collections of the Royal Ontario Museum. We are grateful to all of those mentioned above and it is through the munificence of Gretchen and Donald Ross that their dedication, interest, and support can be celebrated in this catalogue.

As a final note, although posthumous, can words carry the depth of gratitude we owe to Paul Kane, both for his vision and for his tenacity to carry through? How many have benefitted from his wilderness toil and his studio concentration? Over the years thousands of visitors have come to the Royal Ontario Museum to view his work, unknown numbers of scholars have studied his sketched and painted details, and generations of writers have included his images as illustrations in their texts. This intensity will continue into the future for Paul Kane portrayed this country on the cusp of transition. Actions are greater than words and actions embrace our values. They are the radiance of thought, and they are our homage.

LIST OF FIGURES

Unless otherwise noted, sketches in the Royal Ontario Museum Paul Kane collection are a gift of Raymond A. Willis, donated in 1946 in memory of his mother, Emmie à Court ("Chelsea"), daughter of Allan Cassels and granddaughter of the Honourable George William Allan. Also, unless otherwise noted, oil paintings in the Royal Ontario Museum Paul Kane collection are a gift of Sir Edmund Osler.

With the exception of Figures 85 and 89, all Infrared Reflectography photographs were taken and processed by George Bevan, Ian Longo, and Michael Fergusson.

Abbreviations

AGO Art Gallery of Ontario
NGC National Gallery of Canada
ROM Royal Ontario Museum
Stark Stark Museum of Art

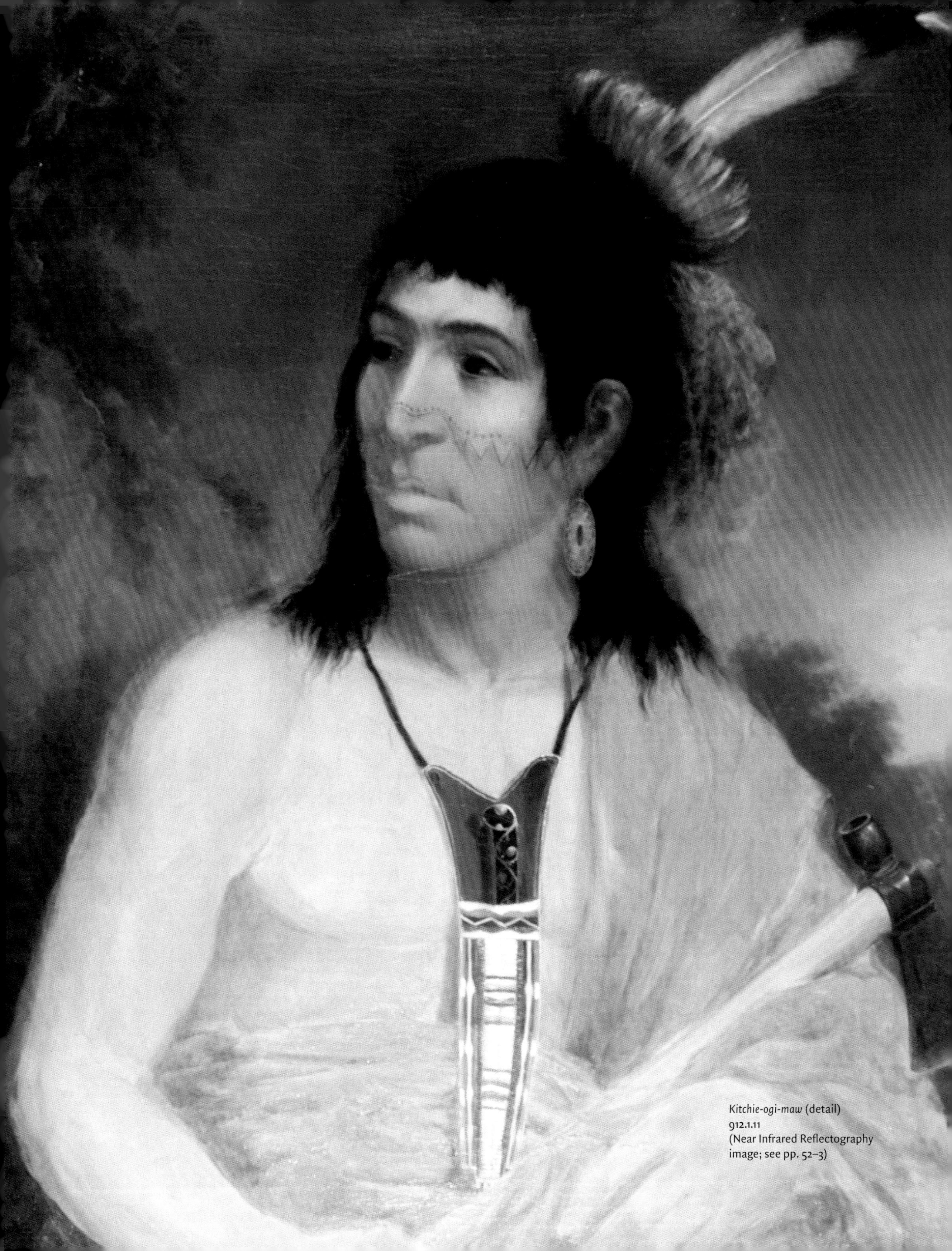

Kitchie-ogi-maw (detail)
912.1.11
(Near Infrared Reflectography image; see pp. 52–3)

INTRODUCTION

Kenneth R. Lister

Contact! That was the single word I desired to see on my computer screen. That morning, Heidi Sobol, paintings conservator at the Royal Ontario Museum (ROM), and Dr. George Bevan and Ian Longo of the Classics department at Queen's University had photographed a Paul Kane painting. A photograph of a Kane painting would not usually excite me, especially when I could easily walk down the hall from my office and view Kane's collection of studio paintings first-hand. However, this was not a usual photograph—Bevan and Longo were using photographic equipment with silicon sensors sensitive to infrared wavelengths of light. As Longo and Bevan explain in their essay, "Infrared Reflectography and the Paintings of Paul Kane," artists' paints have varying degrees of infrared light (IR) reflectance and transmission with the result that pigments opaque in visible light can become transparent in infrared light. With a modified Nikon D200 camera, infrared transmitting filters, and two specialized flash units that give infrared-only illumination, Longo and Bevan photographed the painting below the surface visible to the naked eye. This technique—known as Infrared Reflectography (IRR), or, for reasons they explain, Near Infrared Reflectography (NIRR)—penetrates the surface paint to reveal underdrawings and earlier design iterations that Kane may have rendered in the initial stages of the painting's development. Therefore, when I finally received Heidi's single-word email message, I knew that we had entered a new era of Paul Kane research.

Paul Kane (1810–1871, fig. 1) lived in a century when foreign cultures were expanding across North America, with the result that Native cultures were being pressured to cede their lands to the encroaching governments. Native peoples were encouraged to adopt different world views and alter the way they made a living. They were forced to move to unfamiliar lands and accept foreign settlers on the lands that they knew intimately through generations of experience and storytelling. As discussed in my essay, "Leaves from an American Plant," it was generally believed that due to these foreign pressures and influences, Native peoples were in the process of disappearing. Newspapers of the day reported the treaties that were being signed, the forced relocations, the battles, and the social unrest, and Kane—aware that Aboriginal cultures were changing—set out to produce a visual record of Native peoples and the land they inhabited before such a record could no longer be made.

Between June and December of 1845, Kane travelled in the region of the Great Lakes taking graphite, watercolour, and oil-on-paper sketches of the peoples he met, their cultural practices, and the Great Lakes environment. With the support of the Hudson's Bay Company,[1] in May 1846, he left on a much more extensive journey that lasted through October 1848, during which time he travelled both solo and with the Hudson's Bay Company fur-trade brigades along the fur-trade routes to the Pacific Ocean and back (see fig. 32).[2] When he returned to Toronto, he had in excess of 600 sketches and a large collection of artifacts that were his inspiration for the next seven years of studio work. Beginning shortly after his return in 1848, Kane began to paint oil-on-canvas and oil-on-board paintings as a formal visual record of the people he met and the land he experienced. By 1856 he had completed three major commissions that are now in the collections of the Art Gallery of Ontario (Toronto), the National Gallery of Canada (Ottawa), and the Royal Ontario Museum (Toronto).[3]

In addition to his large collection of oil paintings, the Stark Museum of Art (Orange, Texas), Library and Archives Canada (Ottawa), and the Royal Ontario Museum have almost all of the field sketches Kane created during his 1845–1848 journeys.[4] The sketches—representing the observed record—allow us to compare what he recorded first-hand to the formal views he developed in his studio.[5] The comparison of sketch to oil painting provides us with an objective view of Kane's art. The sketch illustrates the scene Kane rendered with his considerable skill; a critical comparison of the sketch with the oil painting it inspired reveals the accuracy—faithfulness, truthfulness—of Kane's final composition. This comparison shows the witnessed record (sketches completed by 1848) in relation to the final studio paintings Kane released (completed by 1856) that manifest eighteenth- and nineteenth century artistic conventions (Lister 2010, 183–85). Now, with the Near Infrared Reflectography technique, we can "see" the period between, his thinking while struggling with the oil-on-

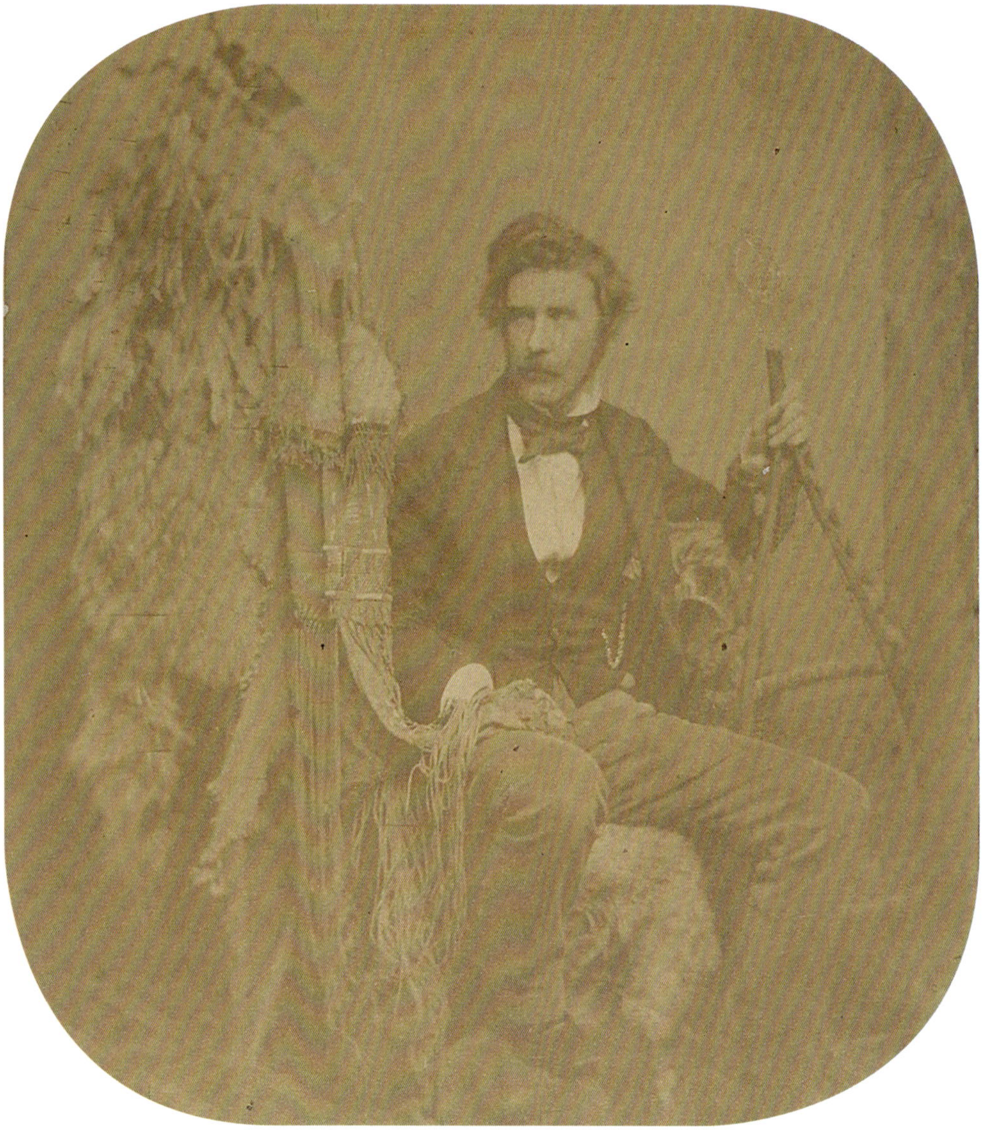

Fig. 1 Paul Kane, post-1848; 976x85.14

canvas compositions in his studio. Beneath the surface of the finished painting lie his initial renderings, the first drawings and painted efforts that expose his original intentions for the painting. Were they true to the sketch? Did he struggle with composition and did his struggle affect "truthfulness"? Did he wrestle with a desire to present in grand fashion, but then resist the temptation? Was there a moment in the studio when a change from faithfulness compromised his historical record?

In March 1856, Kane delivered 100 studio oil paintings to his principal patron, George William Allan,[6] and in 1912 this complete cycle of paintings was gifted to the Royal Ontario Museum.[7] Using the Near Infrared Reflectography technique, described by Ian Longo and George Bevan in this volume, the complete cycle of paintings has been recorded and analyzed. Heidi Sobol, in her essay, "Exploration in Technical Art History: Paul Kane," describes her study of the conservation needs of the Paul Kane collection at the ROM and the value of NIRR to the conservator as a diagnostic tool to help understand Kane's materials and technique. In this light, it is impressive to note that fifty-seven of the paintings—a full 57% of the collection—reveal no initial alterations, no compositional changes, no adjustments. Thus, in these paintings, Kane shows himself to be secure from the beginning and confident in his vision (see figs. 34, 48, and 63). However, in forty-three paintings, NIRR exposes numerous adjustments and alterations as Kane thought through his compositions. Some reveal a struggle with figure dimensions (fig. 66), changes to figure positions (fig. 72), and even eliminations (fig. 69). Others show alterations that relate directly to historical accuracy and bring focus to the nature of his thinking and the truthfulness of his formal record (figs. 46, 51, and 61).

Paul Kane's painting *Dalle des Morts, or the Rapid of the Dead* (fig. 49) was the subject of Heidi Sobol's excited message. We chose this painting for an initial test because in visible light—on the surface we can see—Kane painted a detail that was historically inaccurate, even in relation to the detail he himself had sketched. But under the surface, using the Near Infrared Reflectography technique—contact!

Notes

1 Sir George Simpson, the overseas governor of the Hudson's Bay Company (HBC), was instrumental in the success of Kane's 1846–1848 journey. Just after the beginning of that journey, Kane received a letter from Simpson that instructed HBC employees to provide Kane with, "your kind attentions and the hospitalities of such of the Company's posts as he may visit: and you will be pleased to afford Mr. Kane passages from post to post in the Company's Craft—free of charge" (HBCA E.42/1 fol. 44).

2 See Lister 2010 for a discussion of Kane's journeys, including illustrations of the sketches he took in the field and the oil paintings he developed in his Toronto studio.

3 In 1849 Kane completed a series of oil paintings for Sir George Simpson and through the generosity of Kenneth Thomson this collection is now in the Art Gallery of Ontario (see Laing 1982). In 1851, Kane received a commission for twelve paintings by the Canadian Parliament. He completed this series of paintings in 1856 and eleven of the paintings are now in the collection of the National Gallery of Canada (see Cassels 2010, 41 note 67; and figs. 84 and 88 this volume). Following the death of George William Allan—Kane's principal patron—Edmund B. Osler purchased the collection of Paul Kane oil paintings from the Allan estate. Osler donated this collection to the Royal Ontario Museum when the ROM was formed in 1912. The Paul Kane collection was the first collection accessioned into the Royal Ontario Museum during the year that the Royal Ontario Museum Act (1912) was signed.

4 The first comprehensive compilation of Kane's output of sketches and oil paintings was completed by J. Russell Harper and published in *Paul Kane's Frontier* (1971). Here Harper presented a catalogue *raisonné* that brought together the known collections of Kane's sketches and oil paintings, matching sketches to the oil paintings they inspired. See Lister this volume and Lister 2010 for illustrations of the sketches and discussions of their relationships to the ROM's collection of Kane oil paintings.

5 In 1998–1999 (*Wilderness to Studio: Four Views of Paul Kane*) and 2000–2001 (*Paul Kane: Land Study, Studio View*) two exhibitions were presented at the ROM examining the relationships between the oil paintings Kane completed in his studio and the sketches he took first-hand during his two western journeys. The exhibitions displayed the sketches he used for reference next to the oil paintings he developed, or composed, in his studio. For the first time, in a systematic manner, Kane's cycle of 100 paintings were exposed to review in association with their respective sketches, thus revealing their degree of faithfulness. Similar displays have been mounted more recently in the ROM's Daphne Cockwell Gallery of Canada: First Peoples, and an in-depth analysis of the ROM's Paul Kane collection is presented in the 2010 publication *Paul Kane /the Artist/: Wilderness to Studio* (Lister 2010).

6 For a discussion of George William Allan and his relationship with Paul Kane, see Cassels 2010.

7 See note 3.

INFRARED REFLECTOGRAPHY AND THE PAINTINGS OF PAUL KANE

Ian Longo and George Bevan

The human eye can sense light particles—photons—only in a relatively narrow band of energies within the broader electromagnetic spectrum. Since light is both a particle and a wave (as first demonstrated by Albert Einstein[1]), these energies can also be expressed by their wavelengths, which, for visible light, are between about 390 and 700 nanometres (nm) (fig. 2). Our perception of individual colours is nothing more than the cones in our eyes discerning between wavelengths in this particular band of about 300 nm (Wandell 1995, 3–9). Blues fall in the shorter wavelengths, while yellows, oranges, and reds are in the longer ones. This range of vision has served us well over the course of our evolution, helping us to distinguish between nutritious fruits or alert us to dangerous predators.

The areas of the spectrum beyond this region are wholly invisible to the naked eye. Below 400 nm lies the ultraviolet spectrum (UV), and above 700 nm the infrared (IR) (fig. 2). While some organisms—insects and a few mammals—have evolved eyes sensitive to light in the UV and IR regions, the areas beyond IR and UV, the X-ray and microwave spectra respectively, are wholly invisible to the eyes of any (known) living creatures.

With the advent of new sensor technologies over the past century, these hitherto invisible areas of the electromagnetic spectrum can be made visible to us, and are now widely used in a broad range of applications, not least of which is the technical investigation of works of art. The present project used a part of the near-infrared (NIR) spectrum, from 700 nm to 1100 nm, to reveal features in the paintings of Paul Kane—features that expose aspects of his working method that were thus far known only to the long-dead painter himself. This imaging technique, generally referred to as Infrared Reflectography (IRR), has been used in the art world to document changes in composition, damage, and previous restorations. Most frequently, though, IRR is used to reveal underdrawings on the foundation layer, beneath layers of paint that are opaque in the visible spectrum. These preliminary renderings on the primed support, obscured by layers of paint, may reflect an earlier, different conception of the piece than that represented by the final painting.

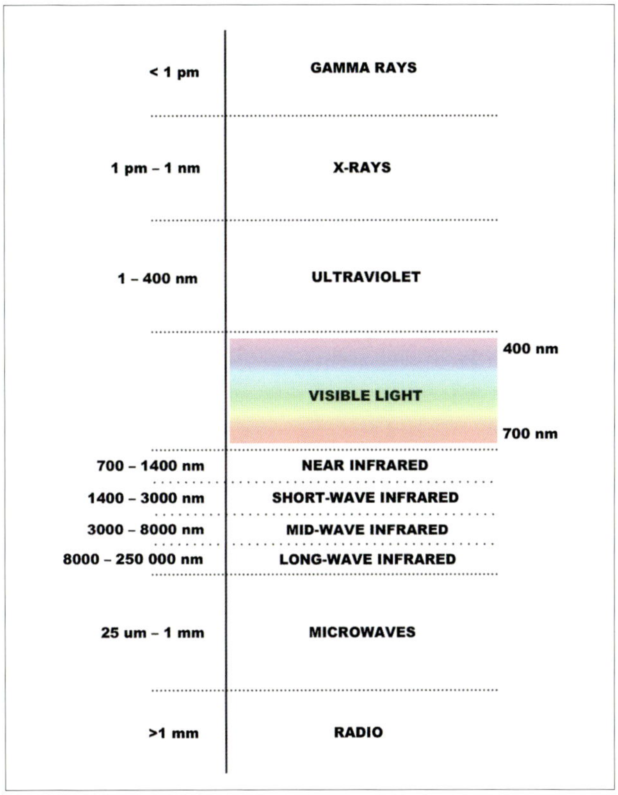

Fig. 2 The electromagnetic spectrum

The History of Infrared Photography

Best known for his discovery of the planet Uranus, Sir Frederick William Herschel, a prominent astronomer of the late eighteenth and early nineteenth centuries, is regarded as the first to have recognized that the light spectrum extends past the range of visible light (Holden 1881, 183).[2] On the 11th of February, 1800, Herschel observed an anomaly when trying to develop filters to observe sunspots. After noticing that the red filters he was testing were all producing more heat, Herschel used a prism on his windowsill to disperse sunlight into the visible spectrum. A thermometer, which was initially intended to act as a control to measure the ambient air of the room, was placed just beyond the red end of the spectrum produced by the prism. When Herschel realized the thermometer was displaying a higher temperature beyond the visible spectrum than in the visible spectrum itself, he concluded that there must be an invisible form of light beyond what can be seen—the infrared.

Photons in the infrared spectrum were not, however, the first invisible part of the spectrum to be recorded on film. After working with cathode rays in his laboratory at the University of Würzburg in Germany, Wilhelm Röntgen noticed a barium platinocyanide screen fluorescing some distance away from the cathode generating tube (Assmus 1995, 10–11). By the end of December 1895, Röntgen had produced a photograph of the bones of his wife's hand.[3] His discovery of photons in the X-ray range of energies earned him the first ever Nobel Prize in Physics (1901). X-rays would soon find applications outside of medicine in both archaeology and art history.

Not until 1910 did the American physicist Robert Williams Wood synthesize photographic plates that recorded infrared wavelengths of light (Dieke 1956, 330–31; Wood 1910a, 1910b).[4] Although the film emulsions capable of recording infrared waves pre-dated Wood, his plates were the first designed with the express purpose of recording infrared. These plates, developed along with plates sensitive to ultraviolet, and intended to observe only the moon and other planets, were prohibitively expensive and required long exposure times, qualities that made them unappealing to the larger commercial market.

It was, however, soon realized that different artists' materials had varying degrees of IR reflectance and transmission (Farnsworth 1938; Lyon 1934). While carbon-based materials like charcoal or graphite were effectively opaque across the UV, visible, and IR spectra, oil paints—essentially ground pigments (e.g. suspended oxides or mineral salts) suspended in a drying oil, such as linseed oil—varied substantially in how much IR light they transmitted, and in which parts of the IR spectrum. It turns out that the longer wavelengths of IR light made pigments that were opaque in visible light transparent. This in turn made underdrawings of highly IR-absorbing carbon clearly visible against the background of a highly IR-reflecting ground layer, such as chalk or gypsum (fig. 3).

In 1930, the Eastman Kodak Company developed the first commercially viable infrared film that was sufficiently sensitive to be exposed in seconds or minutes. By the 1950s, Kodak had introduced their High Speed Infrared film (HIE) in various formats and it was widely adopted for both scientific and art

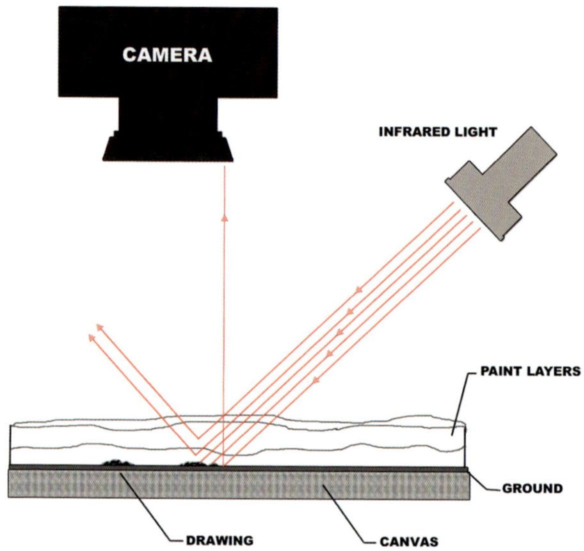

Fig. 3 Cross-section of a painting during Infrared Reflectography

photography (Eastman Kodak 1963). The best IR filter then available, the visibly opaque #87, admitted a broad band from 750 nm up to the maximum sensitivity of the film, a little above 900 nm (Eastman Kodak 2008, 2). Despite its potential, Kodak HIE was not widely deployed in the technical investigation of paintings (Ibarra-Castanedo et al. 2010, 6). The film was difficult to handle—it had to be loaded and unloaded in complete darkness—and the longer wavelength of IR meant that standard focal distances marked on the lenses for the visible spectrum had to be adjusted. This was a particular challenge when opaque IR filters were used, and proper exposure times were difficult to estimate as metering in the visible spectrum did not provide a reliable guide. A study of the underdrawings and pentimenti (see Sobol this volume, p. 33) in the work of Flemish painter Jan van Eyck was one of the only published examples to use Kodak HIE film (Desneux 1958). The Kodak HIE was finally discontinued in all formats in 2007 (Eastman Kodak 2008, 1).

Infrared Reflectography

In the late 1960s, experiments by the Dutch physicist, Rudolph van Asperen de Boer, with raster scanning video units sensitive in the visible and IR spectra led to significant advances in the field (Burmester and Bayerer 1993; Van Asperen de Boer 1968, 1969). In order to differentiate this technique from IR photography with film, the technique was designated Infrared Reflectography (IRR). The new electronic cameras used a vidicon tube—a lead sulphide sensor—that was sensitive from 400 nm to 1900 nm, with some sensors capable of reaching 2400 nm, much deeper in the IR spectrum than the Kodak film (Van Asperen de Boer 1974). The use of electronic sensors had the further advantage of producing a "live view" on a cathode ray tube (CRT) monitor so exposure and focus could easily be adjusted. To capture a still image from the monitor, Polaroid P/N 55 film was used (Van Asperen de Boer 1969, 107). Vidicon images revealed underdrawings during the examination of *Ginevra de' Benci* by Leonardo da Vinci and *The Feast of the Gods* by Giovanni Bellini (Walmsley et al. 1994), Jan van Scorel's *St. Vitus Church,* and Gerard David's *The Rest on the Flight into Egypt* (Van Asperen de Boer 1969).

By the late 1990s new Indium-Gallium-Arsenide (InGaAs) sensors, invented in 1977 by T. P. Pearsall and R. W. Hopson Jr. to replace Germanium photodiodes in physics applications, came to replace the Vidicon for technical art investigation (Baronti et al. 1998; Faries 2005; Fischer and Kakoulli 2006; Liang 2012; Lie 2003; Pearsall and Hopson 1977; Van Asperen de Boer 2003). InGaAs sensors are sensitive to wavelengths between 900 nm and 2500 nm, a range particularly useful for penetrating common pigments like azurite or Prussian blue that are opaque to film. Digital cameras sensitive to longer wavelengths of IR have already produced significant results in the technical examination of paintings such as Picasso's *The Old Guitarist* in the Art Institute of Chicago,[5] as well as in works of the Old Masters. When equipped with variable bandpass filters, InGaAs sensors, with their wide spectral sensitivity, allow what is called multi-spectral imaging. This technique generates a series of images, each of only a narrow part of the IR spectrum, and allows the identification of pigments by the quantitative comparison of these images (e.g., Daffara and Fontana 2011; Walmsley et al. 1994).

While InGaAs sensors are sensitive to longer wavelengths of IR than earlier film techniques, they have drawbacks. First, because each camera sensor is generally low resolution—on the order of 640 × 512 pixels, or 0.3 megapixels—mosaics of many images need to be stitched together, a time-consuming process, although computer techniques have significantly sped up the final assembly (e.g., Bertani and Consolandi 2006; Torres et al. 2008). Second, the sensors are still very expensive, often in the range of US$50,000, an amount beyond the means of many cultural heritage organizations. Third, like earlier video cameras, InGaAs cameras require constant illumination from tungsten or halogen lights that can heat the canvas, and great care is required to ensure that the oil paints are not damaged by long exposure, a problem usually remedied by the use of a rheostat to dim the lights. Finally, longer wavelengths of IR do not penetrate more deeply through paint layers in all instances (Gargano et al. 2007).[6] IR transparency equal to or greater than that found between 1100 and 1900 nm can be seen at shorter wavelengths of IR in such common pigments as vermilion, lead white, and cobalt blue.

As it turns out, the silicon sensors used in consumer digital cameras are sensitive in the NIR range up to 1100 nm (Bulow-Jacobson 2008; Falco 2010; Verhoeven 2008). Fuji manufactured limited-availability cameras that were based on the consumer Nikon D200 DSLR to bring this capability to forensics applications. This IR sensitivity is, however, usually blocked by an Internal Cut Filter (ICF) that is installed by manufacturers in front of the sensor to improve performance in visible light. Several companies offer services to remove the ICF and can turn relatively inexpensive digital cameras into effective NIR imaging systems.[7] While the term "Reflectography," since Van Asperen de Boer, has been confined to imaging with electronic sensors of longer wavelengths of IR, the use of silicon sensors can, we think, be properly designated Near Infrared Reflectography (NIRR).

The Case of Paul Kane

The IR imaging of Paul Kane's oil paintings was intended to clarify the relationship between the sketches he made in the field and the paintings developed in his Toronto studio. In particular, how did the underdrawings differ from the final paintings and how did Kane struggle to rework his sketches into the final painted compositions we now see? What can these changes tell us about Kane's method?

The primary tool used for the project was a Nikon D200 camera with a 3872 × 2592 pixel silicon sensor modified by Life Pixel (fig. 4). A 60 mm quartz-fluorite APO macro lens, made by Coastal Optics, was used not only for its high IR transmission, but because it is the only lens available that is focus-corrected across the IR, visible, and UV ranges.[8] In other words, the focal distance established in visible light can be used in IR without any adjustment. Once the image is crisp in visible light, the opaque IR filter can be quickly swung into place by means of the hinged Nikon AF-1 filter holder.

Two IR filters were used in the project, both from Peca Products Inc.,[9] with different transmission properties: the PECA 912 (#88A) with transmission starting at 700 nm, peaking at 850 nm, and then dropping to less than 50% transmission after 1050 nm; and the PECA 908 (#87B), a high-pass filter, that transmits IR at 90% starting at 900 nm.

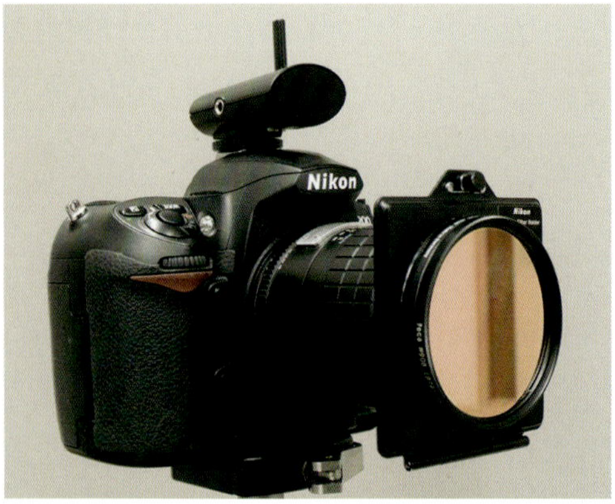

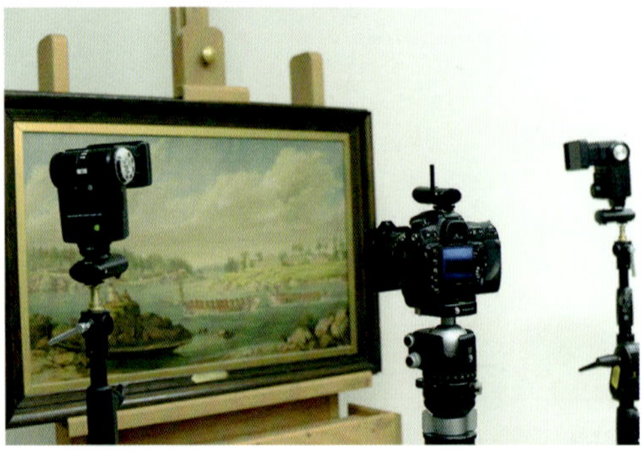

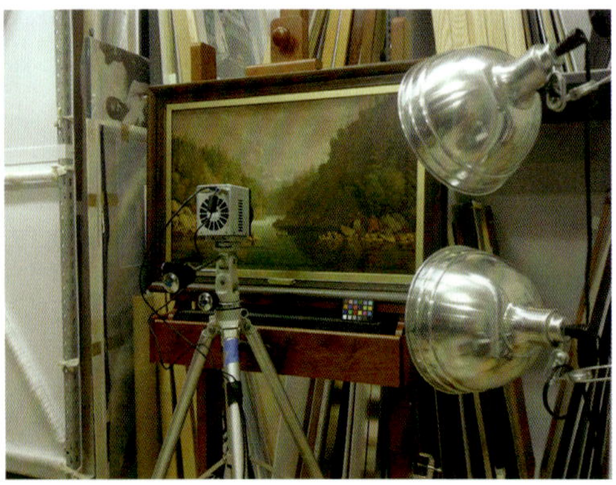

Fig. 4 Nikon D200 camera with the Coastal Optics 60 mm macro lens and PECA 908 filter

Fig. 5 Nikon D200 camera and two Vivitar 285HV flash units

Fig 6 The Xenics Xeva InGaAs camera with two tungsten spotlights. Painting: *Dalle des Morts, or the Rapid of the Dead*

Two Vivitar 285HV xenon flash units were converted with IR filters to provide IR-only illumination without the high heat of spotlights (fig. 5).[10]

In addition to the converted Nikon D200 camera, a Xenics Xeva-1.7-320 InGaAs camera was used with a 35 mm lens for close-up investigations of areas of particular interest (fig. 6).[11] The camera had a resolution of 320 × 256 pixels and IR sensitivity from 900 nm to 1700 nm. Constant illumination was provided by two tungsten spotlights.

Despite the promise of the InGaAs camera, it was found, in general, that comparable results were obtained with shorter wavelengths of IR, even when we expected the InGaAs to provide better images. This result, we believe, may be due to several factors, which should not preclude entirely the use of InGaAs cameras in future investigations. First, Kane is known to have used several pigments, such as lead white, calcium phosphate, and vermilion, that are just as transparent in lower wavelengths of IR as in the higher ones detected by the InGaAs sensor (Gayer 1996, 21; Sirois 1997). Second, even in cases where Kane used pigments that have very low IR transmission at the lower wavelengths, particularly those based on iron oxides, such as red ochre, Van Dyke brown, or Prussian blue, he likely mixed these pigments with the more transparent lead white and applied them as very thin layers, thereby rendering the underdrawing and underpainting visible with NIRR. With the use of digital post-processing to increase contrast, even faint indications could be brought out in such images. A series of examples illustrates when NIRR worked and when it did not, although in the absence of a detailed analysis of the pigments in each painting some speculation is unavoidable at present.

In *The Return of a War Party* (fig. 7), on the left of the painting a war canoe can be identified underneath blue and white pigments of the water, something that cannot be seen in visible light (fig. 8). Where thick brown paint, presumably some form of iron oxide, was applied to build up the foreground rock formation, the continuation of the underpainting cannot be detected. The InGaAs camera did not reveal any further indications of the underdrawing in this area.

Good transmission in the NIR range, however, was observed in the case of Kane's brown pigments in *Red River Settlement* (fig. 9). In the bottom left-hand corner NIRR allows us to see beneath the cow to the original painting of the shed wall (fig. 10). The brown pigments may have been applied so thinly to render the cow—perhaps an afterthought—that transmission in the shorter wavelengths was possible. Interestingly, in another version Kane made of *Red River Settlement*,[12] entitled *Fort Garry and St. Boniface*, the shed wall could not be seen

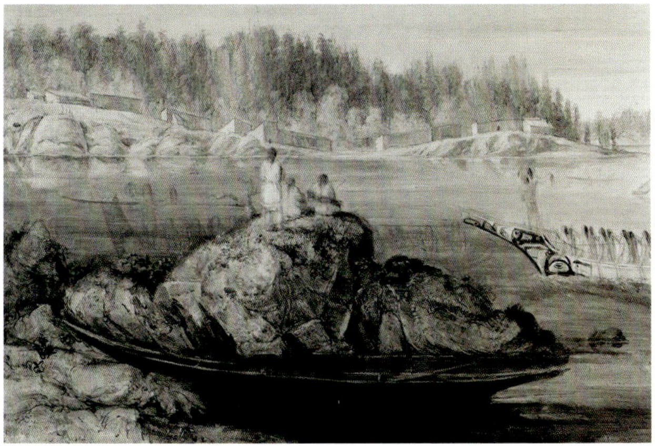

Fig. 7 *The Return of a War Party*, detail (Near Infrared Reflectography image)
Songhees (Central Coast Salish) and Hudson's Bay Company
Songhees village and Fort Victoria, south Vancouver Island, British Columbia; 1849–1856
oil on canvas; 43.0 × 71.0 cm
912.1.91

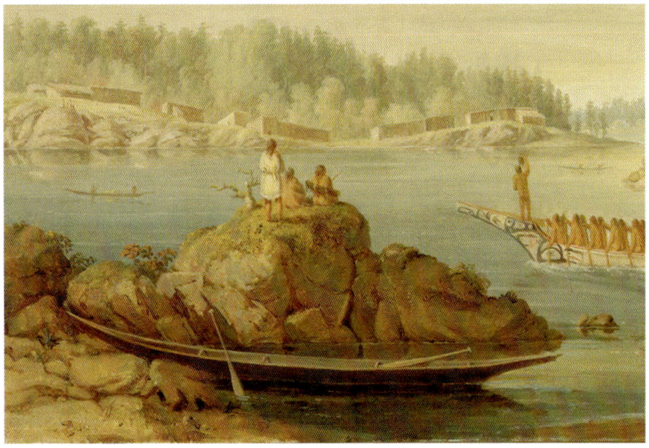

Fig. 8 *The Return of a War Party*, detail
Songhees (Central Coast Salish) and Hudson's Bay Company
Songhees village and Fort Victoria, south Vancouver Island, British Columbia; 1849–1856
oil on canvas; 43.0 × 71.0 cm
912.1.91

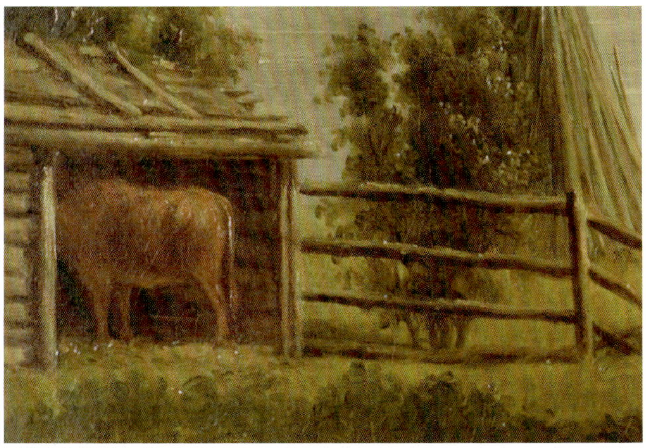

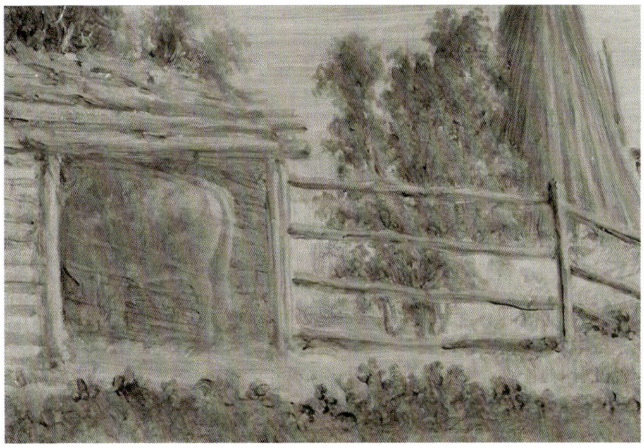

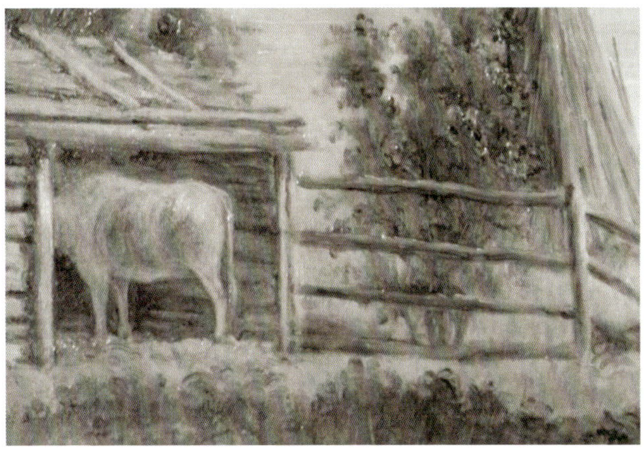

Fig. 9 (top) *Red River Settlement*, detail
Junction of the Red and Assiniboine Rivers, Manitoba; 1849–1856
oil on canvas; 45.8 × 74.3 cm
912.1.23

Fig. 10 (top right) *Red River Settlement*, detail
(Near Infrared Reflectography image)
Junction of the Red and Assiniboine Rivers, Manitoba; 1849–1856
oil on canvas; 45.8 × 74.3 cm
912.1.23

Fig. 11 (right) *Fort Garry and St. Boniface*, detail
(Near Infrared Reflectography image)
Junction of the Red and Assiniboine Rivers, Manitoba; 1851–1856
oil on canvas; 45.9 × 73.6 cm
National Gallery of Canada, Ottawa, no. 102
Transfer from the Parliament of Canada, 1888

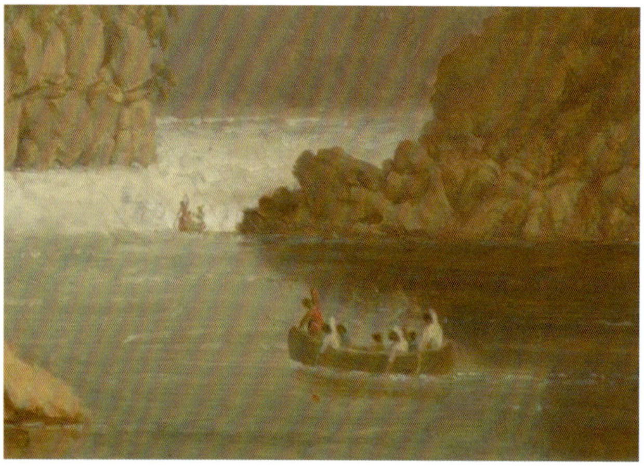

Fig. 12 *Dalle de Morts, or the Rapid of the Dead*, detail
Hudson's Bay Company brigade
upper Columbia River, British Columbia; 1849–1856
oil on canvas; 46.0 × 74.0 cm
912.1.20

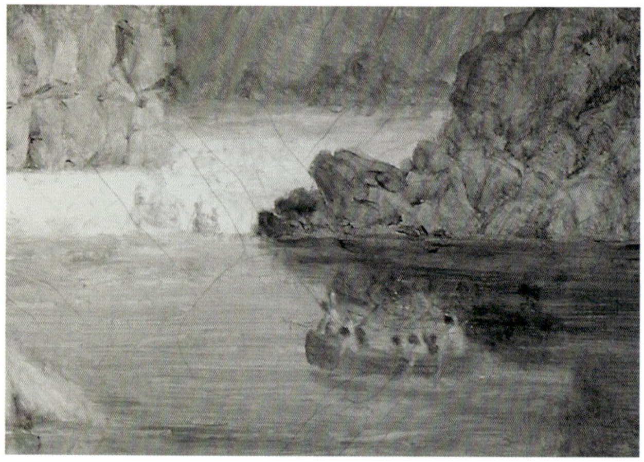

Fig. 13 *Dalle de Morts, or the Rapid of the Dead*, detail
(Near Infrared Reflectography image)
Hudson's Bay Company brigade
upper Columbia River, British Columbia; 1849–1856
oil on canvas; 46.0 × 74.0 cm
912.1.20

under the cow (fig. 11). We speculate that Kane, confident of the composition when he started since his vision for this image had been defined in the previous painting, gave precedence to the cow and did not paint the shed wall beneath. This observation suggests that this second painting was a later version of the first, in which the wall was visible in IR.

In the case of *Dalle des Morts, or the Rapid of the Dead*, the paint layers are so thin that faint images of two bateaux (fig. 12) can already be detected in visible light. With NIRR the details of the two bateaux that were painted initially become much more apparent (fig. 13). In this case, the InGaAs camera did not show any more details than the silicon sensor of the Nikon D200.

Kane's use of graphite to draw on his primed canvas creates a high contrast image that is immediately visible in the NIR range. In the case of *Medicine Mask Dance* (fig. 14), we can see clearly the graphite used to outline the legs of the figures, outlines that cannot be seen in visible light (fig. 15). What is more, we can also observe underpainting on the same canvas. Kane has adjusted the figure on the right by moving his arms and the rattle he is holding.

One of the most striking results from NIRR is seen in *A Babbine Woman*. Here one can identify slight pentimenti in visible light that betray Kane's changes (fig. 16). The NIRR, though, shows that Kane significantly altered the position of the child's head, as well as the hand of the mother (fig. 17). Most importantly, NIRR has revealed that the female figure was first painted as a nude and then later clothed in the final version.[13]

Future Investigation

Our preliminary investigation of the paintings of Paul Kane has shown that even relatively inexpensive NIRR equipment can reveal underdrawings and compositional changes, and provide significant insights into a painter's technique. Indeed, the combination of speed, low cost, and portability of our NIRR set-up meant that almost all of Kane's work in oil, just under 130 paintings in three institutions,[14] could be photographed in a matter of weeks. All documentation, however, is provisional; each year brings new technologies to document works through different means, as well as software techniques to analyze old data in new and surprising ways (Ainsworth 2005). Our journey in the technical evaluation of Kane's work has only just begun.

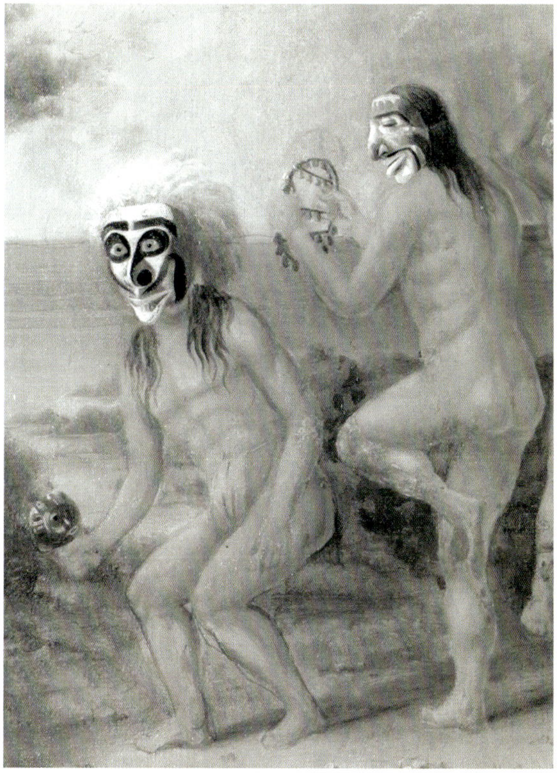

Fig. 14 *Medicine Mask Dance*, detail
(Near Infrared Reflectography image)
Northwest Coast peoples
Vancouver Island–Strait of Juan de Fuca region, British Columbia; 1849–1856
oil on canvas; 45.3 × 73.8 cm
912.1.92

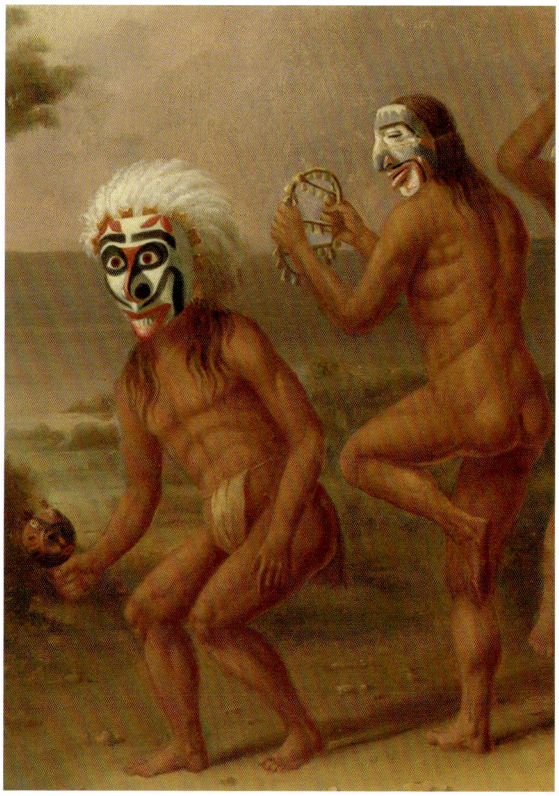

Fig. 15 *Medicine Mask Dance*, detail
Northwest Coast peoples
Vancouver Island–Strait of Juan de Fuca region, British Columbia; 1849–1856
oil on canvas; 45.3 × 73.8 cm
912.1.92

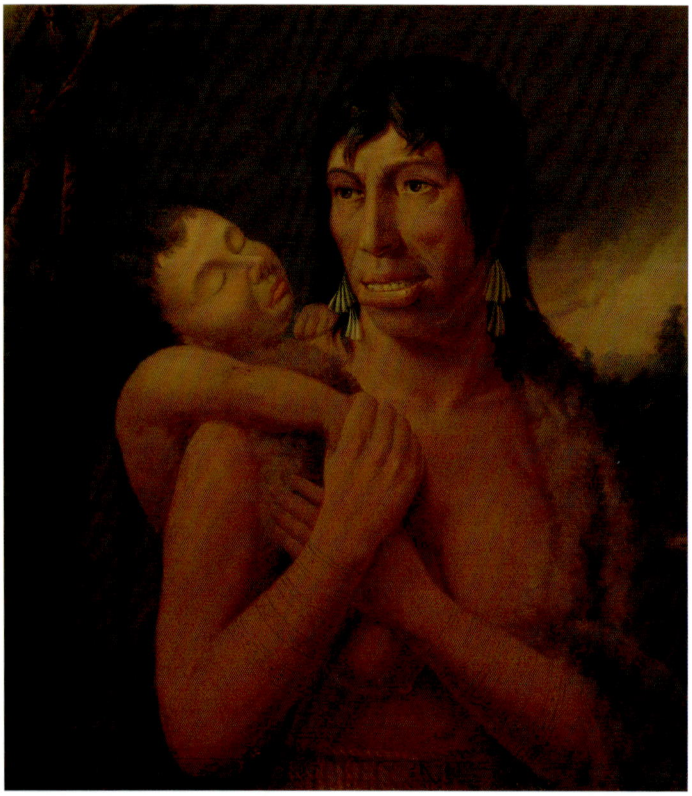

Fig. 16 *A Babbine Woman*
Tsimshian
Skeena River region, northwest British Columbia
1849–1856
oil on canvas; 76.1 × 63.0 cm
912.1.88

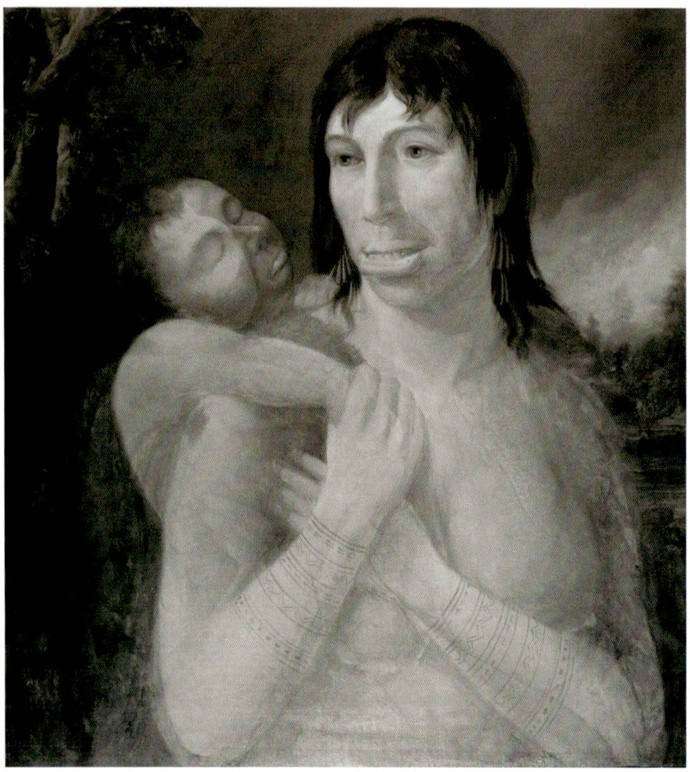

Fig. 17 *A Babbine Woman*
(Near Infrared Reflectography image)
Tsimshian
Skeena River region, northwest British Columbia
1849–1856
oil on canvas; 76.1 × 63.0 cm
912.1.88

Notes

1 We owe our modern understanding of light as a particle to Albert Einstein. In 1905, his miraculous year of scientific productivity at the age of only 26, while still a patent clerk, he demonstrated that light, up to that point seen only as an electromagnetic wave, consisted of discrete packets with fixed energy states (quanta). This packet would later be called the "photon." Rigden 2005 offers a readable account of this and Einstein's other groundbreaking discoveries in 1905.

2 Herschel, who began his career as a musician and composer, not a scientist, termed these rays "calorific" after their ability to heat. The term "infrared" was not used until eighty years later (White 2012). While such heating, we now know, is produced only by long-wave infrared, Herschel's insight that these "calorific rays" were a form of light was monumental and prompted questions in physics that would only be satisfactorily answered a century later.

3 The cathode tubes Röntgen was experimenting with were glass vacuum tubes through which an electrical current flowed between electrodes. An aluminum window in the tube permitted the new rays to escape and expose film. So alarmed was Anna Bertha Röntgen upon seeing the bones of her hand revealed by these mysterious new rays that she was said to have exclaimed, "I have seen my death!" Poor Anna could not yet have forseen the tremendous life-saving potential of X-rays in medical diagnostics. The standard biography of Röntgen is Nitske 1971.

4 Robert Williams Wood, a professor at Johns Hopkins University, published the first infrared photographs in the *Journal of the Royal Photographic Society* in 1910. The images of landscapes, which would appear a year later for a general audience in the *Illustrated London News*, demonstrated how chlorophyll in vegetation was a strong reflector in the infrared. Dark green leaves appeared strikingly bright white in Wood's images. Wood would soon use his new emulsions to produce photographs of Jupiter and Saturn, results he published in 1916. Wood's other contributions to science, including the first UV photography, as well as his character as a practical joker, are treated at length in Seabrook 1941.

5 Revealing Picasso Conservation Project http://www.artic.edu/collections/conservation/revealing-picasso-conservation-project. Here an Inframetrics InfraCAM was used with a Platinum Silicide detector sensitive to wavelengths between 3 and 5 microns.

6 The reflectance and absorption spectra for many commonly used pigments in European art have been conveniently measured and put online by Lawrence Berkeley National Laboratory as part of the Cool Colors Project: http://coolcolors.lbl.gov/assets/docs/PAC-2003-03-11/Pigment-Charts-2003-03-09.pdf.

7 LDP LLC www.MaxMax.com, 220 Broad Street, Carlstadt, NJ 07072 USA, www.maxmax.com; and Life Pixel Infrared Conversion Services, 13024 Beverly Park Road, Suite 103, Mukilteo, WA 98275, USA. http://www.lifepixel.com.

8 http://www.jenoptik-inc.com/coastalopt-standard-lenses/uv-vis-nir-60mm-slr-lens-mainmenu-155/80-uv-vis-ir-60-mm-apo-macro.html.

9 Peca Products Inc., 471 Burton Street, Beloit, WI 53511, USA. http://www.ir-uv.com.

10 The IR filters for the conversion were provided by Shane Elen of Tacoma, WA. http://www.beyondvisible.com/BV4-UV285.html.

11 http://www.xenics.com/documents/XB-003_04_Xeva-1.7-320_Scientific_LowRes.pdf. The camera was generously loaned by Channel Systems Inc., P.O. Box 188, S2-24 Aberdeen Avenue, Pinawa, Manitoba R0E 1L0, Canada.

12 This version of *Red River Settlement* was completed by Kane as part of a commission of twelve paintings granted by the Canadian Parliament in 1851. The extant paintings from that commission are now in the National Gallery of Canada collection (see Cassels 2010, 41 note 67).

13 This is consistent with the oil-on-paper sketch that inspired the oil painting where Kane rendered the figure without clothing (see Lister 2010, 298 fig. a).

14 The works of Paul Kane photographed using Near Infrared Reflectography were in the collections of the Art Gallery of Ontario (Toronto), National Gallery of Canada (Ottawa), and Royal Ontario Museum (Toronto).

EXPLORATION IN TECHNICAL ART HISTORY: PAUL KANE

Heidi Sobol

Introduction

One of the Royal Ontario Museum's most iconic collections is the Paul Kane cycle of 100 oil paintings. Kane created this collection of oil-on-canvas and oil-on-board paintings after his 1845–1848 journeys as far west as the Pacific Ocean to sketch Canada's Native peoples and the North American landscape. Throughout their long history, the paintings have undergone a range of restoration and conservation treatments. While some are virtually pristine, others have undergone complex treatments to address minor and major damages. Thus, a conservation survey was necessary in order to assess the condition of the collection. Beginning in the spring of 2007, I led a conservation survey of sixty-seven paintings in the Kane cycle. The level of condition assessment was randomly applied: some paintings received extensive assessment, some intermediate, and some cursory. The remaining thirty-three paintings from the collection had been assessed and/or treated just prior to the 2007 survey and so were not included. During the conservation survey, it was estimated that 28% of the entire cycle of 100 Kane paintings required major treatment. Major treatment may include the removal of varnish; overpaint removal [1] and filling/inpainting;[2] or structural work, namely lining [3] and frame upgrades. The remaining 72% of the paintings were considered in stable condition—treatment required was estimated to be minor or moderate. Such treatment is primarily considered to be aesthetic with little to no structural work required.

From *Brigade of Boats* to *Indian Horse Race*: Samples from the Conservation Survey

With the survey completed, I had the opportunity to work on a number of paintings within the Kane 100-painting cycle. A key painting in the cycle, *Brigade of Boats* (fig. 18), is typical of the paintings within the major-treatment group identified in the survey. Many of the paintings in this group, including *Brigade of Boats*, exhibited some degree of physical damage (i.e., tears, water damage) that had already been restored. However, with cumulative restoration campaigns, paintings can often exhibit "restoration fatigue": surfaces that look abraded and old damages that are not ameliorated despite the number of restoration attempts.

Brigade of Boats was treated in the paintings laboratory of the ROM in 2008. The primary focus of the treatment was two-fold: first, to address structural concerns relating to delamination between the original canvas and lining support, and second, to ameliorate aesthetic issues involving discoloured varnish and mismatched overpaint. The structural concerns emanated from at least two previous lining procedures: a lining with glue in 1934 and a re-lining with wax-resin in 1970.

In an attempt to remove glue residue prior to the application of wax-resin, the verso of the original canvas was "sanded down," likely during the 1970 treatment. Unfortunately, the original canvas was too thin and the mechanical action resulted in the formation of holes (visible in both conservation photos, figs. 19 and 20). Additionally, the painting suffered from paint loss and in turn those areas were covered with overpaint.

Conservation treatment involved the removal of the discoloured synthetic varnish (from 1970) and the removal of all overpaint. Now the viewer sees as much of the original painting as possible. All losses were secured with adhesive and inpainted with a removable paint system. Finally, a new synthetic varnish was applied to the surface.

Significantly, during the survey a small number of paintings were found to be in a "pristine state." While it is possible that after they left Kane's studio these paintings received minor conservation treatments, those treatments would have been relegated to a singular campaign of surface cleansing, varnish removal, minor inpainting to address discrete/minute surface damages, and re-varnishing. These paintings have not been lined, nor removed from their stretchers. In this cache of paintings there was no evidence of significant damages, such as tears or paint loss; consequently these paintings did not exhibit significant amounts of overpaint or retouching.

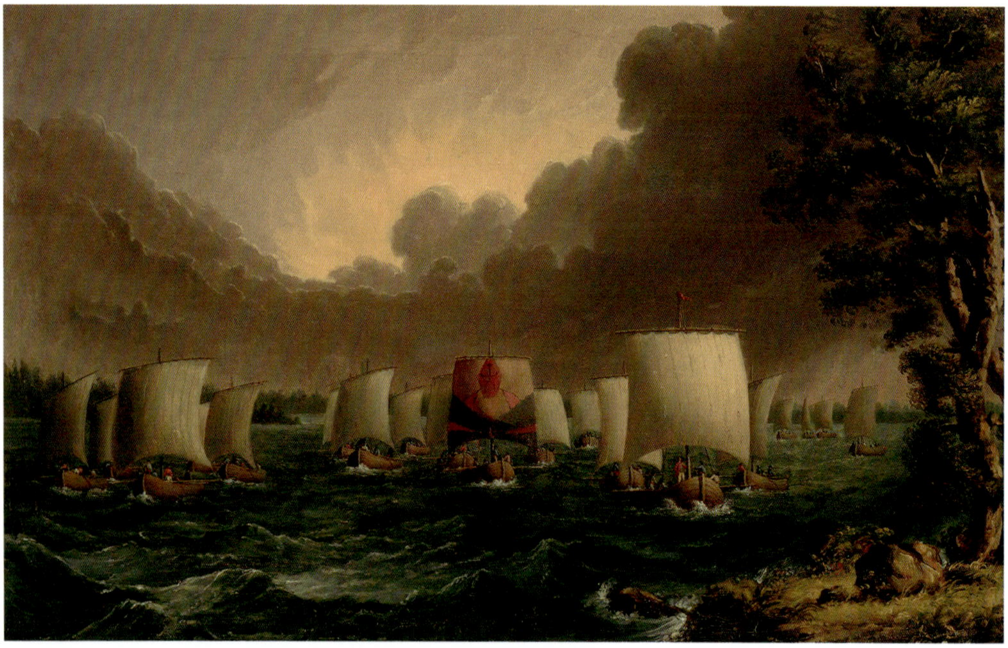

Fig. 18 *Brigade of Boats*
Hudson's Bay Company brigade
Saskatchewan River–Cedar Lake region, Manitoba
1849–1856
oil on canvas; 46.4 × 74.2 cm
912.1.31

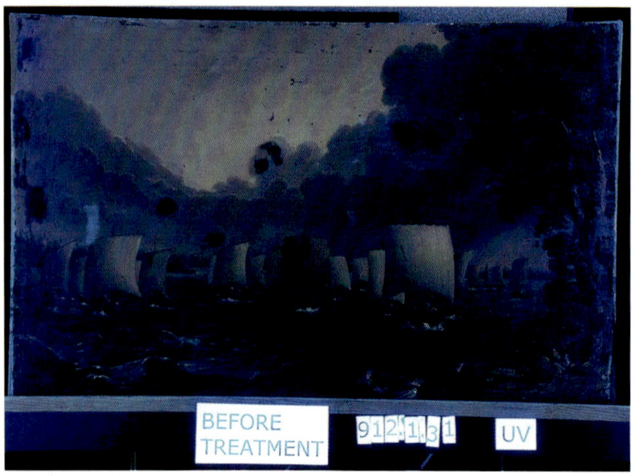

Fig. 19 *Brigade of Boats*
Hudson's Bay Company brigade
Saskatchewan River–Cedar Lake region, Manitoba; 1849–1856
oil on canvas; 46.4 × 74.2 cm
912.1.31
Before-treatment image during UV examination, recto surface.

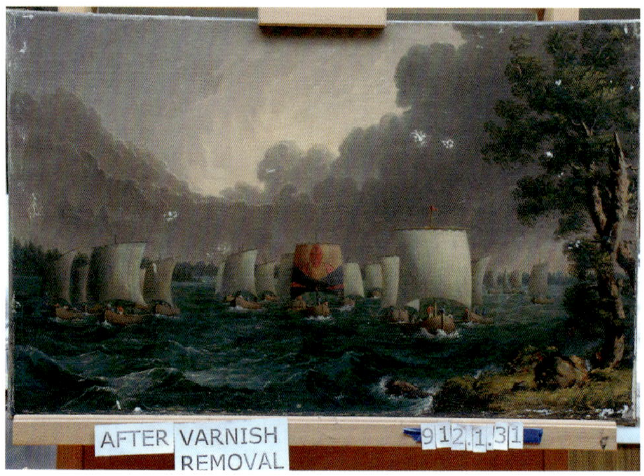

Fig. 20 *Brigade of Boats*
Hudson's Bay Company brigade
Saskatchewan River–Cedar Lake region, Manitoba; 1849–1856
oil on canvas; 46.4 × 74.2 cm
912.1.31
During-treatment image showing the recto surface after varnish and overpaint removal.

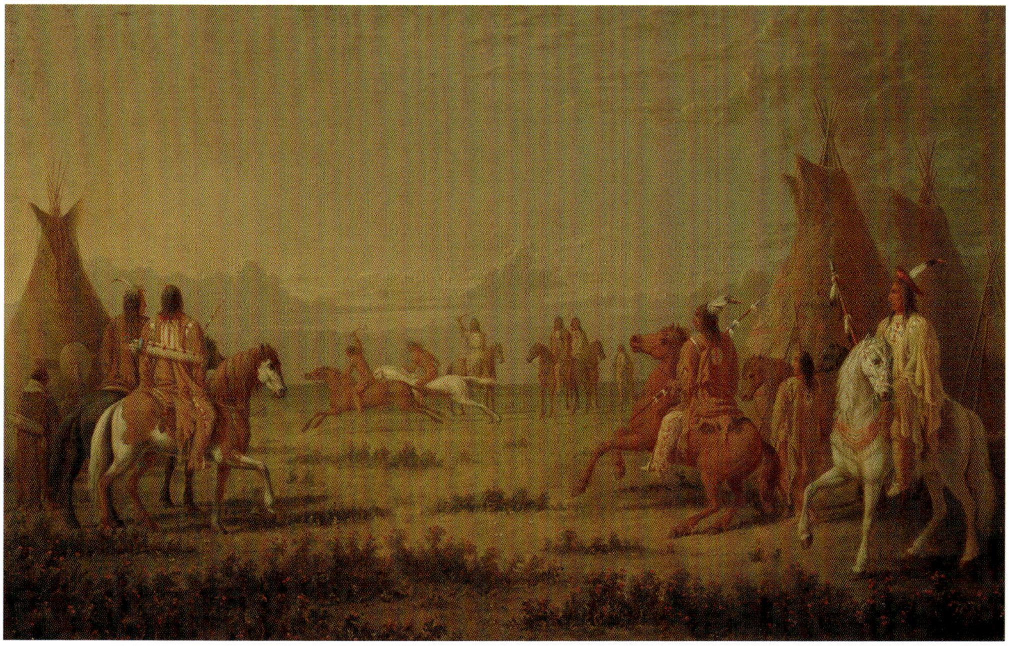

Fig. 21 *Indian Horse Race*
Blackfoot
Fort Pitt region, North Saskatchewan River, Saskatchewan; 1849–1852
oil on canvas; 46.2 × 74.0 cm
912.1.51

Indian Horse Race (fig. 21) is one of the pristine paintings identified during the survey. The painting depicts an animated outdoor scene and it is warm in tonal values. Paint application is typical of this series of works, with lean oil paint application and very slightly impastoed areas. The commercially primed linen canvas (estimated) is stretched on a wood stretcher with metal tacks. This is likely the original attachment of the canvas to the stretcher, as evidenced by an intact tacking margin and well-anchored metal tack heads. Critically, the image layers are in good condition with minimal evidence of damage, that is to say, there are minor abrasions in the top corners that have been locally overpainted, though the overpaint is somewhat mismatched. It is estimated that this painting possesses the original varnish layer, or at the very least, has experienced only one campaign of removal and re-varnishing.

Concurrent Analytical Work: Paul Kane's Paintbox and Early Portraiture

During this period, analysis had been completed by the Canadian Conservation Institute (CCI) on a painting attributed to Paul Kane that had been acquired by the ROM in 2011 (fig. 22). The painting, entitled *Eliza Cory Clench*, is dated circa 1836—twenty years before the completion of the 100 studio paintings inspired by his ethnographic sketches. Eliza Clench is depicted at approximately five years of age, holding a bonnet of flowers, in a three-quarter profile. The oval portrait shows a somewhat stoic Eliza, who would incidentally go on to become Paul Kane's sister-in-law as he married Eliza's older sister, Harriet. Kane may have been working as an apprentice furniture painter in Cobourg, Ontario, for Eliza and Harriet's father, Freeman Schermerhorn Clench (see Cassels 2010, 39 note 27).

Prior to his residency in Cobourg, the young Paul Kane studied art with drawing master Thomas Drury (or Drewry) at Upper Canada College (Cassels 2010, 39 note 23; Davis 1982, 45). While in Cobourg, and during his subsequent travels through Canada and the United States, Kane garnered increasing praise for his paintings, which through to the 1840s were predominantly portraiture.[4]

Art conservators primarily rely on analytical results derived from actual artworks attributed to the artist. Also of benefit though are the results obtained from analysis of material remnants from artists' studios.[5] Significantly, one critical artifact from his workshop remains: the studio paintbox attributed to Kane that is now in the collection of the National Gallery of Canada (fig. 23). Despite his peregrinations, Kane likely used this attributed paintbox for a rather lengthy period

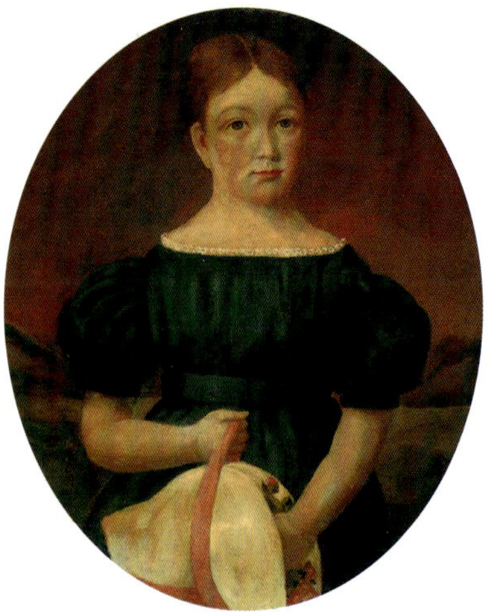

Fig. 22 *Eliza Cory Clench*
Attributed to Paul Kane; c. 1836
oil on canvas; 60.2 × 50.2 cm
2011.10.1.1-1.2. Gift of Mrs. Janet Shirley

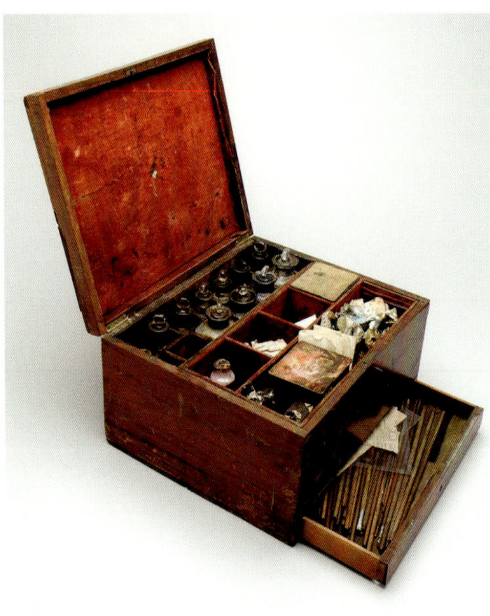

Fig. 23 Paul Kane's paintbox
Wood veneer, brass hinges, tin, velvet
Contents include apothecary jars and colours of Van Dyke brown, ivory black, Naples yellow, yellow ochre, traditional Prussian blue, lead white, rose madder, hematite, shell gold, and vermillion. Medium elements include drying oil, mastic, turpentine, and rosin. Metal syringes partially filled with dried oil paint and more than fifty paintbrushes and paintbrush handles are included, with conté crayons, charcoal, and chalk.
Height: 21.0 cm, Width: 38.3 cm, Depth: 33.5 cm
National Gallery of Canada, Ottawa, ST35
Photo © NGC

spanning 1820–1860 (Sirois 1997, 6). This would mean that cumulative remnants of pigments, drawing media, and tools from this paintbox are available for analysis, providing insights into Kane's painting practice from his time as an apprentice in the furniture factory of W. S. Conger in the late 1820s (Cassels 2010, 28) to when his art production generally ceased in the late 1850s. Analytical studies of artists' paintboxes provide compelling information about the history of their methods and materials and can assist in provenance investigations and authentication. The CCI study of Paul Kane's studio paintbox was completed as part of a study of the portraits of Eliza's parents, *Freeman Schermerhorn Clench* and *Eliza Clarke Cory Clench*[6] (Gayer 1996), which are contemporaneous with the portrait of their subjects' daughter. Scientific analysis confirmed correlations between pigments found in the paintbox and analytical evidence from the elder Clenches' portraits. Contained within the paintbox are pigments that were "powdered and wrapped in fragments of newspaper from Mobile, Alabama: one was dated 1844" (Sirois 1997, 6). The paintbox also contains labelled jars from New York (likely courtesy of Mr. Conger, who had made a trip there) and from London (which Kane likely purchased himself during his stay in England in 1842–1843). Taken together, the jars and the paint analysis provide illustrative information about Kane's materials, as well as confirmation of his affiliations and travels.

The anchor, in a sense, in the painting practice of Paul Kane throughout the 1830s and all the way through to the 1860s was not a singular studio location, but rather his multi-segmented wood paintbox. Correlations between the elder Clenches' portraits, Kane's paintbox, and the portrait *Eliza Cory Clench* are manifest in the analytical results presented by CCI's research (Moffatt and Poulin 2010). There is evidence of the following pigments in all four sources (three paintings and the paintbox): lead white ($2PbCO_3{\times}Pb(OH)_2$), calcium carbonate ($CaCO_3$), carbon-based black, vermillion, and Prussian blue. In the portrait of Eliza Clench, there were a number of trace elements detected that may constitute additional pigments shared between the elder Clenches' portraits and the paintbox (e.g., yellow ochre). Drying oils were detected in all three portraits. Thus, while there are some divergences in pigments used, there are similar materials in all three portraits.

This evidence, coupled with evidence from Kane himself,[7] provides a skeletal idea of how Kane worked, but there exists no definitive written record of his studio practice. Aside from lessons with Mr. Drury, Kane did not have formal art training or aspire to align himself with any artist groups or clubs aside from association with the Canadian Institute, where he presented papers.[8] The information gained from technical study and analysis can provide new insights into his methods based on what the paintings themselves tell us. For example, examination of the paint stratification (cross-sectional analysis) reveals how Kane constructed the painting in terms of the physical application of media. With more cross-sections of more paintings from different times in Kane's art career we will be able to chart similarities and differences in his painting methodology.

From Survey to Near Infrared Reflectography: Establishing the Paul Kane NIRR Project

Many of Kane's paintings exhibited pentimenti—signs of the artist's changes to a painting's design—and include textural pentimenti, which are a result of heavy layers of paint dimensionally showing through upper and often thinner layers of paint.[9] Pentimenti are visible to the naked eye and can be anything from a faint ghosting that hints at the artist's early design struggle, to a remnant from a completely different composition. A pentimento (singular) can occur as a result of the increasing transparency of the upper paint layers as a painting ages. The visibility of these changes can also be related to the physical thinness of the paint layers themselves. Kane's pentimenti initially appeared to be stylistic changes made during the painting's evolution in his studio. For instance, a tree may have been redrawn in the foreground or an incongruent figure readjusted to sit properly in the composition. The clarity of the pentimenti suggested that there might have been only one or two significant changes before the final image was allowed to dry. Kane, though, was not scraping down his canvas after a displeasing painting campaign, nor, conversely, struggling with numerous changes, both of which can typically result in a blurry infrared image. Rather, it seemed he was executing a first draft with a fair amount of paint body and modelling, allowing it to dry, and then coming back for a second (and most often final) repainting. Important, though, we still did not have a comprehensive understanding of Kane's painting practice, nor were we able to determine the "intermission time" between campaigns.

During the conservation survey, paintings were examined under different wavelengths of light and infrared reflectography provided increasingly compelling information. What further information would infrared reflectography yield as more and more paintings were evaluated? At the time of the survey, the ROM Conservation department was transitioning from traditional film photography to digital IRR imaging. During this transition period, familiarity with the new digital procedures was growing, but was not universal and effortless.

A couple of years after the survey, I was approached by Dr. George Bevan, who was working with various types of digital multi-spectral imaging. He specifically inquired as to whether I might know of good candidates for study with Near Infrared Reflectography within the ROM's collection. Dr. Bevan had been exploring recent applications for a converted multi-spectral, digital single-lens reflex camera (DSLR). This camera had potential to capture infrared images, or reflectograms, of art objects, in a studio set-up that would efficiently and accurately capture materials lying just below the surface in question and not visible to the naked eye, such as graphite pencil, a frequent initial drawing medium that has been employed by painters for centuries.

With the recent survey fresh in mind, I suggested that we take a look at some of Kane's paintings. First, I felt that the cycle offered a finite group of paintings on which a comprehensive NIRR survey could be based. Second, we were assured some degree of success in terms of NIRR imaging as the pentimenti were a harbinger of things to come. Third, and most intriguing, not only did the ROM have the paintings, but the ROM, Library and Archives Canada, and the Stark Museum of Art had hundreds of field sketches that Kane had referenced for the paintings. The sketches, in many cases, could act as frameworks for what we might find a few microns below the surface. As well, possibilities for comparisons between the ROM's paintings and similar versions in the collections of the Art Gallery of Ontario and the National Gallery of Canada widened the scope of the prospective project.

Observations and Future Directions

When interpreting infrared reflectograms, the conservator's eye seeks out information about the materials and techniques used to construct the image layers in a work. In the case of our NIRR imaging, we can say with some confidence that many of the underdrawings appear to have been executed in graphite pencil. The weight and appearance of the mark-making and the fluidity of graphite pencil stroke are evocative of the media Kane would have used in other pursuits (i.e., sketching). We note that the underdrawings of the original paintings have a somewhat sketch-like quality and exhibit changes in design. Where there are underdrawings of the later versions, however, they appear confident and evenly-weighted; very different in appearance from the infrared images of the originals. This suggests that Kane may have used some type

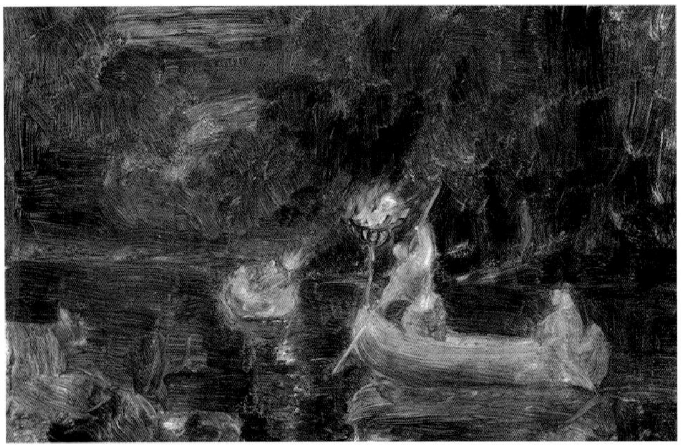

Fig. 24 *Fishing by Torch Light*
(Near Infrared Reflectography image)
Menominee
Fox River, Wisconsin; September 1845
oil on paper; 24.5 × 31.1 cm
2011.58.1

This acquisition was made possible by the generous support of the Louise Hawley Stone Charitable Trust, Gretchen and Donald Ross, the Daphne Cockwell Gallery of Canada: First Peoples Acquisition Fund, Mr. and Mrs. Albert Milstein, Friends of the Canadian Collections, and contributions from Laura Adams and Michael Serbinis, Gyrus Investment Management, Flavia Redelmeier, the Frank and Emily Riddell Memorial Fund, Mark and Mary-Ann Schmeer, the Elizabeth Walter Endowment Fund, and Susan Witteveen; certified by the Canadian Cultural Property Export Review Board under the terms of the Cultural Property Export and Import Act.

of copying method to transfer the original design to the subsequent version (see fig. 85).

Kane's pictorial paint applications are clear and almost always singular in attempt, as evidenced throughout the NIRR study of the paintings. This might suggest that Kane initially executed his paintings, lived with them in his studio environment during the "painting years" of 1849–1856, and in that same time frame, made another pass at their appearance.

Maude Cassels, the daughter of Kane's primary patron, George William Allan, provides evidence for another supposition. In her thirty-two-page manuscript detailing recollections of her childhood interactions with Paul Kane, she notes: "After his [Kane's] return he scarcely used his brush again except for a few small pictures, and to retouch some of those at Moss Park, . . ." (Cassels 2010, 33). Cassels is speaking of a period of time after 1858 but before 1871, the year in which Kane died. This would suggest that the paintings had several years between their creation and the subsequent retouching. The paintings commissioned by George William Allan were housed in his home, Moss Park (located on 100 acres of land between Queen and Bloor Streets on the west side of Sherbourne Street, Toronto), and if indeed Kane was retouching the Moss Park paintings, then the cycle of 100 paintings would have been among them. The compelling question about why Kane chose to retouch is difficult to answer. Was he retouching them at the behest of his patron, George William Allan, or was he acting on his own initiative?

Sadly, this period of Kane's life was marked by a deterioration of his eyesight. It can be theorized that perhaps Kane, frustrated by loss of vision, sought refuge in his earlier landscapes and portraits. While he was unable to execute a new painting or a copy of a painting, the act of revisiting his earlier works by retouching distinct elements may have provided a comforting sense of activity and ownership.[10]

In disseminating the information yielded by our NIRR reflectograms during this study we have not only added to the ethnographic understanding of Paul Kane's paintings, but also shed light on his physical painting practice. In one particular instance, the clarity of the infrared reflectogram of an oil-on-paper sketch, *Fishing by Torch Light*, illuminates this dark painting (fig. 24). The NIRR image is an almost grey-scale version of a primarily black sketch. Though atypical of Kane's canvas paintings, the brushwork revealed in the oil sketch is exceptionally confident and expressionistic. Combined with the knowledge that Kane executed the oil sketch with haste in situ,[11] the NIRR image reveals a stylistic departure from Kane's studio practice. The 100 paintings in the cycle are consistently uniform in their appearance: smooth brushwork, defined edges, and thin paint applications. In the *Fishing by Torch Light* sketch, the wider brush marks are animated, with greater impasto, giving the impression of an inspired paint application.

To further understand Kane's media and paint construction, scientific analysis of the paint layers in the 100 Kane paintings would provide a wealth of information that could be evaluated against the analytical information from the study of the three early-career Clench portraits and Kane's paintbox. The information obtained by cross-sectional analysis would allow us to compare paintings throughout his career and may assist in making connections between his later works and the use of his paintbox. While sampling all 100 paintings is not feasible, selections from a smaller but varied range of paintings would be possible.

Conclusion

The Paul Kane NIRR project represents the triangulation of science, research, and conservation—all key pillars in art historical study. Though the interpretations and insights were derived from individual expertise, all parties shared the objective of increasing our understanding of Paul Kane, the artist. The uniqueness of the knowledge and perspective of the contributors lent itself to creating a productive collaboration. A NIRR image provides us with a temporal experience insofar as it is essentially a snapshot of the creation of the piece and opens the pathway to deeper insight into its greater context. Additionally, as demonstrated by *Fishing by Torch Light*, NIRR reflectograms—in their monotone and somewhat ethereal appearance—often have a unique beauty.

In the case of Paul Kane, our documented history of his painting practice is scant. It therefore becomes necessary to turn to the artworks themselves. Technical study can provide insights into the materials and the construction of the artist's work, documenting aspects of process and intention that cannot otherwise be known. As the remainder of this catalogue details in numerous dramatic examples, NIRR has proven to be a particularly fruitful investigative tool in the study of Kane's works.

Notes

1 Overpainting occurs when paint applied to an area of damage or loss extends beyond the area.

2 Inpainting is the application of paint to areas of loss or damage. Paint is applied discretely, only where needed, without covering any of the original surface of the painting.

3 Paintings made on a flexible surface or support (e.g., canvas) can become frail, torn, or warped over time. They can be stabilized by the addition of a lining: a piece of fabric attached with an adhesive to the entire verso, or back, of the painting's support.

4 In *Paul Kane's Frontier*, J. Russell Harper notes source material from both the May 1855 *Anglo-American Magazine* (quoted in Harper 1971, 11) and an article in the Mobile, Alabama *Commercial Register* for March 20, 1841 (Harper 1971, 336–37) that indicates Kane was actively painting portraits at this time in cities such as Detroit, Michigan, and Mobile, Alabama.

5 Intact artists' studios that are made available to archivists, conservators, and affiliated professionals (e.g., architects) yield a wealth of information about the artists' materials and techniques. Refer to the relocation of Francis Bacon's studio to the Hugh Lane Gallery, Dublin, circa 2001. Unfortunately, there is no definitive record of the set-up of Paul Kane's studio at his home on Wellesley Street, nor is there information about the studio he rented in the Wellington Buildings at 64 King Street West, Toronto (Robson 1938, 14).

6 The portraits of Freeman Schermerhorn Clench (NGC, 30486) and Eliza Clarke Cory Clench (NGC, 30487) are both in the National Gallery of Canada collection.

7 See Paul Kane's 1846–1848 journal (Kane 1989) and his published narrative, *Wanderings of an Artist among the Indians of North America*, published in 1859, which document his travels and associated art production during his westward travels in the late 1840s.

8 Kane was invited to become a member of the Toronto Society of Arts in March 1849, but he declined, stating, "it is impossible for me to give that attention to the interest of the Society which it deserves without great personal inconvenience to myself" (HBCA E.42/1 fol. 16d).

9 "Pentimenti" is derived from the Italian word *pentirsi*, meaning "to repent."

10 According to Maude Cassels, the daughter of George William Allan, due to Kane's failing eyesight, her mother was concerned about what Kane might do to the paintings if he kept them too long (Cassels 2010, 35).

11 In *Wanderings of an Artist*, Kane writes about his experience of witnessing Menominee fishermen spearing fish at night: ". . . although very tired with my long day's paddling, I sat down by the fire, and while my companion was cooking some fish in a moh-cock, Indian fashion (for we had lost our kettle), I made the sketch No. 4" (1859, 32).

"LEAVES FROM AN AMERICAN PLANT"

Kenneth R. Lister

"ere they depart"

> *In that period I executed numerous portraits of chiefs, warriors, and medicine-men of the different tribes among whom I sojourned, and also of their wives and daughters. The Indian fishing and hunting scenes, games, dances, and other characteristic customs, also occupied my pencil; while I was not forgetful of the interest which justly attaches to the scenery of a new and unexplored country, and especially to such parts of it as were either intimately associated with native legends and traditions, or otherwise specially connected with the native tribes as their favourite fishing or hunting grounds, the locations of their villages, or the burying-places of the tribes. The whole of these sketches are now in my possession, and I have already been honoured by a commission to execute a series of paintings from them for the Legislature of the Province of Canada, which now have a place in the Library of the Provincial Parliament. A much more extensive series of oil paintings had been executed by me, from my sketches, for George W. Allan, Esq., of Moss Park, the liberal patron of Canadian art.* (Kane 1859, ix–x)

The above sentences detailing Paul Kane's sojourn and commissions for his art were published in the preface to his book, *Wanderings of an Artist among the Indians of North America*. The book was published in 1859, the same year Charles Darwin published *The Origin of Species.* It was published fourteen years after Kane started out on the first of two journeys to sketch this country's Aboriginal peoples and the North American landscape. This was eleven years after he exhibited 240 sketches in Upper Canada's first-ever solo art exhibition and seven years after he displayed eight studio oil paintings at Toronto's Provincial Agricultural Show that were so enthusiastically reviewed by Susanna Moodie ([1853] 1959, 237). It was three years after Kane delivered to his patron, the Honourable George William Allan[1], 100 oil canvases that are now part of the Royal Ontario Museum's Paul Kane collection. And within fours years of its English publication, Kane's book had been translated into French (1861), German (1862), and Danish (1863), giving him international recognition. And it was only twelve years before he died at the age of sixty-one (P. J. Kane 2010, 49).[2]

Wanderings of an Artist was published when Kane was forty-nine years old and is the narrative of an artist who travelled across Canada and south of the 49th parallel along the Columbia River at a time when Native cultures were under increasing pressure to cede their lands, move away from their traditional home territories, and adopt foreign views and ways of life. In September 1810, the month that Paul Kane was born in County Cork, Ireland, it was reported in London's *Evangelical Magazine* (September 1, 1810) that the Cherokee nation in the American southeast was embracing civilization as evidenced by the existence of "13 grist-mills, 3 saw-mills, 3 salt petre works, and one powder mill. They have 30 wagons, nearly 500 ploughs, 1600 spinning wheels, 467 looms, and 49 silversmiths." The article goes on to note, however, "there is no church erected; and few feel the impressions of grace." This was twenty-eight years before that same nation—despite being acclaimed as the "model of a civilized Indian nation" (Dippie 1982, 57)—was forced to move from its home territory in the State of Georgia across the Mississippi River to Indian Lands in the present State of Oklahoma (King 2004, 359).

In 1819, the year the Kane family moved to "muddy York" on the shores of Lake Ontario, it was reported in the *Republican Compiler* (February 17, 1819) of Gettysburg, Pennsylvania, that the planned establishment of an American settlement in the area of the Yellowstone and Missouri Rivers would instigate a war with the Indians of that territory. This, however, the article states, "would be productive of great injury to themselves and corresponding good to us." The view was that the Indians would be forced to respect the American character and thereby transfer their allegiance from the British to the American governments. Subsequently, the focus of trade would transfer from Montreal to St. Louis. This, it was thought, would "probably be the last Indian war of consequence."

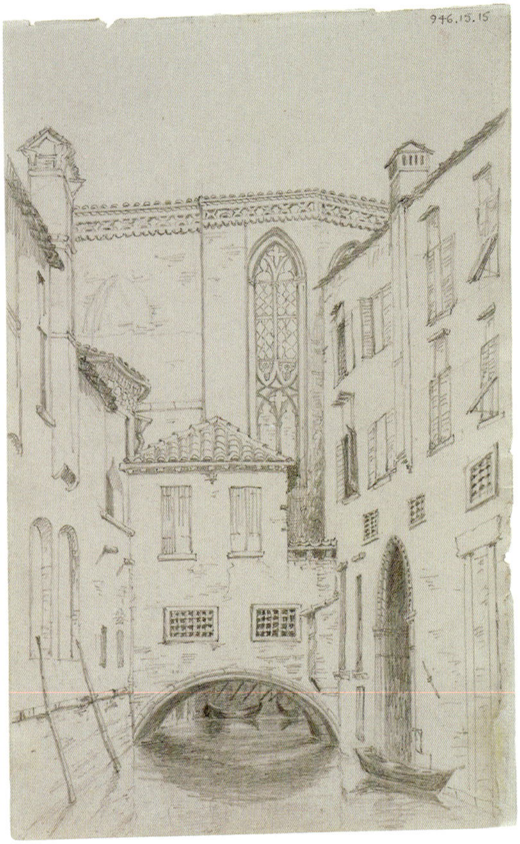

Fig. 25 *Canal Scene*, Paul Kane
Rio del Santissimo and Chiesa di San Stefano from Calle Spezier Venice, Italy; August–September 1842
graphite on paper; 21.5 × 13.8 cm
946.15.15

When Paul Kane left Canada in 1836 for an extended tour of the United States that saw him travel the length of the Mississippi River painting portraits, the Saugeen First Peoples on the shores of Lake Huron surrendered 1.5 million acres of their territory to the British, thereby leaving their land limited to the area of the Bruce Peninsula (Aborigines' Committee 1839, 19–20). Likewise, the same year, in a treaty signed at Cedar Point on the Fox River, the Menominee of Wisconsin ceded four million acres of their land to the United States government, receiving in exchange about seventeen cents an acre (Fay 1970, 23–27; Keesing 1987, 137).

In September 1842, as Paul Kane was sketching on the canals of Venice, Italy (fig. 25) during his own grand tour, *The Hagerstown Mail*, Maryland (September 2, 1842), announced that hostilities had ceased with the Indians in the territory of Florida. Farther north in Wisconsin, the *Wiskonson Enquirer* (September 1, 1842) informed the public about the death of a Menominee woman at the hands of her drunken husband. When the husband became sober he was so distraught he wrapped himself in a blanket and lay down beside his dead wife. He was in that position when his brother-in-law arrived and did to him what he had done to the man's sister. The article ended by expressing regret that the man who had sold the whisky to the Indian was not also one of the dead.

On May 9, 1846, the day Paul Kane left Toronto on a two-year journey for the purpose of sketching the country's Aboriginal peoples, *The Wisconsin Democrat* reported that the Texas House of Representatives had passed a resolution stating that the State of Texas recognized no title to any portion of the State's soil by the Indians living within its boundaries. Additionally, the resolution stated that the State of Texas recognized no right in the Government of the United States to make treaty with the Indians of the State. On November 17, 1848, the same day that *The British Colonist* in Toronto reported on the "truthfulness" of Paul Kane's sketches during this country's first solo art exhibition, the *Alton Telegraph* of Alton, Illinois, wrote about a delegation of twelve Chippewa Indians who were travelling to Washington to meet with the president in a bid to purchase back lands previously ceded to the United States. Their intent, the article stated, was to build homes and cultivate the fields of their reclaimed land and become "industrious citizens of the United States, instead of roaming hunters of the forest."

On January 18, 1856, just as Paul Kane was preparing to deliver his cycle of 100 oil canvases (fig. 26) to his patron, the *New York Daily Times* reported on the "Indian War" taking place in Oregon and Washington. The article stated that the purpose was not so much to win a victory—"that could be easily effected"—but to bring the Indian nation "to such proper subjection that they will respect the law, and leave our settlers unmolested." This conflict, the reporter wrote, will be "the last stand made by the North American Indian against the progress of civilization, and the more determined his resistance the more complete will be his overthrow."

In the month of February, 1871—two days before Paul Kane died of liver disease[3]—it was reported in the *Janesville Gazette*, Wisconsin (February 1, 1871), that President Ulysses S. Grant supported the development of a government structure by the "civilized Indians" of the Indian Territory that would be compatible with the Constitution of the United States. The president stated that this was the first time that the Aboriginal population had expressed desire for an American form of government and, he noted, "it is highly desirable that they become self-sustaining, self relying, Christianized and civilized." Interestingly, it was under this president's watch that five years later the 7th Calvary, under the command of Lieutenant Colonel George Armstrong Custer, charged into a Sioux encampment on the Little Big Horn River, Montana, only to be annihilated (Wilson 2007, 281–97).

This was the world of Paul Kane! Over the course of Paul Kane's life, North America experienced the War of 1812–1814, the Canadian Rebellions of 1837–1838, and the American Civil War (1861–1865), in addition to the Indian wars, such as the Whitman massacre and the Cayuse War (1847–1850), the Dakota War of 1862, and the Battle of Sand Creek (1864). Think also of the arts and literature of that time—Albert Bierstadt, George Caleb Bingham, George Catlin, and Thomas Cole in the arts and Ralph Waldo Emerson, Henry David Thoreau, Herman Melville, and Walt Whitman in literature. And if we were to be invited into Paul Kane's library in his Toronto home on Wellesley Street, we could select from his shelves the *Illustrated Magazine of Art*; volumes of Shakespeare's plays; John Richardson's *Arctic Searching Expedition*; volumes of poetry by Robert Burns and Lord Byron; George Simpson's *Narrative of a Journey around the World*; and Daniel Wilson's *Prehistoric Man*.[4] In the latter, Wilson, professor of History and English Literature at University College, acknowledges the significant contributions of Paul Kane to his own understanding of Canadian Aboriginal culture: "To Mr. Paul Kane, the author of *Wanderings of an Artist among the Indians of North America* for sketches made during his travels, as well as for information derived from recollections of the incidents, and observations of a highly privileged sojourner among the Indian tribes of the Hudson's Bay territory" (Wilson 1862, xv).

It is within the context of the nineteenth century's political, cultural, and artistic worlds that we need to view Paul Kane's art. And one of the most profitable references to that view is in the writing of Margaret Fuller. Fuller was a writer and activist colleague of the transcendentalists, Ralph Waldo Emerson, Henry David Thoreau, and Bronson Alcott. In 1843, while Paul Kane was a portrait artist living in Mobile, Alabama, Fuller journeyed around the Great Lakes. In her book, *Summer on the Lakes*, she describes the journey and laments the decline of the North American Native:

> *Yet, ere they depart, I wish there might be some masterly attempt to reproduce, in art or literature, what is proper to them, a kind of beauty and grandeur which few of the every-day crowd have hearts to feel, yet which ought to leave in the world its monuments, to inspire the thought of genius through all ages. Nothing in this kind has been done masterly* .... ([1844] 1970, 96–97)

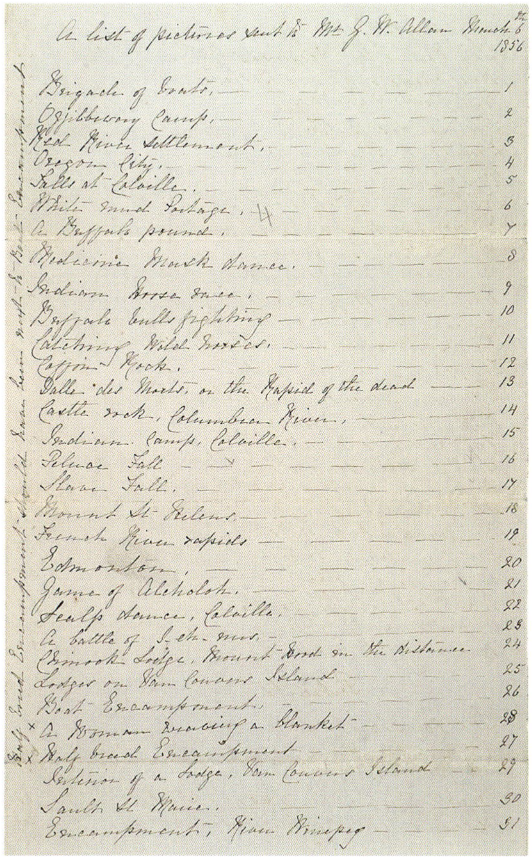
A list of pictures sent to Mr G. W. Allan March 6th 1856

Brigade of Boats, 1
Ojibbeway Camp, 2
Red River Settlement, 3
Oregon City, 4
Falls at Colville, 5
White Mud Portage, 6
A Buffalo pound, 7
Medicine Mask dance, 8
Indian Horse race, 9
Buffalo bulls fighting 10
Catching Wild horses, 11
Coffin Rock, 12
Dalle des Morts, or the Rapid of the dead 13
Castle rock, Columbia River, 14
Indian Camp, Colville, 15
Pelouse Fall 16
Slave Fall, 17
Mount St. Helens, 18
French River rapids 19
Edmonton, 20
Game of Alcholoh, 21
Scalp dance, Colville, 22
A battle of [illegible] 23
Chinook Lodge, Mount Hood in the distance 24
Lodges on Vancouver Island 25
Boat Encampment, 26
A Woman weaving a blanket 28
Half breed Encampment 27
Interior of a Lodge, Vancouver Island 29
Sault St. Marie, 30
Encampment, River Winnipeg 31

Fig. 26 First page of "A List of Pictures Sent to Mr G. W. Allan, March 6, 1856." Prepared by Harriet Kane. Paul Kane collection, ROM. Gift of Raymond A. Willis

That was 1844! By the spring of 1845 Paul Kane was back home in Toronto, and in June of that year he began the first of his two journeys sketching the Aboriginal peoples he met and the landscapes he experienced (see fig. 32). It is not known if Paul Kane read Margaret Fuller's book, or even if he was aware of her "wish"; however, he certainly concurred with her mindset and recognized that Native culture was suffering due to Euro-American advances to take Native lands; pressure to adopt Euro-American beliefs, practices, and government; the social destruction that came with alcohol; and the decline of Native populations caused by diseases. Whether Kane had read Fuller's words or not, he would have been well aware of the news and the social attitudes expressed in the papers.

Thus, in the atmosphere that prompted Margaret Fuller's challenge, he set himself the goal to reproduce in art "what is proper to them" before, as Fuller writes, "they depart."

"excellent ethnographical studies"

> *Kane, . . . we have reason to believe, succeeded in individualizing his Indian likenesses, so that his paintings are excellent ethnographical studies from this point of view as well as from every other. Few artists have displayed the same amount of care in the details of dress and decoration that he was always careful to bring out. It is noticeable that in all his work we find very little that is overcharged with color [sic], and the colors [sic] he does use are as nearly as possible those of the things themselves, that is to say, he made no attempt to idealize in this or in any other respect.*
> (David Boyle quoted in *The Globe*, March 22, 1904)

The above view from David Boyle, archaeologist with the Ontario Provincial Museum, was his response to an exhibition of 100 of Paul Kane's studio oil paintings placed on display in the gallery of William Scott & Sons located at the corner of Yonge and Adelaide streets, Toronto (fig. 27). The exhibition, sponsored by the Woman's Canadian Historical Society of Toronto, with proceeds going to the Victoria Memorial Hall fund, was on display between March 5 and March 19, 1904. This was the first time that all 100 of the paintings in the cycle completed for George William Allan had been available at one time for general public viewing. Titled *Pictures of Indians and Indian Life*, the exhibition of paintings was on loan from the collection of Edmund B. Osler, who had recently purchased the cycle of paintings from Allan's estate.[5] At the opening of the exhibition, Osler was praised by Lieutenant-Governor Mortimer Clark for his "patriotism" in preserving Kane's cycle of paintings in Canada, "when," he stated, "so many individuals and institutions on the United States side of the line would have eagerly bought them up had they the chance" (*The News*, March 1904). The Lieutenant-Governor and David Boyle were of like mind, for Mortimer Clark—we are told in *The News* report—also praised Kane for the "faithfulness" of his art.

Throughout his lifetime and well into the twentieth century, Kane received positive affirmations for his art. Even prior to his return to Toronto from his western journey in October 1848, he received praise for his "masterly delineations." James Douglas, chief factor for the Hudson's Bay Company at Fort Vancouver wrote (June 30, 1847), his "Indian Portraits and

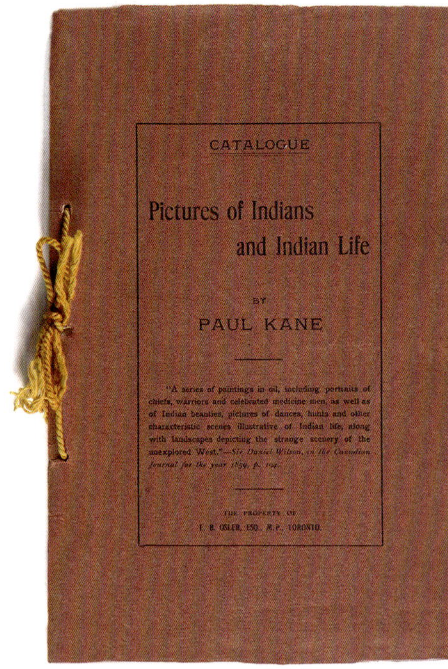

Fig. 27 *Pictures of Indians and Indian Life by Paul Kane*. The Property of E. B. Osler, Esq., M. P., Toronto. This is the cover of the published catalogue for the 1904 exhibition of 100 Paul Kane paintings held at the William Scott & Sons gallery, Toronto.

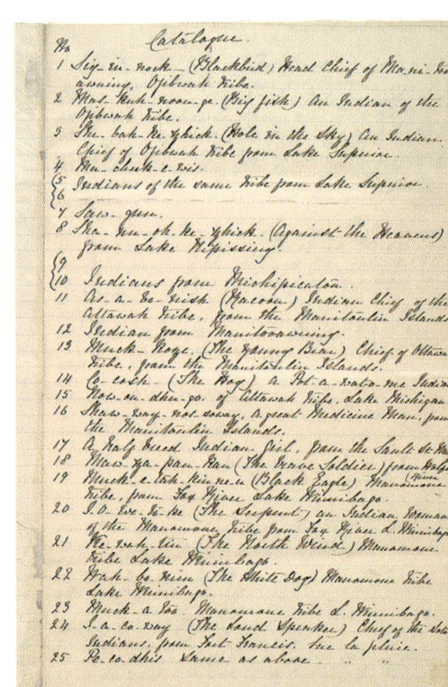
Catalogue

Fig. 28 First page of "Catalogue of Sketches of Indians and Indian Chiefs, Landscapes, Dances, Costumes, &c. &c. by Paul Kane." Toronto, November 1848. Prepared by Harriet Peek Clench. Paul Kane collection, ROM. This catalogue was published by Scobie and Balfour, Toronto (See Kane 1848).

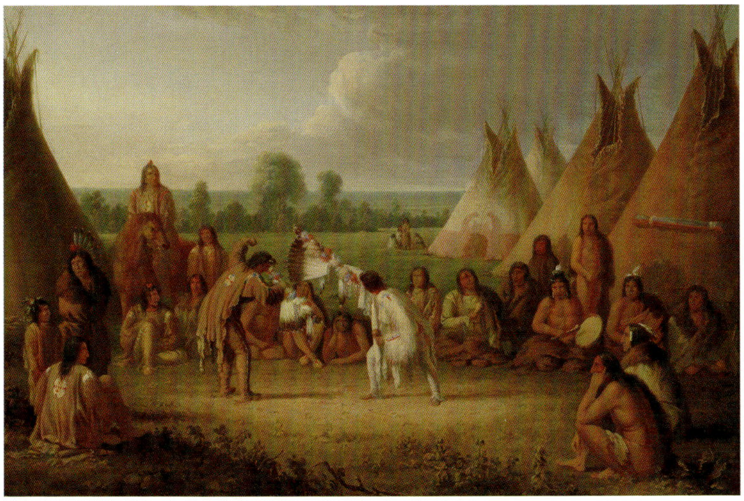

Fig. 29 *Medicine Pipe Stem Dance*
Blackfoot
east of Fort Pitt, North Saskatchewan River, Saskatchewan; 1849–1852
oil on canvas; 48.9 × 74.5 cm
912.1.56

Costumes are perfect and it is impossible to give a better idea, than they convey, of the dress and appearance of the Native inhabitants of this Country" (HBCA E.42/1 fol. 52). One month later (July 30, 1847), William McBean, clerk in charge of Fort Walla Walla in the Columbia District, expressed similar sentiments when he remarked that Kane's landscapes and portraits are "admirably and happily executed, with an exact and strong similitude to the original" (HBCA E.42/1 fol. 54). These praises, undoubtedly given in response to Kane's desire for letters of verification, are akin to the reviews he received in the Toronto press for an exhibition of 240 sketches he placed on display one month after his return (fig. 28). "So very extraordinary and interesting a collection" was the view of the *British Colonist* (November 10, 1848). *The Globe* (November 15, 1848) followed by stating his sketches were "exceedingly well executed" and "perfectly accurate."

This praise is notably similar to the commendation Kane received for the paintings in the 1904 exhibition at the William Scott & Sons gallery. However, the 1904 praise was not for the art that Kane recorded first-hand from direct observation, in sketches of graphite, watercolour, and oil. Rather, that praise—albeit similar in nature—was for the formal studio oil paintings that were inspired by his sketches. Indeed, his studio paintings were being recognized as early as 1851, when a committee of the Legislative Assembly of the Province of Canada granted Kane £500 for twelve paintings inspired by his sketches, "in a style and size best suited to the subject." Referring to Kane as "an Artist of the first merit," the committee visited Kane's Toronto studio and "were highly gratified by the inspection of the splendid Paintings" (Canada 1851, 310).[6] However, it was his display of eight oil paintings at Toronto's Provincial Agricultural Show in 1852 that set the tone for subsequent reviews and attention.[7] Susanna Moodie, in her book *Life in the Clearings*, praised Kane's paintings by stating, "For correctness of design, beauty of colouring, and a faithful representation of the peculiar scenery of this continent they could scarcely be surpassed" ([1853] 1959, 237). *The North American* (September 17, 1852) praised Kane's "finely executed Indian scenes" and the review in *The Canadian Journal of Industry, Science, and Art* (1852, 60–61) highlighted Kane's "eight beautiful paintings" and granted him foremost status in redeeming the "distressing mediocrity of a large proportion of the contributions" on display. Finally, the *Anglo-American Magazine* (1852), in a review that commented on all eight paintings individually, praised Kane's eye for composition, such as the "harmony" and care in rendering the foreground in *Medicine Pipe Stem Dance* (fig. 29); his colouring, characterized as "very correct and chaste" in *White Mud Portage* (fig. 81); the details that are "skilfully and truthfully represented in *Indian Horse Race* (fig. 86); and his depictions of Indian customs, such as in *Flat Head Woman and Child, Caw-wacham* (fig. 30).

George William Allan sent four paintings from his Paul Kane collection to the Paris Exhibition of 1855, including *Six Black Feet Chiefs* (fig. 31). Although the Canadian report from the Exhibition was not enthusiastic about Canada's art contributions, an exception was made for Kane's work stating that his paintings were "a remarkably interesting

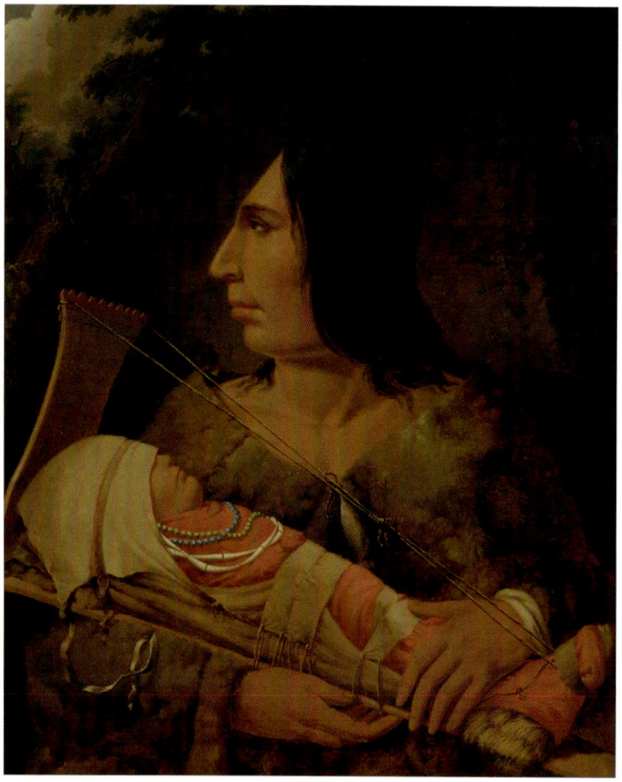

Fig. 30 *Flat Head Woman and Child, Caw-wacham*
Cowlitz
Cowlitz Farm region, Cowlitz River, Washington
1849–1852
oil on canvas; 75.9 × 63.3 cm
912.1.80

collection of views and scenery of western America" (Taché 1856, 202). In the *New York Daily Times* (February 27, 1855), the correspondent agreed, noting the general "mediocrity" of the Canadian art submissions with the exception of "representations of Indian life" by Paul Kane. Daniel Wilson, in his review of Kane's *Wanderings of an Artist*, noted that through his art Kane showed "a keen appreciation of every striking minutiae of detail" (1859, 187), emulating the 1852 *Anglo-American Magazine* review that stated, "nothing short of the most intimate acquaintance with each subject" could have "produced the accuracy of detail with such striking effect of light and shade" (1852, 372). In a letter to Daniel Wilson following Kane's death, in 1871, George William Allan submitted the opinion that Kane's portraits were "painted with great vigour and spirit" and "his landscapes are very carefully and well painted" (1871, 4). He also described Kane's paintings as "truthful." Thirty-three years later the *Toronto Daily Star* (March 5, 1904) concurred and, foreshadowing David Boyle's testimony relating to the exhibition in the William Scott & Sons gallery, reported that from an "ethnological standpoint" Kane's paintings "are of the greatest importance."

Kane's oil paintings, however, did not totally escape criticism from those who saw in them the characteristics of the Old World. Nicolas Davin, writing in 1877, opined that Kane's oil paintings did not portray the "glory and beauty of Canadian landscape": "The Indian horses are Greek horses; the hills have much of the colour and form of those of Ruysdael,[8] and the early European landscape painters; the foregrounds have more of the characteristics of old pictures than of our out-of-doors" (Davin 1877, 616). But this was also noticed much earlier by the reviewer for the *The Canadian Journal of Industry, Science, and Art* (1852, 60) who, in a review of the eight paintings Kane displayed at the 1852 Provincial Agricultural Show, commented upon the artist's "fondness for browns and yellows, which threatens to give a monotony to his otherwise most spirited and faithful pencil." Curiously, this is at odds with Susanna Moodie's review of the same paintings where she expresses exuberance over their "beauty of colouring" ([1853] 1959, 237).[9] But, George William Allan himself also lamented Kane's tendency toward the sombre colours: "There is a great predominance of light browns & yellows the foregrounds are often weak and there is a certain sameness in tone and colouring which I attribute to their being painted in the studio from his sketches instead of out of doors on the spot" (1871, 5).

Notwithstanding Kane's affinity for browns and yellows and his portrayal of traits that reflect on the European-art tradition, in the views of his critics the "truthfulness" of his art was not affected. The Canadian artist Charles W. Jefferys, quoted by Lawrence J. Burpee in the introduction to the 1925 edition of Kane's *Wanderings of an Artist* (and reprinted in subsequent editions), noted that the atmosphere of Kane's paintings is "essentially European" and the "actions and gestures" of his Indian subjects are "conventional" (Burpee 1968, xliv); however, Jefferys goes on to state that even in the light of these "conventions and limitations," Kane's paintings represent "authentic records":

> *But with all of these conventions and limitations, he possesses an original and personal quality, he has much genuine poetry, he reveals an accurate observation of facial type, of details of costume, of geological structure and natural growth; and the technical excellence of his pictures elevates these authentic records to the rank of works of art.*

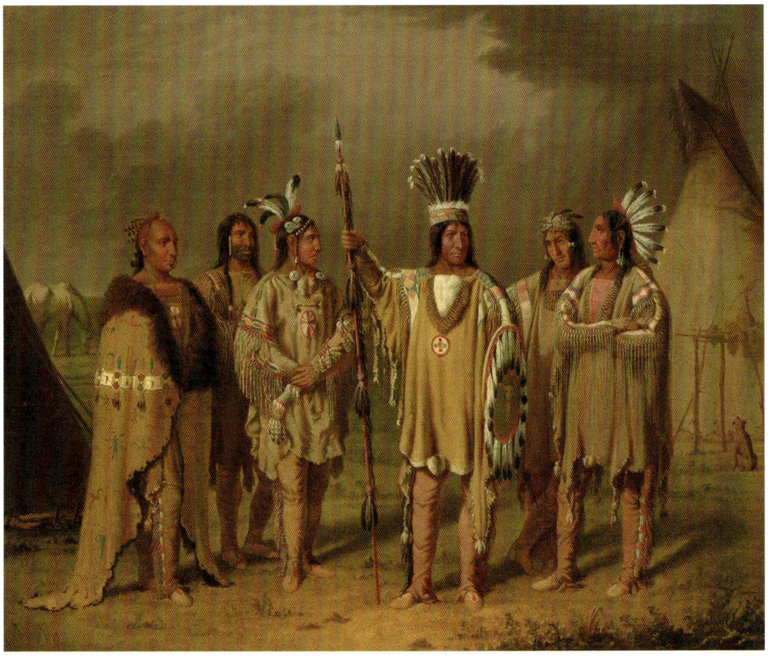

Fig. 31 *Six Black Feet Chiefs*
Blackfoot
Fort Pitt region, North Saskatchewan River, Saskatchewan
1849–1855
oil on canvas; 65.5 × 78.5 cm
912.1.50

G. W. Allan wrote in a letter to Daniel Wilson: "Several of his paintings from my collection I allowed to be sent to the . . . Paris Exhibition and they attracted a good deal of attention there—especially a group of Blackfeet Flathead and Blood Indians which I think is one the best things he ever painted." (Allan 1871, 5–6)

Jefferys, and like-minded critics, saw beyond the convention and recognized that the landscapes Kane painted with romantic skies and the portraits he rendered as from an academic studio were from the witness of his era. Convention, despite its perceived limitations, does not belie beauty and humanity.

"I don't think Kane had much imagination."

> *His portraits of Indian Chiefs and members of different tribes both male and female are painted with vigour and spirit, and are I imagine very truthful for I don't think Kane had much imagination but he most faithfully and accurately represented what he saw whether in portraiture or landscape.* (Allan 1871, 5)

In his 1871 letter to Daniel Wilson, George William Allan expressed the opinion that Kane's studio paintings were "truthful." The intrigue of his statement is that Allan's view was not based on in-depth knowledge of the art in his possession, but rather on his perceived understanding of the man. "I don't think Kane had much imagination," he wrote, and to him this character trait portended the truthfulness of Kane's art. Allan, though, was the one man with the ability to understand the nature of Kane's art; in 1871 he possessed Kane's cycle of 100 studio paintings, as well as his total collection of field sketches. Kane wrote in the preface to *Wanderings of an Artist* that his series of studio paintings commissioned by George William Allan were "executed" from his field sketches;[10] therefore, the truthfulness of his oil paintings could be gauged through sketch-to-oil-painting comparisons. Although Allan and his family were in the best position to objectively confirm the "truthfulness" of Kane's paintings, it seems that this potential endeavour was not realized. The opportunity was lost in 1901 when Allan died, with the paintings subsequently sold to Edmund Osler. At that time, the collection of sketches remaining with the Allan family was separated from the oil paintings.[11] Osler donated the Allan collection of 100 Kane paintings to the Royal Ontario Museum in 1912, but the sketches stayed in the private possession of the Allan family. After 1848, when Kane displayed 240 of them in a public exhibition, his field sketches remained largely unknown and unseen until Allan's great-grandson, Raymond Willis, made them publicly available in 1946 by donating them to the ROM.[12]

To gauge Kane's art is to gauge his truthfulness. As Brian Dippie notes with reference to the art of George Catlin—

Kane's contemporary and perhaps inspiration[13]—there was little critical distance between the art and the subject (2007, 22). The subject was Kane's objective and the recognition of his faithful renderings was the measure of his art.

The title of this essay, "Leaves from an American Plant," is the last phrase written in the *Anglo-American Magazine* review of the eight Paul Kane paintings displayed at the 1852 Provincial Agricultural Show (1852, 374). The reviewer used the phrase to solidify—in the minds of his readers—Kane's work in the North American narrative. Indeed, Kane's sketches, his oil paintings, and his book—*Wanderings of an Artist*—representing his main contributions to the record of mid-nineteenth century Native culture and landscape are wholly American. But this story is not only about Kane. This essay began by placing Kane within the context of Euro-American and Native relations. This was the world within which Kane found his calling. Reviews of Kane's work, and especially those that espoused the truthfulness of his art, were reflections of a larger desire to record and preserve the peoples and the lifeways of cultures that were changing due to foreign pressures. Kane's supporters, such as the Hudson's Bay Company, and his patrons, such as the Canadian Parliament and George William Allan, were instrumental in helping Kane realize his vision. Philanthropy, as espoused by Edmund Osler and Raymond Willis, preserved the record that can now be analyzed and measured against the views of our predecessors. To adapt the metaphor, all of these elements are leaves in an American narrative rooted in Paul Kane's story of travel, art, historical documentation, exhibition, patronage, philanthropy, and museum preservation, display, and study. "Leaves from an American plant" encompasses the celebration of Kane's successful struggle and years of dedicated work; the recognition of his contribution to the documentation of Native life and the North American landscape; the vision of those who saw his work worthy of preservation and provided for its realization; and the continuing significance of his art. This art commands our attention, reveals beauty and grace, and, through new and continued study, instructs our history.

Notes

1 George William Allan (1822–1901) was a lawyer called to the bar in 1846. Over the length of his career, he was an alderman, mayor of Toronto (in 1855), chancellor of Trinity College (between 1877 and 1901), and president of the Western Canada Savings and Loan Company. He served in the Legislative Council of Canada and in the Senate, where he was Speaker between 1888 and 1891, and as commissioner of the Canada Land Company. Allan was also Paul Kane's principal patron and was recognized by Kane in the dedication to his book, *Wanderings of an Artist* (see Cassels 2010 for a discussion of the relationship between the artist and the Allan family).

2 For a discussion of Paul Kane's chronology and family history, see P. J. Kane 2010.

3 In the 1871 Census of Canada, "Liver Complaint" is written under "Disease, or other cause of Death."

4 Copy of "Inventory" of Paul Kane's Estate, Surrogate Court, Country of York, Number 1336, 1872. Paul Kane collection, Royal Ontario Museum.

5 Sir Edmund Boyd Osler (1845–1924) was a large influence in the founding of the Royal Ontario Museum. He was president of the Dominion Bank, director of the Canadian Pacific Railroad, and a conservative representative for West Toronto in the House of Commons (see Cassels 2010, 43 note 115).

6 The paintings that Kane completed for the Canadian Parliament were initially intended for display in the Library of the Legislature. They have now been transferred to the collection of the National Gallery of Canada. See Cassels 2010, 41 note 67, for a discussion of this commission and Kane's relationship with the Legislative Assembly of the Province of Canada.

7 The eight paintings that Kane placed on display at the Provincial Agricultural Show were *The Midday Woman*; *A Sketch on Lake Huron* (see figs. 76 and 79); *Buffalo Bulls Fighting; A Buffalo Pound* (fig. 44); *Flat Head Woman and Child, Caw-wacham* (fig. 30); *Indian Horse Race* (fig. 86); *Medicine Pipe Stem Dance* (fig. 29); and *White Mud Portage* (fig. 81).

8 Jacob van Ruisdael (c.1628–1682), Dutch landscape painter.

9 David Boyle likewise would not agree. See his statement that opened this section.

10 "A much more extensive series of oil paintings had been executed by me, from my sketches, for George W. Allan, Esq., of Moss Park, the liberal patron of Canadian art" (Kane 1859, ix–x).

11 As part of the commission that George William Allan gave to Kane, Allan received Kane's total collection of field sketches. This collection remained intact until 1887 when, at the request of Kane's widow, Harriet Kane (née Clench), Allan agreed to return 221 sketches to the Kane family. These sketches remained in the Kane family until Paul Kane III of Winnipeg sold them to H. J. Lutcher Stark of Texas in 1957. They are now in the Paul Kane collection at the Stark Museum of Art, Orange, Texas (see MacLaren 1997).

12 An exception occurred in 1922, when Paul Kane III—who had the Kane family sketches in his possession—placed 196 of the sketches on display in the Art Gallery of the Board of Trade Building, Winnipeg (HBCA MG 14 C23/2/42).

13 In the 1830s, the American painter George Catlin (1796–1872) travelled in the Great Lakes and Midwest regions painting Native peoples also with the belief that North America's indigenous peoples would soon disappear. During the early 1840s, Catlin displayed his paintings in a variety of English towns and it is possible that Kane had the opportunity to view Catlin's "Indian Gallery" before returning to America in 1843.

THE EXHIBITION:

THE FIRST BRUSH: PAUL KANE AND INFRARED REFLECTOGRAPHY

Kenneth R. Lister

The exhibition looks into Paul Kane's thinking and artistic processes between the years 1849 and 1856 as he painted in his Toronto studio. Divided into four sections, and exhibited over four separate periods, the exhibition first explores the issue of truthfulness in Kane's art ("'to paint their likenesses': Great Lakes to North Saskatchewan River" and "'to paint their likenesses': Columbia River to Vancouver Island") and then his struggle for composition ("a most faithful representation"). In the last section, the exhibition delves into comparisons between painted versions of the same scene and reveals the initial painting and the copy ("out of a series of Paintings"). Additionally, these comparisons expose Kane's response to external pressures, as well as his steadfastness to a realized vision.

The titles for the exhibition sections are drawn from the writings of Kane and his patrons. In *Wanderings of an Artist* (1859, 62) Kane writes that he was met by Native peoples who arrived to see the artist who "made Indians" and was travelling "to paint their likenesses." George William Allan (1871, 6), in a letter to Daniel Wilson following Kane's death, wrote of the value of Kane's cycle of paintings as "a most faithful representation" of peoples and a country that were rapidly changing. And finally, "out of a series of Paintings" is a phrase taken from the *Journals of the Legislative Assembly of the Province of Canada* (Canada 1856, 556) wherein Kane's justification for his tardy completion of the Canadian Parliament commission was detailed as a concern over copyright.

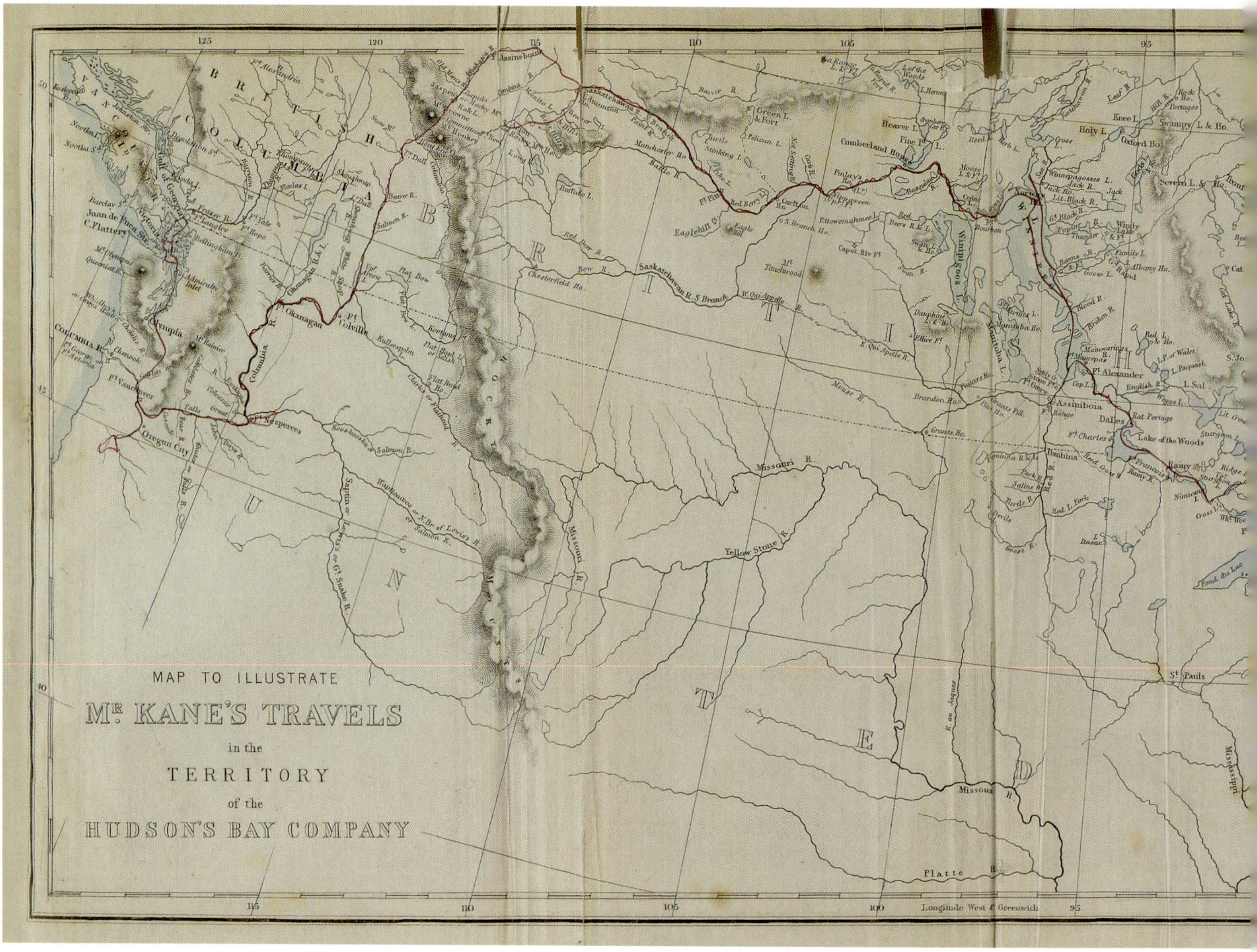

Fig. 32 Map of routes taken by Paul Kane during his 1845–1848 journeys. Published in *Wanderings of an Artist*, 1859.

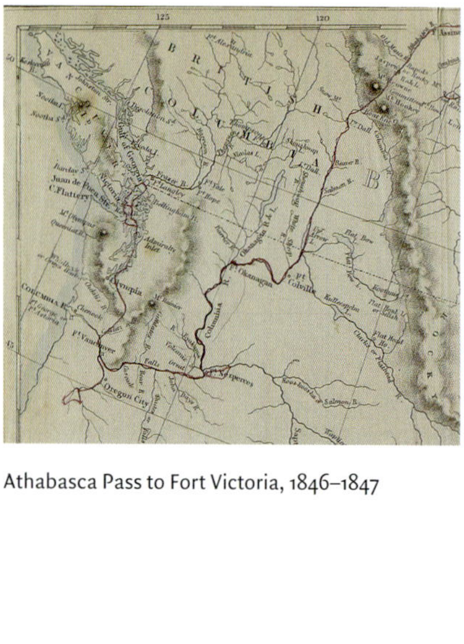

Athabasca Pass to Fort Victoria, 1846–1847

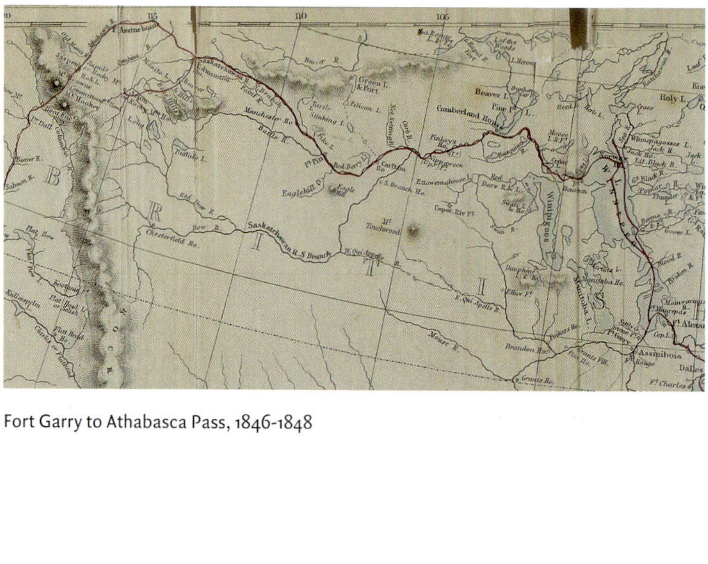

Fort Garry to Athabasca Pass, 1846-1848

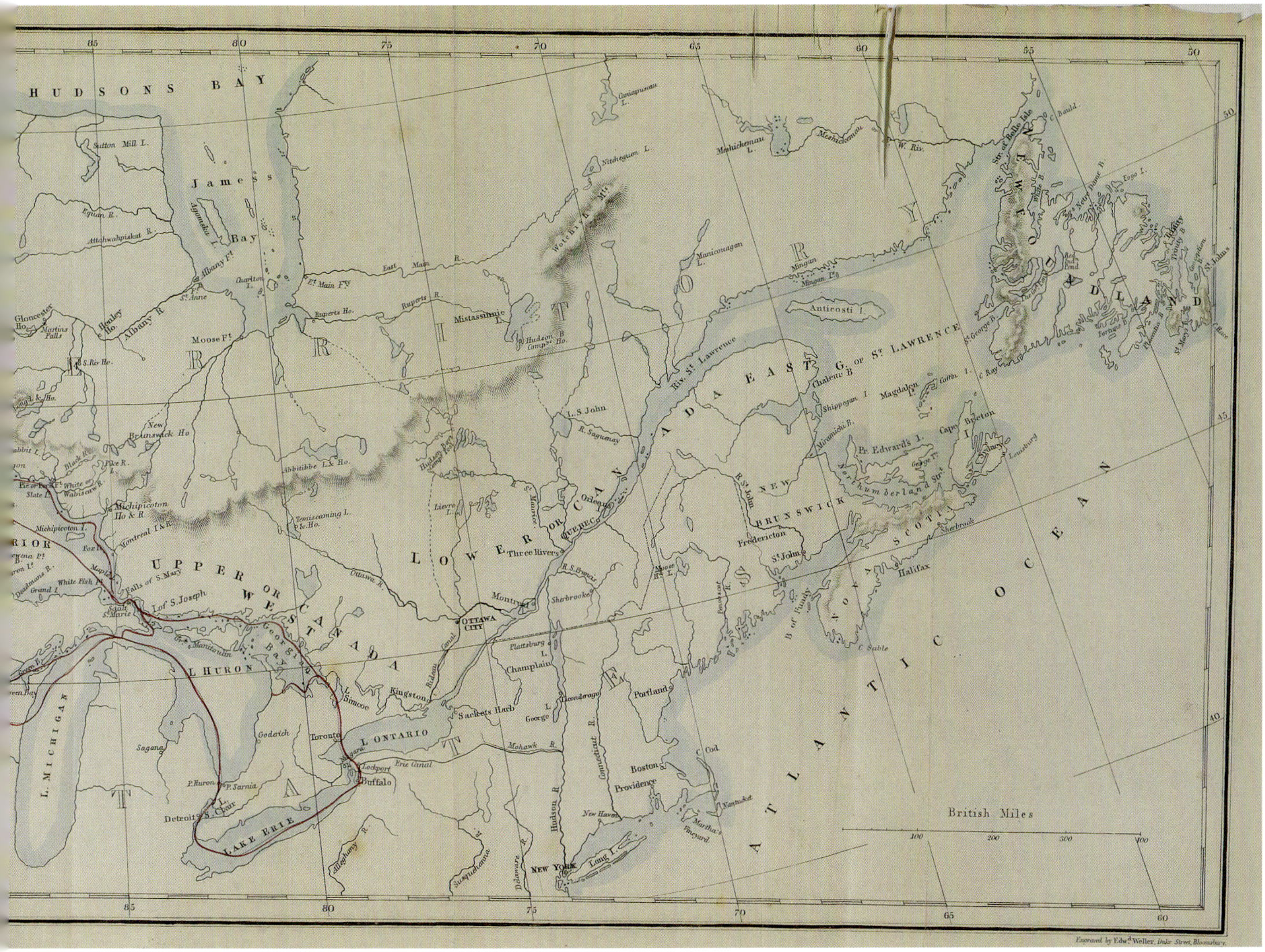

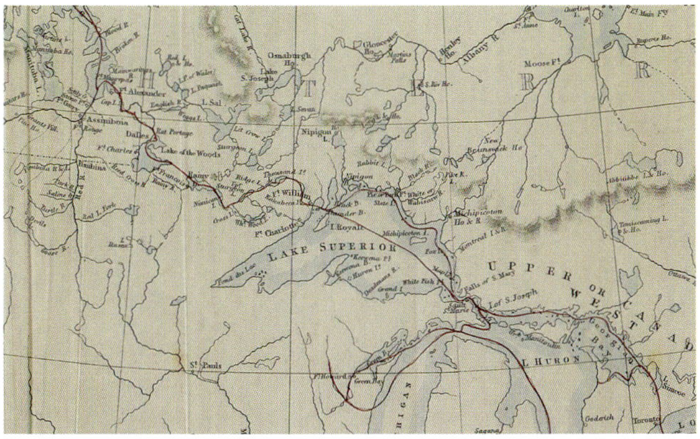

Sault Ste. Marie to Fort Garry, 1846 and 1848

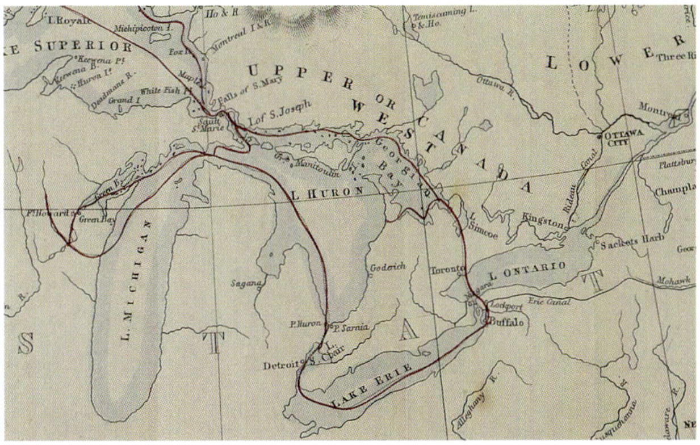

Great Lakes, 1845

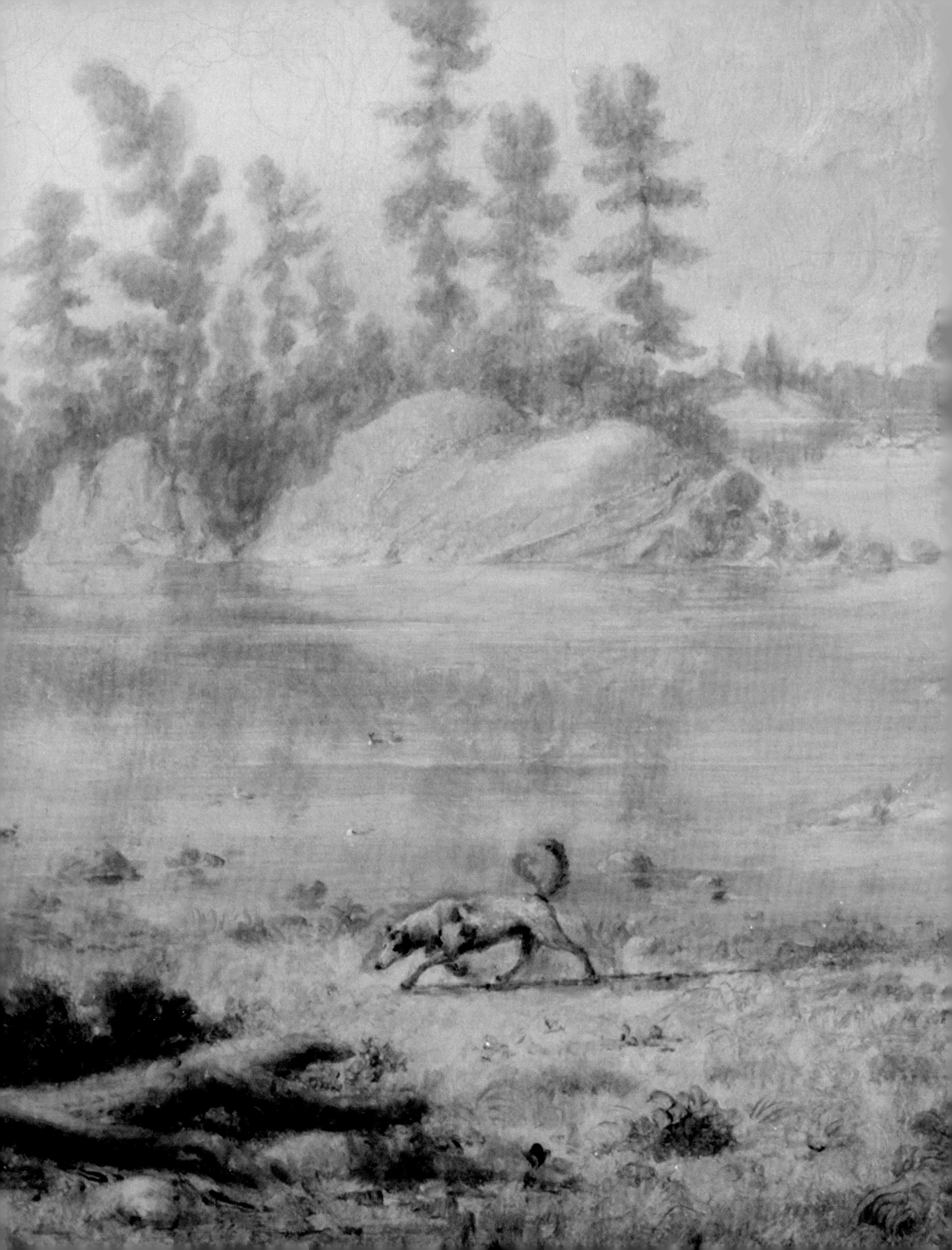

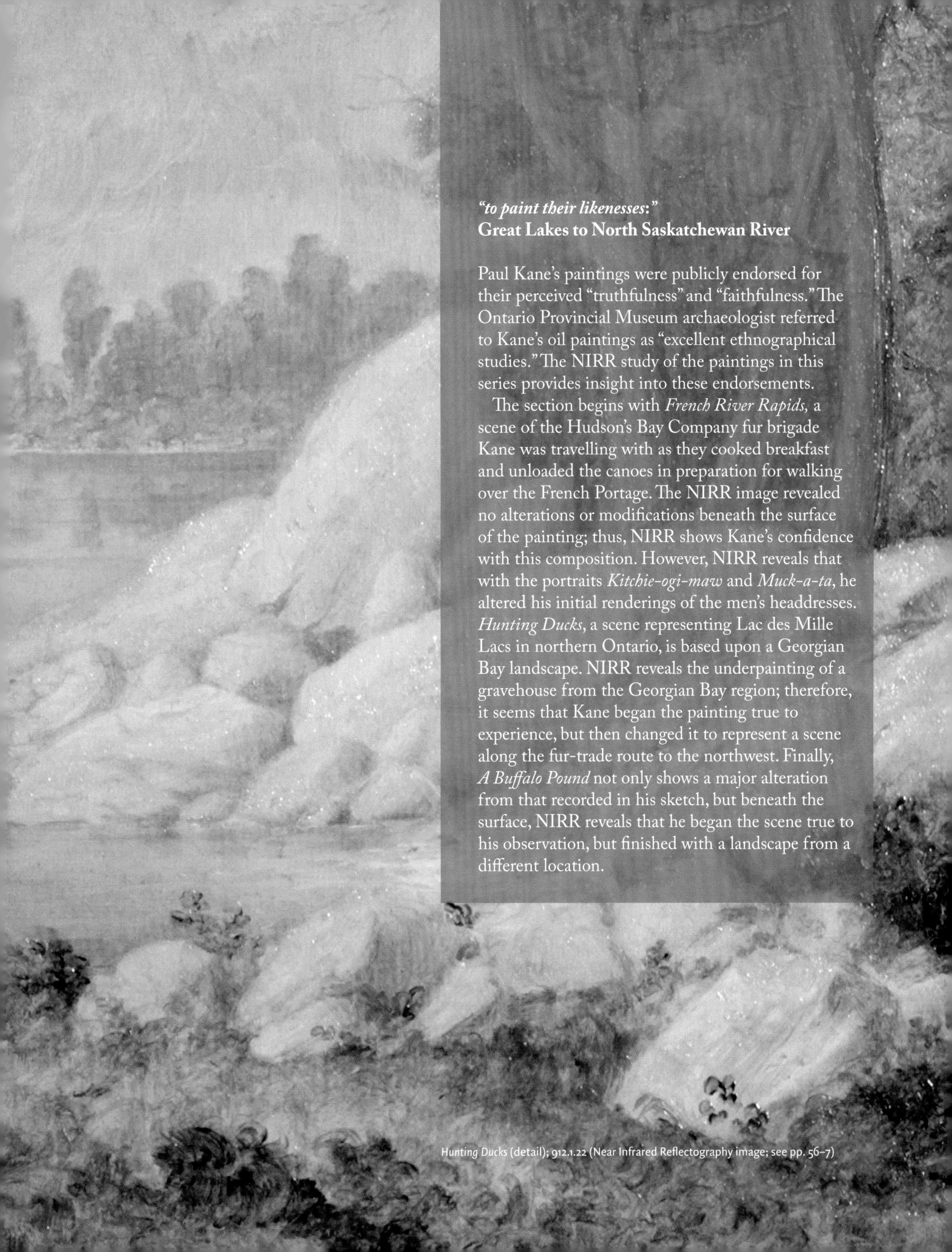

"to paint their likenesses:" Great Lakes to North Saskatchewan River

Paul Kane's paintings were publicly endorsed for their perceived "truthfulness" and "faithfulness." The Ontario Provincial Museum archaeologist referred to Kane's oil paintings as "excellent ethnographical studies." The NIRR study of the paintings in this series provides insight into these endorsements.

The section begins with *French River Rapids,* a scene of the Hudson's Bay Company fur brigade Kane was travelling with as they cooked breakfast and unloaded the canoes in preparation for walking over the French Portage. The NIRR image revealed no alterations or modifications beneath the surface of the painting; thus, NIRR shows Kane's confidence with this composition. However, NIRR reveals that with the portraits *Kitchie-ogi-maw* and *Muck-a-ta*, he altered his initial renderings of the men's headdresses. *Hunting Ducks*, a scene representing Lac des Mille Lacs in northern Ontario, is based upon a Georgian Bay landscape. NIRR reveals the underpainting of a gravehouse from the Georgian Bay region; therefore, it seems that Kane began the painting true to experience, but then changed it to represent a scene along the fur-trade route to the northwest. Finally, *A Buffalo Pound* not only shows a major alteration from that recorded in his sketch, but beneath the surface, NIRR reveals that he began the scene true to his observation, but finished with a landscape from a different location.

Hunting Ducks (detail); 912.1.22 (Near Infrared Reflectography image; see pp. 56–7)

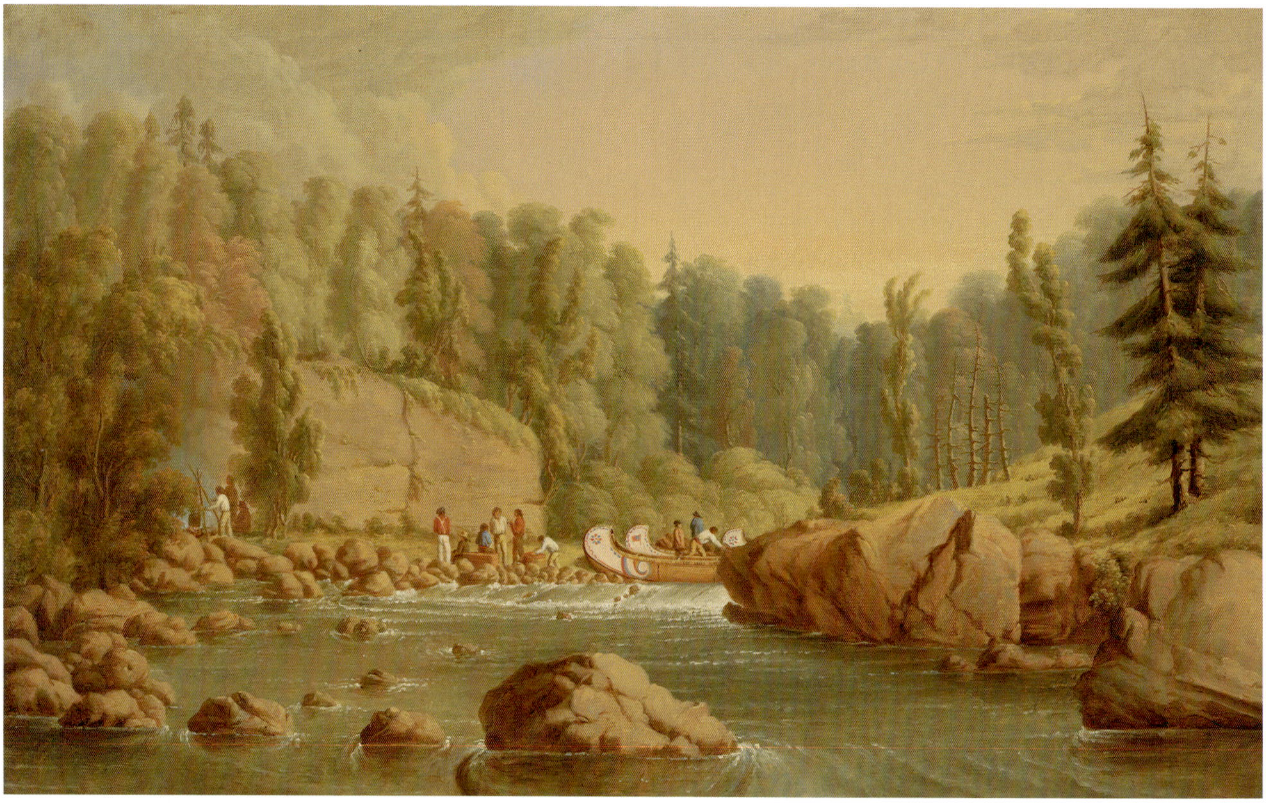

Fig. 33 *French River Rapids*
Hudson's Bay Company brigade
French River at the eastern end of the French Portage, northern Ontario
1849–1856
oil on canvas; 45.9 × 73.8 cm
912.1.2

May 30th. We made an early start, reaching the "French Portage" by breakfast-time. Here we lightened the canoes of the principal part of the baggage, and carried it across the portage, a distance of three miles, in order that we might be able to send the canoes round by the river, which had now become very shallow, to meet us at the further end of the portage. (Kane 1859, 57–58)

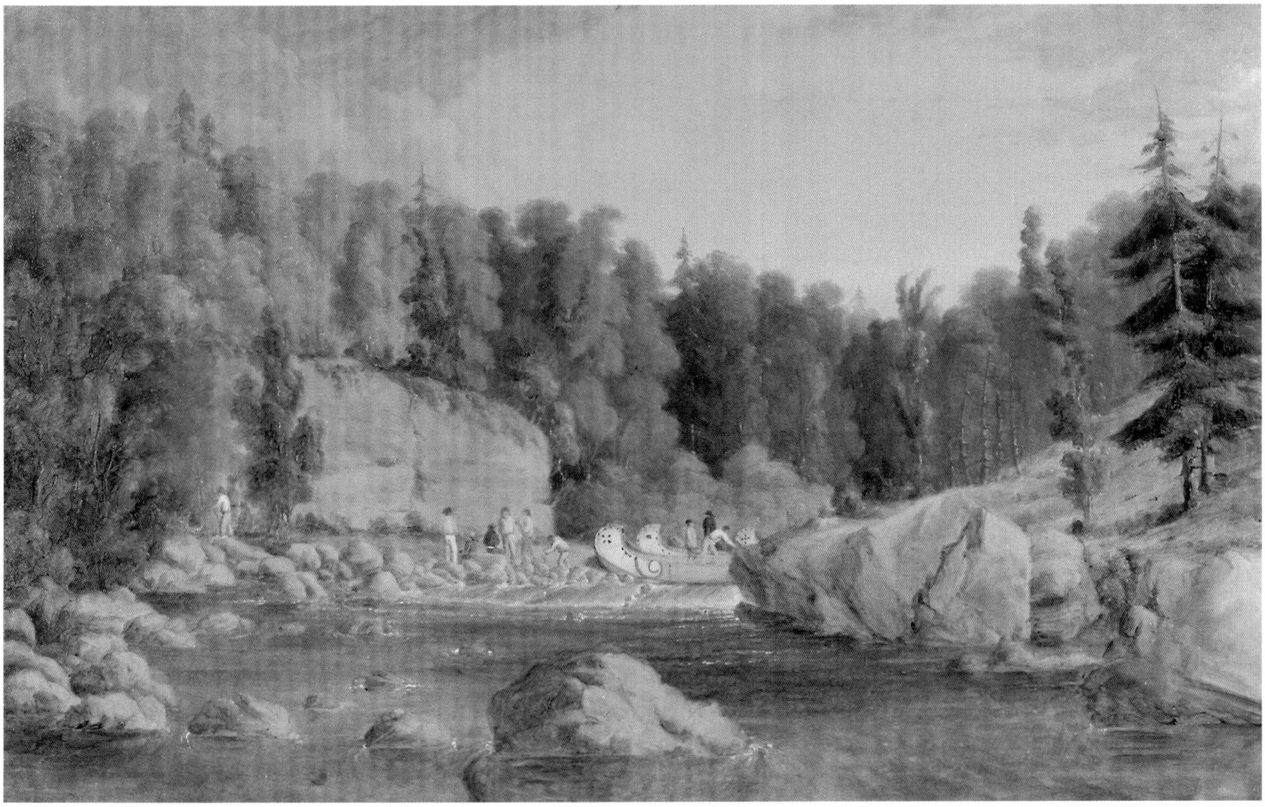

Fig. 34

Kane shows his confidence with this composition as the NIRR image reveals no alterations or modifications.

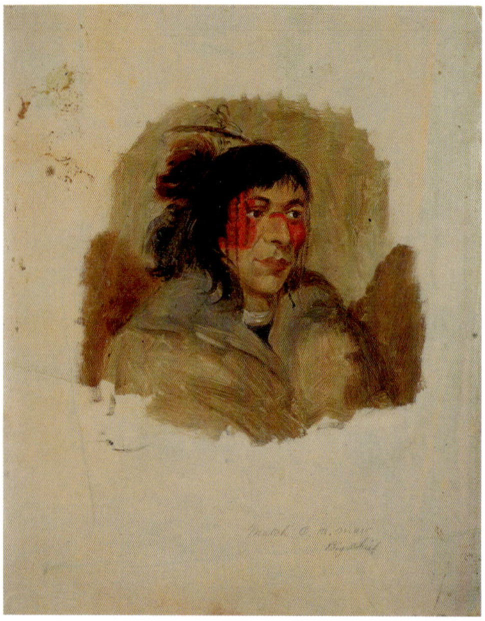

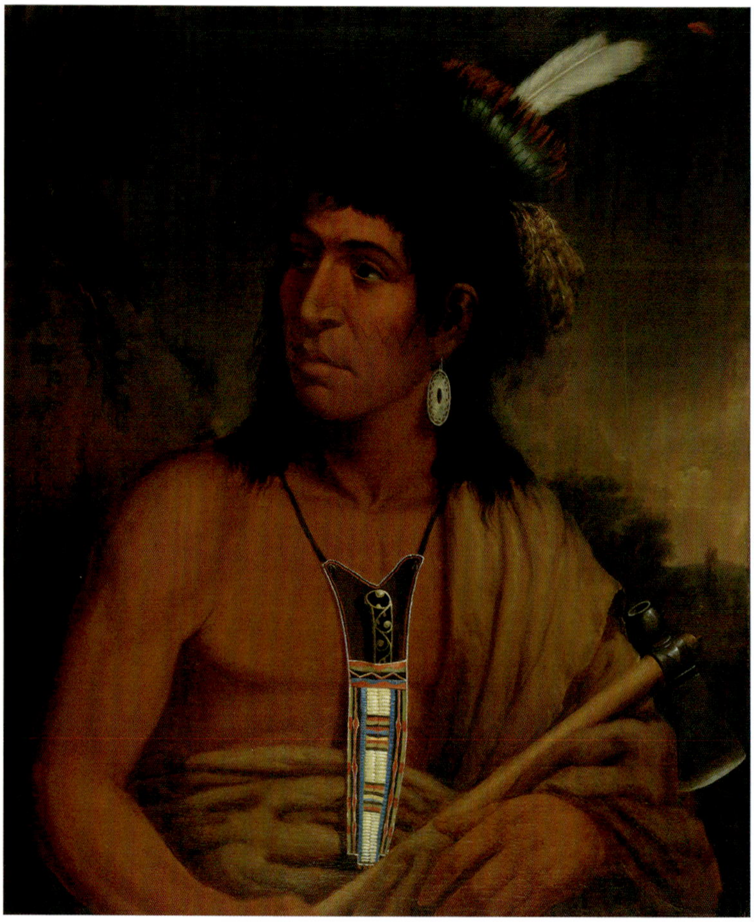

Fig. 35 (Top) *Match-o-kee-maw or "Big Chief"*
Menominee; Fox River, Wisconsin
mid–late September 1845
oil on paper; 31.4 × 24.8 cm
Stark Museum of Art, Orange, Texas
31.78.142

Fig. 36 (Right) *Kitchie-ogi-maw*
Menominee; Fox River, Wisconsin
1849–1856
oil on canvas; 76.1 × 63.5 cm
912.1.11

> *Among other Indians whose likeness I took, is that of Kitchie-ogi-maw, or, "the Great Chief," a Manomanee, who was celebrated among his tribe for many acts of daring.* (Kane 1859, 36)

In 1845, when Paul Kane paddled up the Fox River to witness the Menominee receiving their treaty payments, they had already signed a number of treaties ceding land to the United States government. In 1836, by the Treaty of the Cedars, more than four million acres were ceded and just three years after Kane's visit the Menominee sold all of their remaining Wisconsin lands (Beck 2002, 96–173; Fay 1970; Hoffman 1896, 20–31; Ourada 1979, xi). Thus, by the mid-nineteenth century, the Menominee were responding to American influences as witnessed by treaty payments that included clothing, livestock, and farm equipment, in addition to the grist and saw mills built for their benefit on the Fox River (Fay 1970, 10).

Kane spent three weeks during the fall of 1845 among the Menominee and witnessed the bustle of the treaty payment period that included opportunistic traders displaying their "finery" (Kane 1859, 32). During these weeks he had the opportunity to sketch a number of portraits providing a record of clothing styles and adornment.

Based upon fieldwork among the Menominee in the early twentieth century, Alanson Skinner (1921, 109–13) describes three types of men's headdresses: bands of fur often embellished with rosettes of beads and eagle feathers;

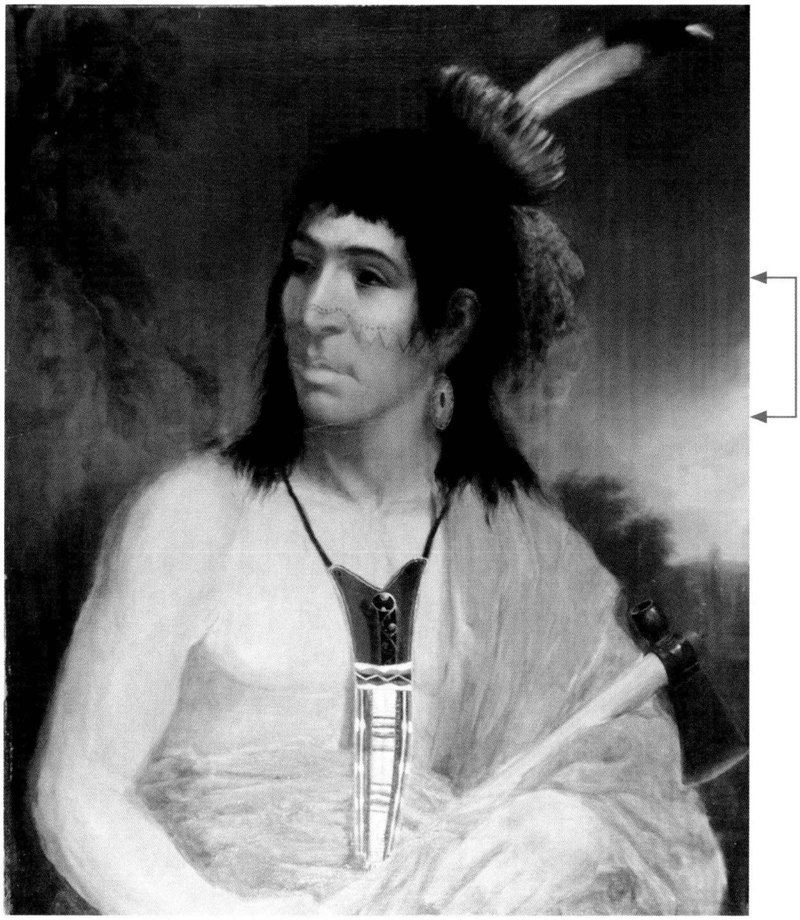

Fig. 37

a yarn sash twisted around the brow adorned with feathers; and a crest or roach of dyed deer hair. Although Skinner was among the Menominee sixty years after Kane, and their lifeways, clothing, and adornment had changed considerably over those years, Kane's images, in addition to portraits by other nineteenth-century artists, such as James Otto Lewis (Horan 1972, 351), Charles Bird King (Viola 1976, 77, 100), and George Catlin (Truettner 1979, 203–7), nevertheless corroborate Skinner's observations.

The headdress type illustrated by Kane is a roach of dyed hair where the hair is made to spread and stand erect through the addition of a bone, antler, or silver spreader. Often an eagle feather, as shown in the painting, is held upright by a bone tube attached to the roach spreader (Skinner 1921, 111–13). In the painting, Kane embellishes the back of the head with a cluster of feathers attached to the bottom edge of the roach. This addition seems to be unusual when compared to other nineteenth-century depictions, although it is important to note that Kane does include such a cluster of feathers in his field sketch of the subject. The NIRR image shows the cluster of back feathers to have been originally more extensive; Kane later chose to shorten its length by merging the end portion into the background sky.

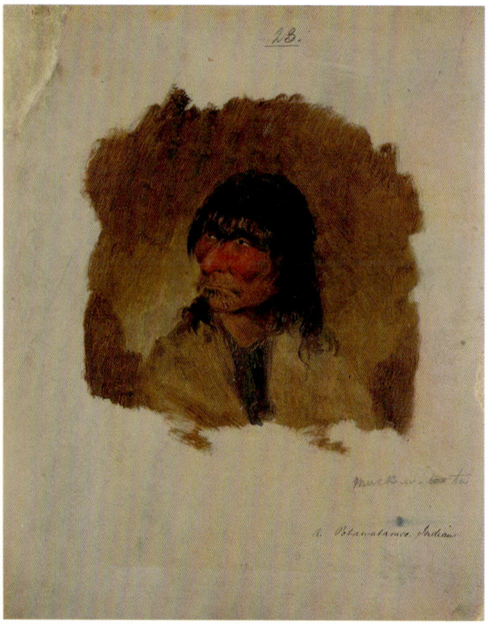

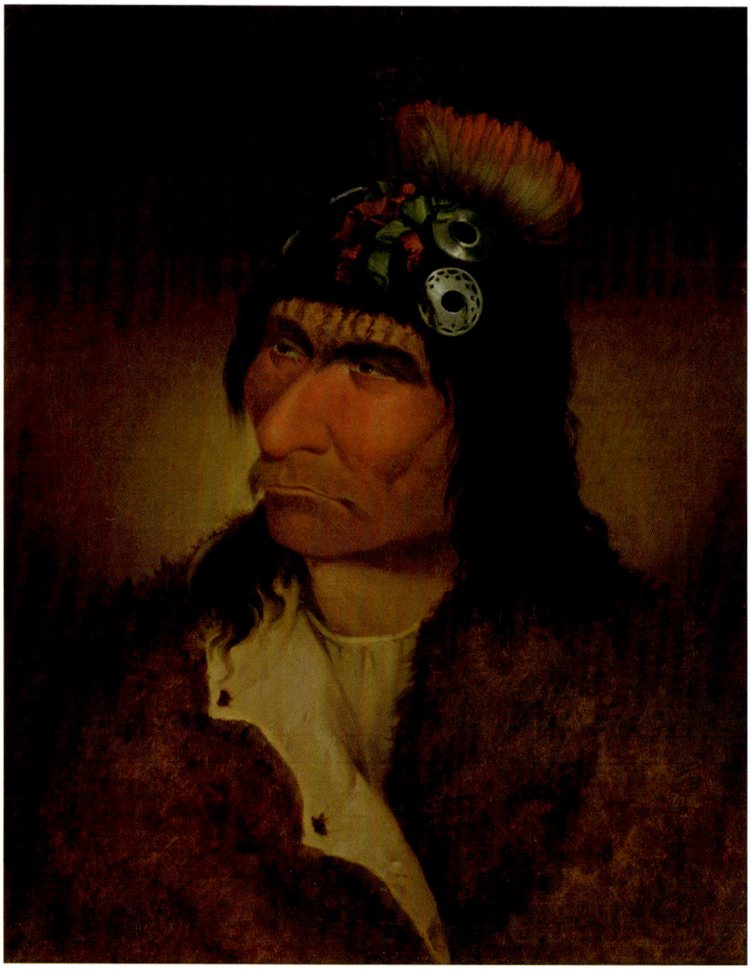

Fig. 38 (Top) Muck-a-ta
Menominee; Fox River, Wisconsin
mid–late September 1845
oil on paper; 31.1 × 24.4 cm
Stark Museum of Art, Orange, Texas
31.78.180

Fig. 39 (Right) Muck-a-ta
Menominee; Fox River, Wisconsin
1849–1856
oil on canvas; 63.5 × 50.8 cm
912.1.12

> *Hearing that I was taking sketches of the most noted Indians in the camp, a fellow named Muck-a-ta paid me a visit. He was one of the most ill favoured of any that had been the subjects of my pencil, and by all accounts his physiognomy did not belie his character.*
> (Kane 1859, 40–41)

Kane's portrait of Muck-a-ta is notable for the ribbons flowing down the subject's forehead and for the round silver brooches embellishing his hair. Silver ornaments in a variety of forms—ring brooch, round brooch, heart-shaped brooch, star brooch, cross, Masonic emblem—were created for the fur trade by European and colonial silversmiths. Often these adornments were worn in quantity on jackets and dresses, headdresses and sashes, and in the hair (Fredrickson and Gibb 1980).

As in his portrait of Kitchie-ogi-maw, Kane shows Muck-a-ta wearing a dyed-hair roach although in this portrait the erect eagle feather and the cluster of back feathers are missing. It is interesting to note also that Kane's field sketch of Muck-a-ta shows him without the hair embellishments of ribbons, silver brooches, or roach.

Comparison of Kane's field sketch of Muck-a-ta to his studio painting shows Kane to have followed the sketch closely in rendering the subject's orientation, facial characteristics and expression, face paint, and hair style. The hair ornamentation of coloured ribbons and silver brooches along with the dyed-hair roach, however, were added to the studio painting. Although Kane did not record his field subject wearing such

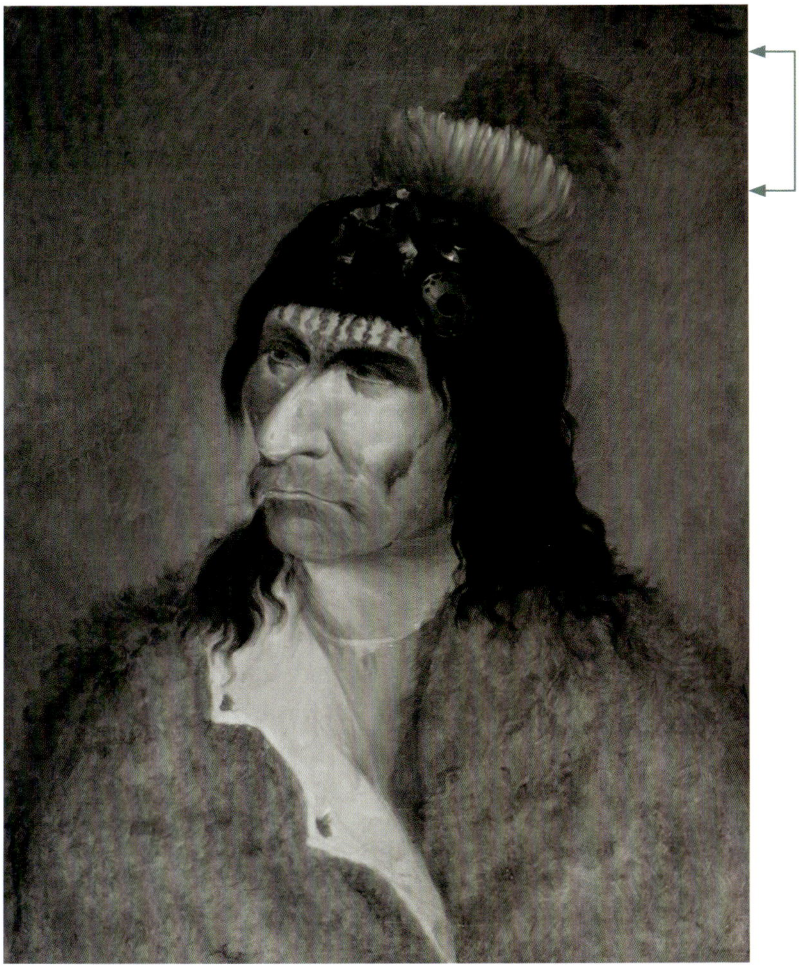

Fig. 40

ornamentation, by reference to some of Kane's other sketches of Menominee subjects, embellishments of ribbons, silver, and the hair roach were clearly observed, and thus he was being accurate culturally, if not accurate to this specific subject.

In the finished studio painting, the hair roach is shown simply as dyed hair spread open and erect. The upright eagle feather and additional cluster of back feathers, such as rendered in the *Kitchie-ogi-maw* painting, are not included and the NIRR image of the painting indicates that Kane did not initially intend to include these elements. He did, however, initially paint a cluster of feathers extending out of the central section of the roach. Clusters of feathers worn on the top of the head have been illustrated by George Catlin and Kane himself (Kane 1846–1848, 26), but such an element as part of a roach headdress is questionable. It is not known if Kane decided to eliminate this element of the headdress for reasons related to composition, or for his desire to uphold historical accuracy.

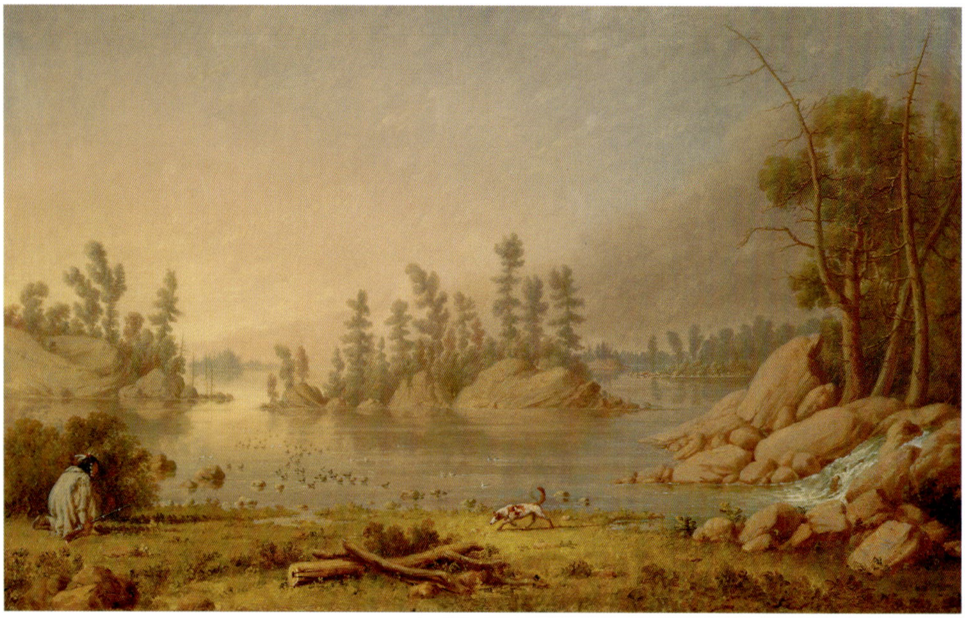

Fig. 41 *Hunting Ducks*
Northern Algonquian (Ojibway)
Lac des Mille Lacs, northern Ontario
1849–1856
oil on canvas; 43.1 × 71.0 cm
912.1.22

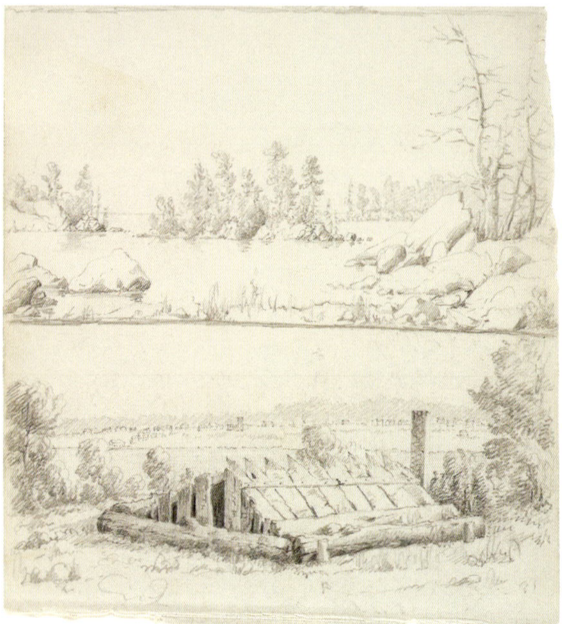

Fig. 42 *Island Landscape and Gravehouse*
Southern Algonquian
Manitowaning Bay, Manitoulin Island?, Ontario
mid-July–early August 1845
graphite on paper; 21.9 × 13.7 cm
946.15.51

> *A young dog is trained by dragging a piece of meat attached to a string up and down the edge of the shore several times, and putting the dog on the scent, who follows it rapidly, wagging his tail. After the dog has followed it for some time, he is given the meat; this is done repeatedly until the dog will do so whenever he is ordered, and his motions attract the ducks swimming in the distance to within reach of the Indian, who lies concealed on the banks.*
> (Kane 1859, 57)

From May 24 to June 4, 1846, travelling with the Hudson's Bay Company brigade, Kane paddled and portaged along the Kaministiquia–Dog Lake fur-trade route between Fort William on Lake Superior and Fort Frances on the Rainy River. After passing over the Height of Land and the Prairie Portage west of Dog Lake, the brigade eventually reached the Savanne River and entered the island-studded Lac des Mille Lacs. They quickly paddled the length of the lake, and by the end of the day on May 29 they were beyond the lake, having travelled, Kane writes, fifty-six miles (Kane 1859, 57).

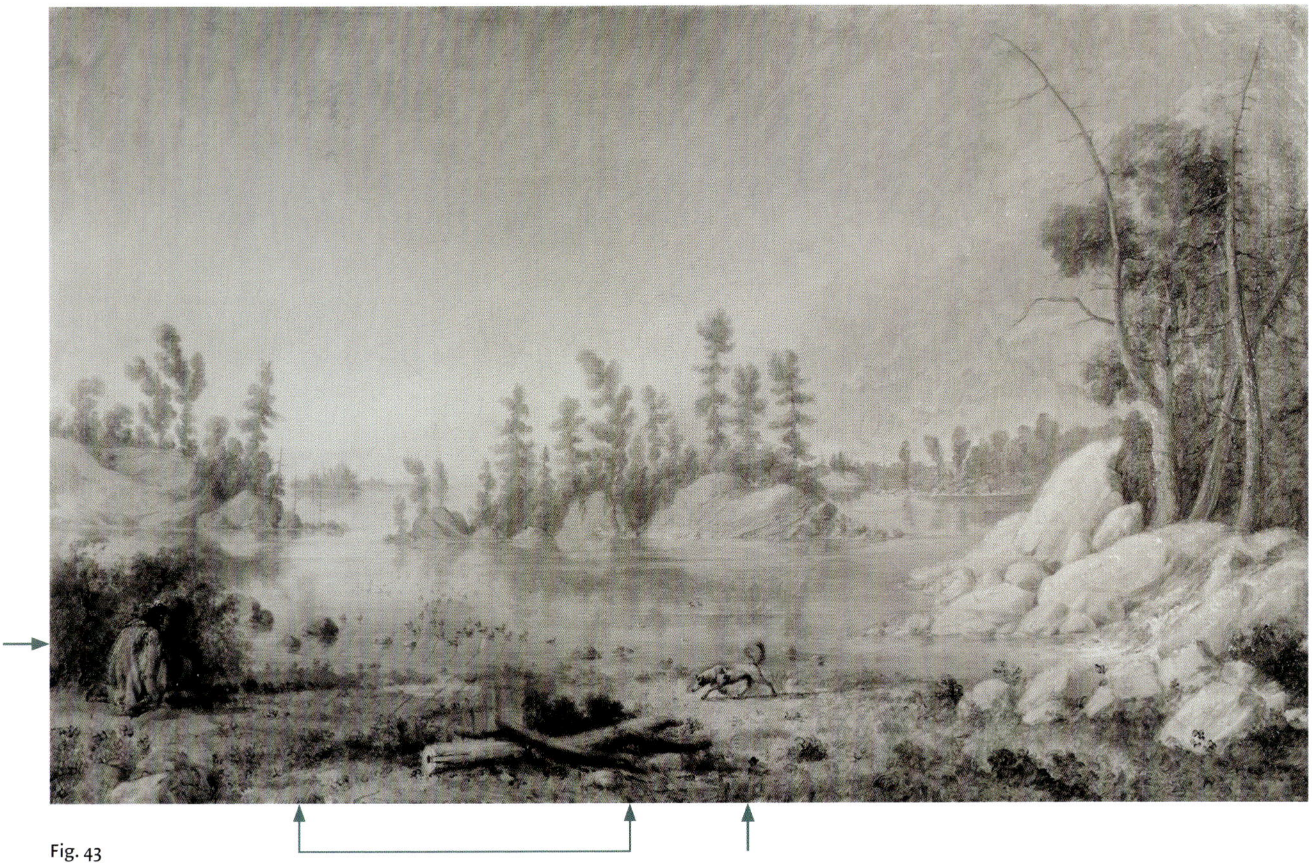

Fig. 43

Although Kane wrote about the lake's "truly beautiful" scenery, he was unable to take a sketch due to the fact that he was travelling on the brigade's schedule and the paddle along the lake was undertaken rapidly. Kane, though, would have noted the similarity of the lake's island landscape to that of the Thirty Thousand Islands in Georgian Bay. Thus, he chose a scene he sketched there in 1845 to represent the landscape of Lac des Mille Lacs in *Hunting Ducks*.

Study of the NIRR image shows that Kane was very secure with his rendering of the painting's setting. The overall scenery shows minimal alterations or adjustments and he followed the scene of the sketch with fair precision. He was less secure with the positioning of the dog and the hunched Indian hunter, however. He repositioned the dog's tail and head, moved the Indian hunter farther back behind the cover of the bush, and altered the details of the hunter's feather headdress.

More significant than these adjustments is what the NIRR image reveals in the central foreground: details of the Algonquian gravehouse that Kane sketched in 1845 while travelling in the Georgian Bay region. The NIRR image shows the outlines of the vertical boards forming the gravehouse's front wall, the foundation logs along the front and side, the outlines of its angled roof boards, and the upright grave post at the rear. Grave posts were inscribed with the totemic identities of the deceased and the spiritual essence of the totem helped direct the deceased spirit on its path (Johnston 2004, 232; Waugh, n.d.). The large horizontal log in the foreground of the painting was initially painted as the front foundation log for the gravehouse as seen in the sketch. Kane chose to leave the log in the foreground of the finished painting. The log that lies on top of it, over the outlines of the gravehouse, was added later and gives a more interesting composition to the log grouping.

The initial painting of the gravehouse suggests that Kane intended to paint the cultural scene that he recorded in 1845 on this canvas. It appears that he changed his mind about the subject of the painting, deciding that the landscape he had sketched in 1845 (immediately above the sketch of the gravehouse) could represent a cultural scene that he experienced the following year some 730 kilometres to the northwest.

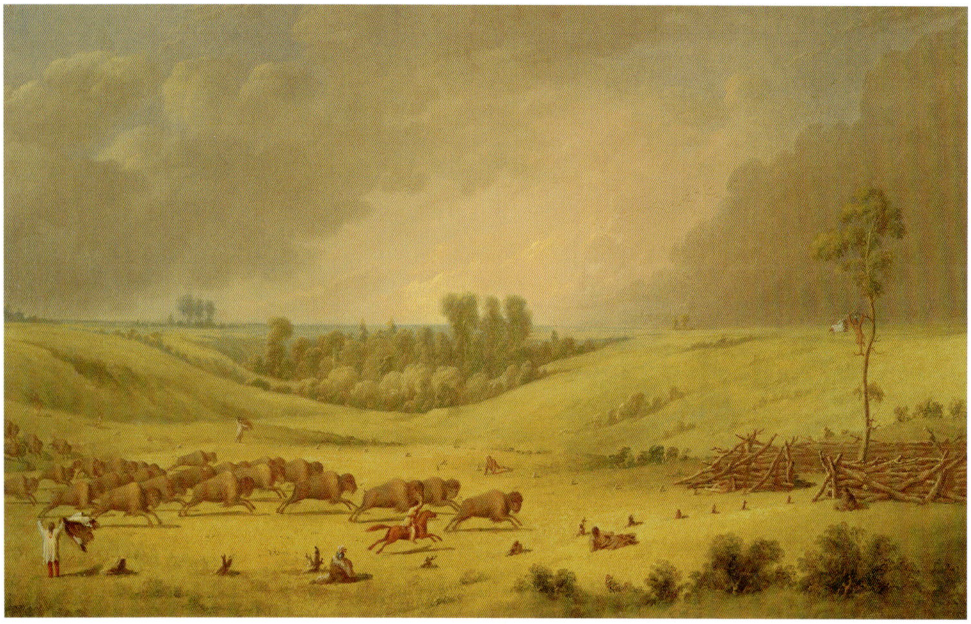

Fig. 44 *A Buffalo Pound*
Plains Cree
Fort Carlton region, North Saskatchewan River, Saskatchewan
1849–1852
oil on canvas; 43.0 × 71.0 cm
912.1.33

Fig. 45 *A Buffalo Pound near Fort Carlton*
Plains Cree
Fort Carlton region, North Saskatchewan River, Saskatchewan
September 12, 1846
graphite on paper; 14.0 × 24.0 cm
946.15.104

> *These pounds can only be made in the vicinity of forests, as they are composed of logs piled up roughly, five feet high, and enclose about two acres. At one side an entrance is left, about ten feet wide, and from each side of this, to the distance of half a mile, a row of posts or short stumps, called dead men, are planted, at the distance of twenty feet each, gradually widening out into the plain from the entrance.* (Kane 1859, 117–18)

By September 1846, Kane was travelling along the North Saskatchewan River toward Fort Edmonton. Now he was on horseback, and with a group of Plains Cree hunters he visited the site of a bison pound close to Fort Carlton. In his graphite sketch of the scene, he recorded the fundamental characteristics of the pound structure including the stumps, or "dead men" as he called them, forming a chute that extended obliquely out into the distance.

Hunters directed bison toward the mouth of the chute by slapping their robes on the ground. As the bison stampeded, funnelled by the gradually decreasing width of the chute, they were unaware of the danger of the pound, as just before the pound's entrance the chute was designed in a curve. As the bison approached, men continued to jump and wave their robes thus encouraging the frenzy and forcing the animals to charge around the curve and through the pound entrance (Mandelbaum 1940, 189–91).

Careful study of Kane's graphite sketch shows the funnel shape of the chute with its sides outlined by stumps. The chute leads toward a stand of trees, where it turns to curve into the pound entrance. The oil painting, on the other hand, is at variance with the sketch as here the chute directs the stampeding bison directly toward the pound entrance. This detail parades Kane's willingness to forfeit the historical

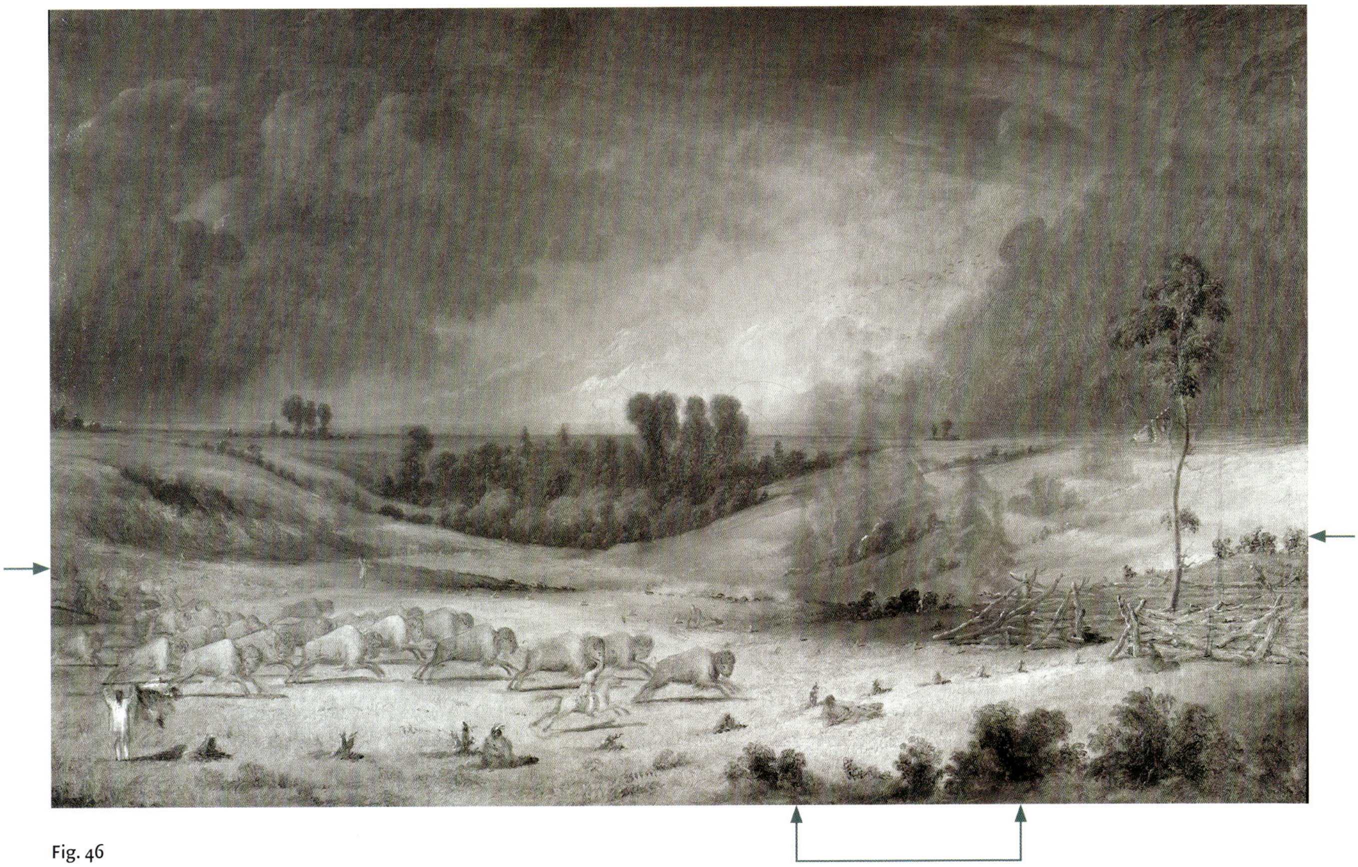

Fig. 46

accuracy recorded in his sketch which is further enhanced by his alteration of the landscape setting.

Comparison of Kane's graphite sketch to his finished studio oil painting reveals discrepancies between the two as they relate to their renderings of the chute and pound structures and the landscape settings. However, the NIRR image clearly shows that Kane originally painted the stand of trees where his sketch illustrates the curve of the chute; thus, he began to paint true to what he had observed. An oil painting in the Art Gallery of Ontario collection completed for Sir George Simpson, the overseas governor of the Hudson's Bay Company—the painting that Kane likely regarded as the prototype for the ROM's oil painting—illustrates the observed landscape of the graphite sketch including the stand of trees bordering the chute and pound (see Lister 2010, 234 fig. e). Nevertheless, after he had started this canvas—apparently following the lead of his former painting—he altered his plans, painted over the stand of trees, and took the landscape from an unrelated sketch to be the setting for *A Buffalo Pound* (see Lister 2010, 234 fig. a). The NIRR image, therefore, demonstrates that Kane began his process of developing the painting, as he did in a previous piece, using the field sketch as his inspiration. But, at some point in his studio, he made the alteration and finished with a painting that inaccurately represents this hunting method.

In the process of developing this oil painting, Kane also shows that he reworked some of the details: the central tree standing in the middle of the pound was moved and a number of bison in the back of the stampeding herd on the left side of the canvas were painted over.

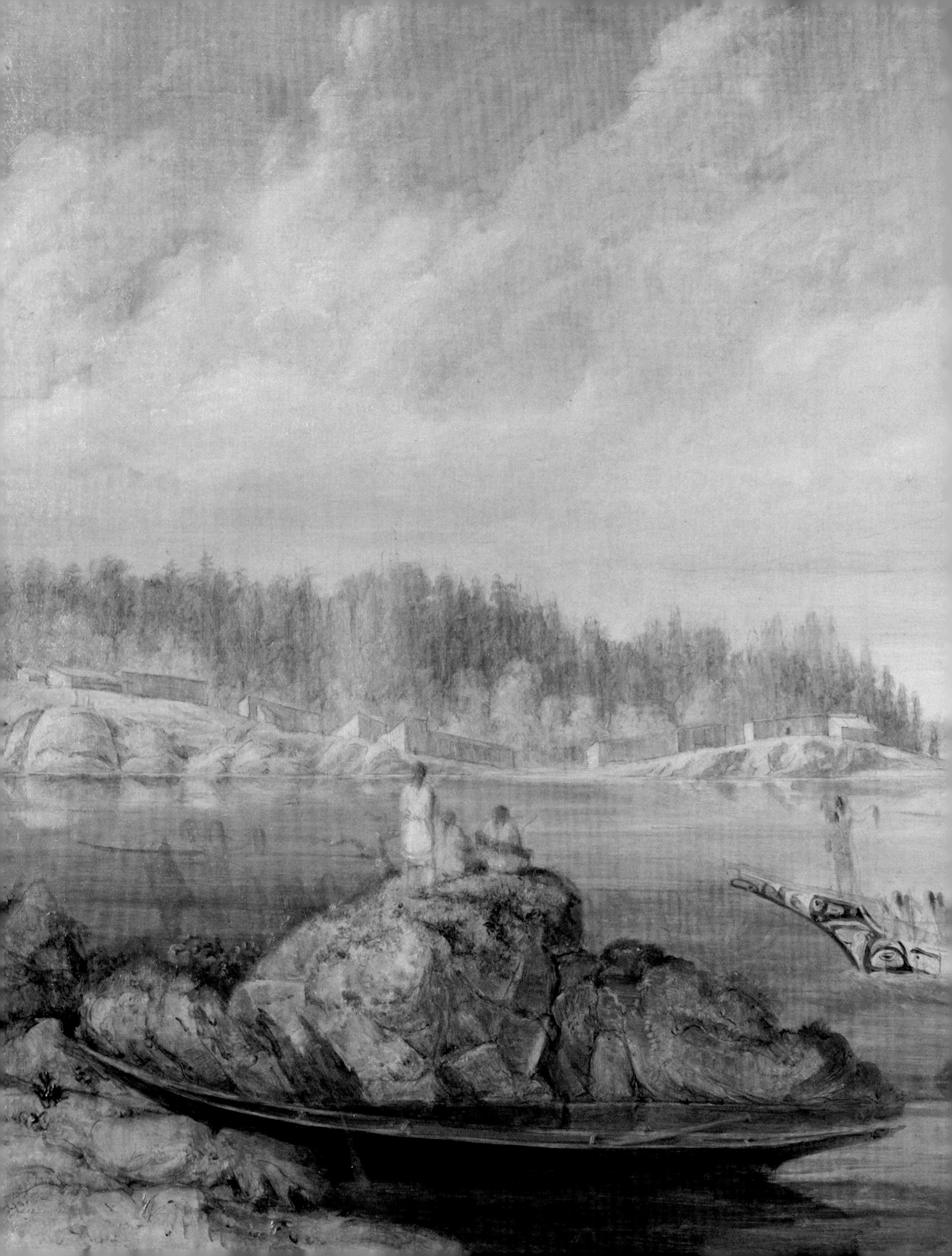

"to paint their likenesses:" Columbia River to Vancouver Island

The section begins with *Castle Rock, Columbia River*, a scene on the lower Columbia River. NIRR revealed that Kane made no modifications from his initial renderings and, thus, he was clearly confident with his vision for the scene. This is likely because he had worked out the details of the composition in two previous works, a watercolour sketch, as well as an oil painting completed for Sir George Simpson (see Lister 2010, 302 fig. d). This is not the case though with the other paintings in this series. *Dalle des Morts, or the Rapid of the Dead*, shows that Kane was initially inspired by his sketch and painted the Hudson's Bay Company brigade entering the rapids in two bateaux. However, in a curious modification shown clearly by NIRR, he later painted over the bateaux and in their places painted canoes. In *The Return of a War Party*, NIRR reveals an initial rendering of three war canoes that resembles a watercolour sketch. But Kane subsequently painted over one of the canoes, changed the context, and created a fictional landscape in its place.

In *An Indian of the Dalles, Columbia River*, NIRR reveals that Kane altered his initial rendering of the headdress for this portrait, similar to his alterations of Menominee headdresses in the previous section. NIRR of *A Nesperces Indian* indicates that Kane did not initially intend to paint the figure with a central forelock, showing evidence that for this portrait he was working out the details as he was developing the composition. NIRR, in combination with the study of his sketches, reveals that for this portrait Kane amalgamated details from two different sketches and two different cultural groups.

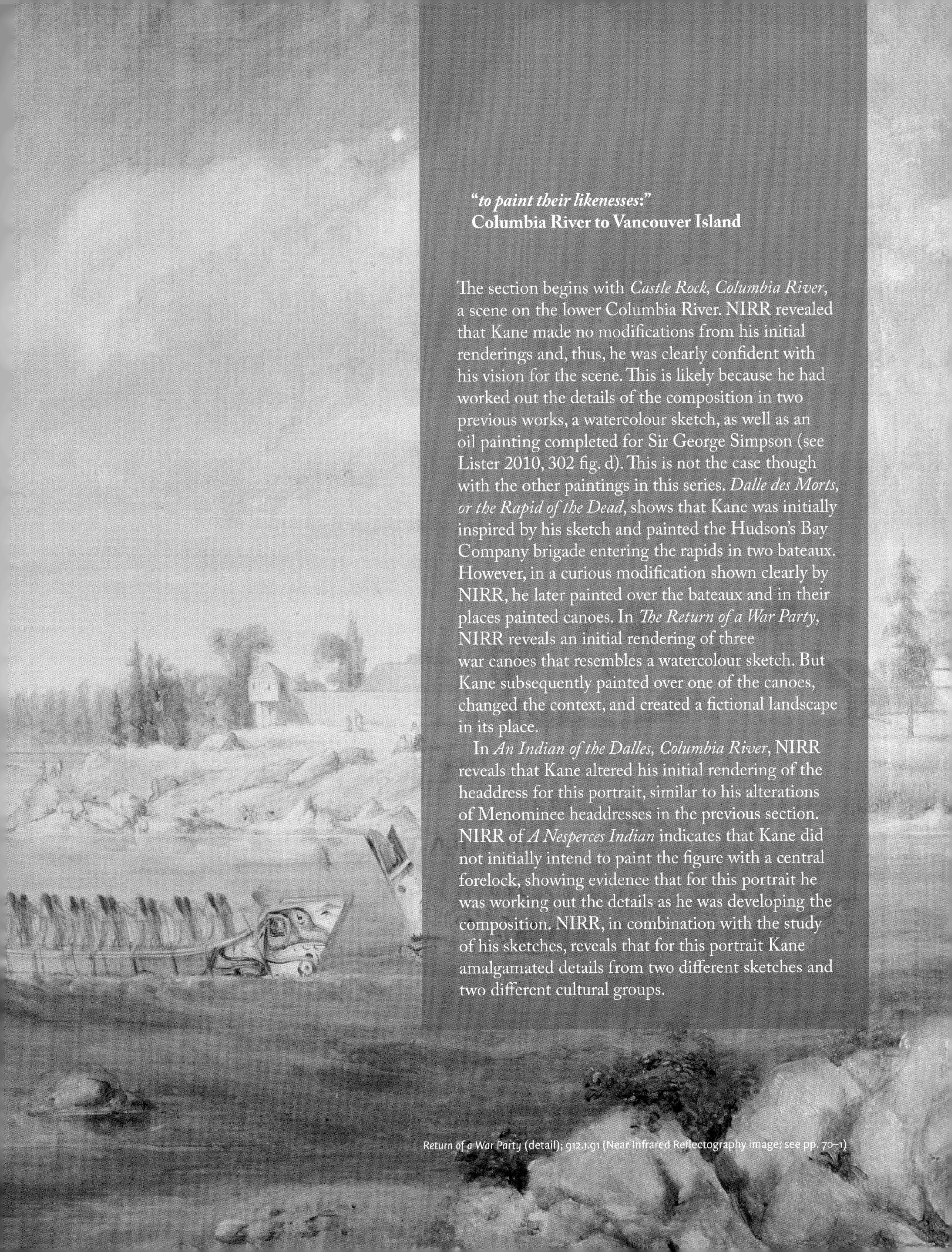

Return of a War Party (detail); 912.1.91 (Near Infrared Reflectography image; see pp. 70–1)

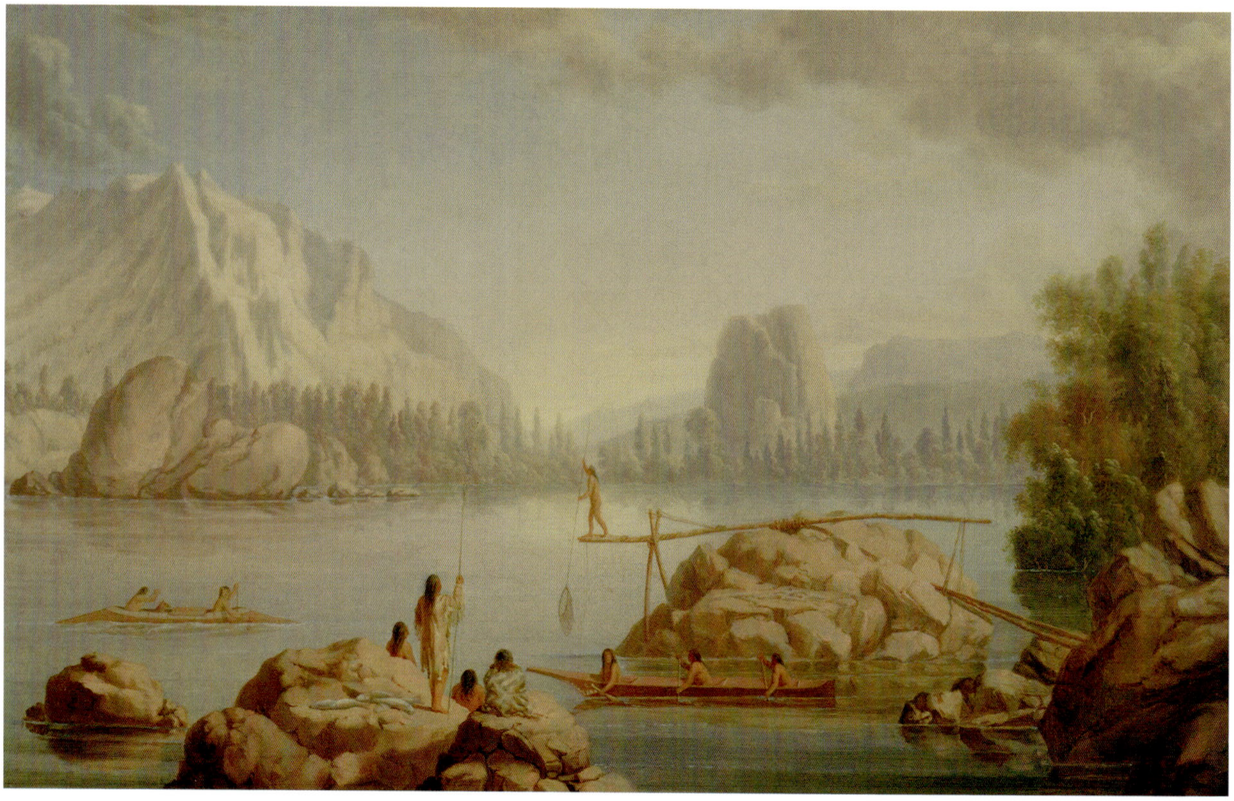

Fig. 47 *Castle Rock, Columbia River*
Cascade (Easterly Chinookan)
Beacon Rock below the Cascades,
Columbia River, Washington
1849–1856
oil on canvas; 45.9 × 74.0 cm
912.1.68

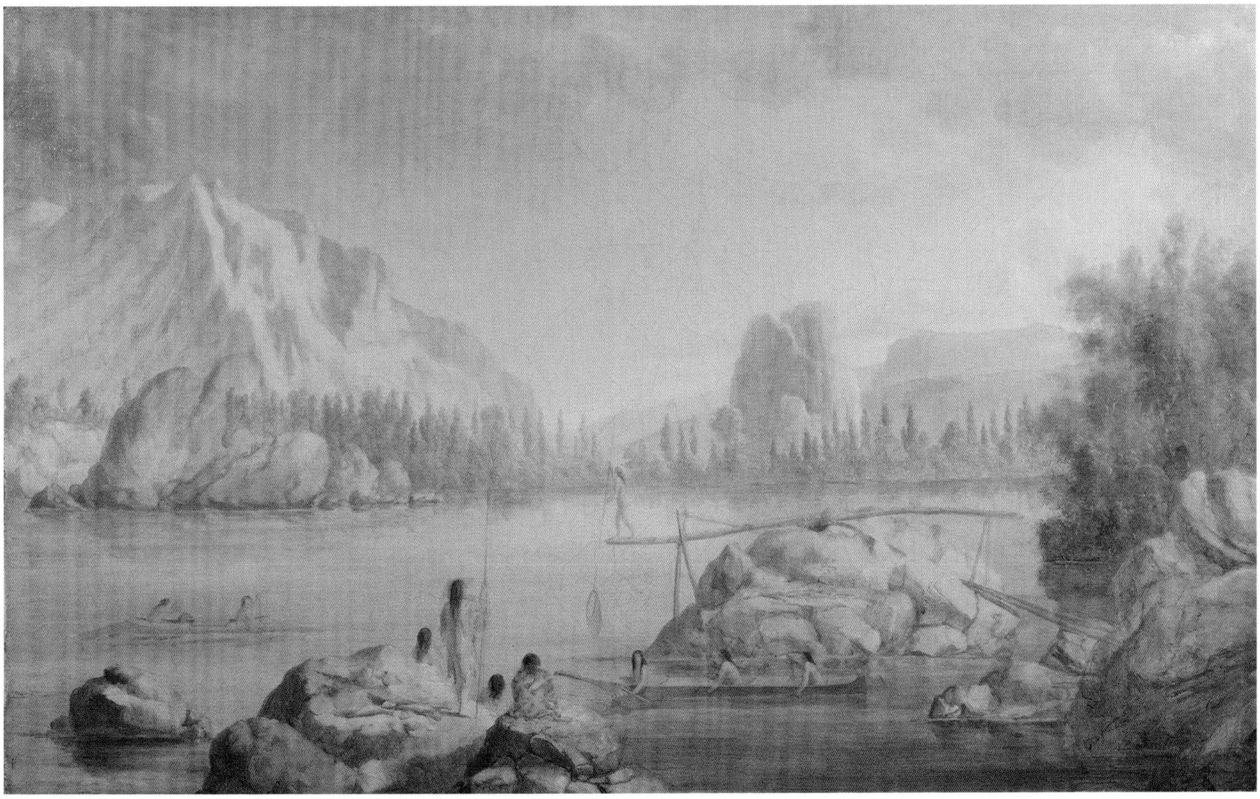

Fig. 48

Kane shows his confidence with this composition as the NIRR image reveals no alterations or modifications.

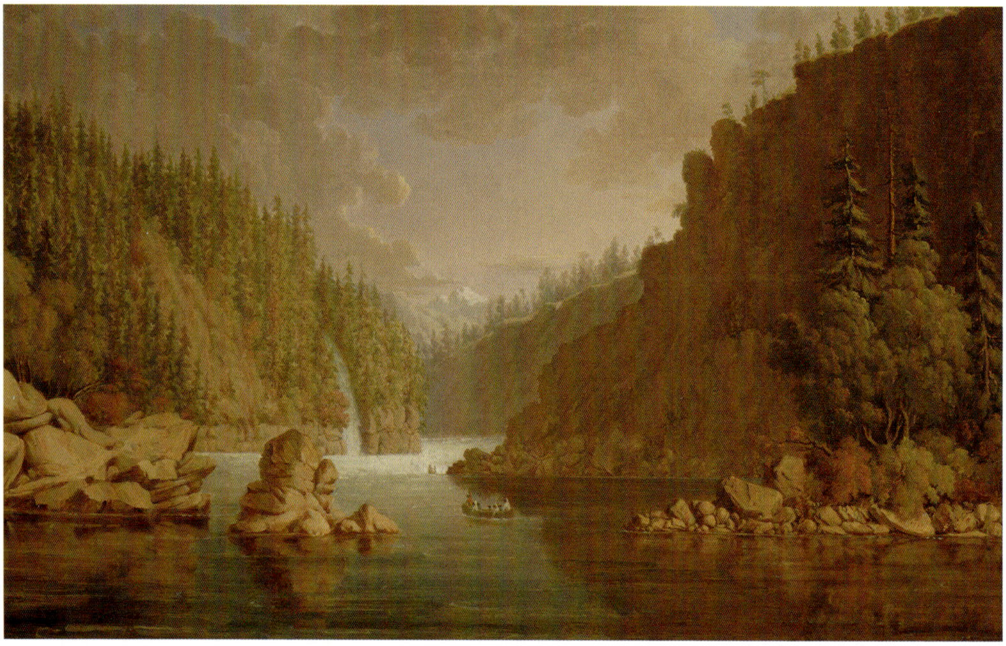

Fig. 49 *Dalle des Morts, or the Rapid of the Dead*
Hudson's Bay Company brigade
upper Columbia River, British Columbia
1849–1856
oil on canvas; 46.0 × 74.0 cm
912.1.20

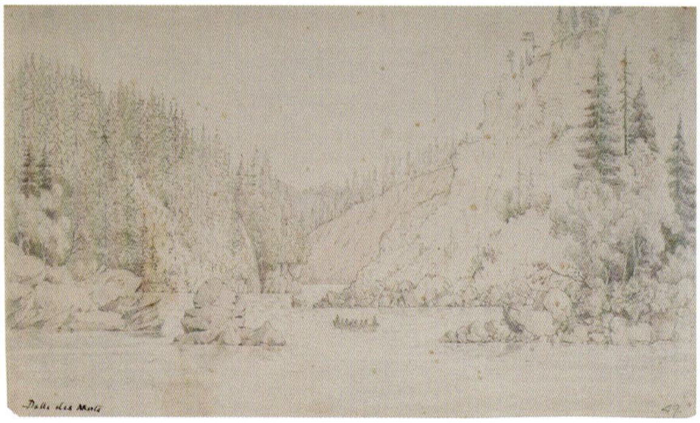

Fig. 50 *Dalles des Morts*
Hudson's Bay Company brigade
upper Columbia River, British Columbia
October 6, 1847
watercolour on paper; 14.0 × 23.8 cm
Stark Museum of Art, Orange, Texas
31.78.19

> *About three hours after our departure, we shot the celebrated "Dalle de Mort." It is about three miles long and is the most dangerous of all the rapids on the Columbia.* (Kane 1859, 166)

When Paul Kane crossed over the Athabasca Pass and reached Boat Encampment (see figs. 67 and 68) on the upper Columbia River in November 1846, he was taking part in a well-established transportation system for moving furs, trade goods, and personnel across the Rocky Mountains. The day following his arrival at Boat Encampment, Kane wrote in his journal, "got the conews decicy and imbarked" (Kane 1989, 36). The important word is "conews" (i.e., canoes) and when his oil painting is examined Kane clearly painted two canoes entering the rapids. However, examination of his field sketch shows not canoes paddled by voyageurs, but rather two bateaux, or wood boats, being rowed.

Kane's sketch of the Hudson's Bay Company brigade entering the rapids of the Columbia River in bateaux is consistent with the historical record. In 1811, North West Company explorer David Thompson, in the absence of suitable birchbark, developed a clinker-style wood boat for navigating down the river (Nisbet 1994, 178; Tyrrell 1916, 454–55). Within twenty years, Fort Colvile—the Hudson's Bay Company establishment at Kettle Falls in Washington—became the main boatyard for the construction of fur-trade bateaux west of the Rocky Mountains (Chance 1986, 81); during the 1830–1831 boat-building cycle, the boat builders at Fort Colvile produced ten bateaux for fur-trade transportation (HBCA B.45/a/1).

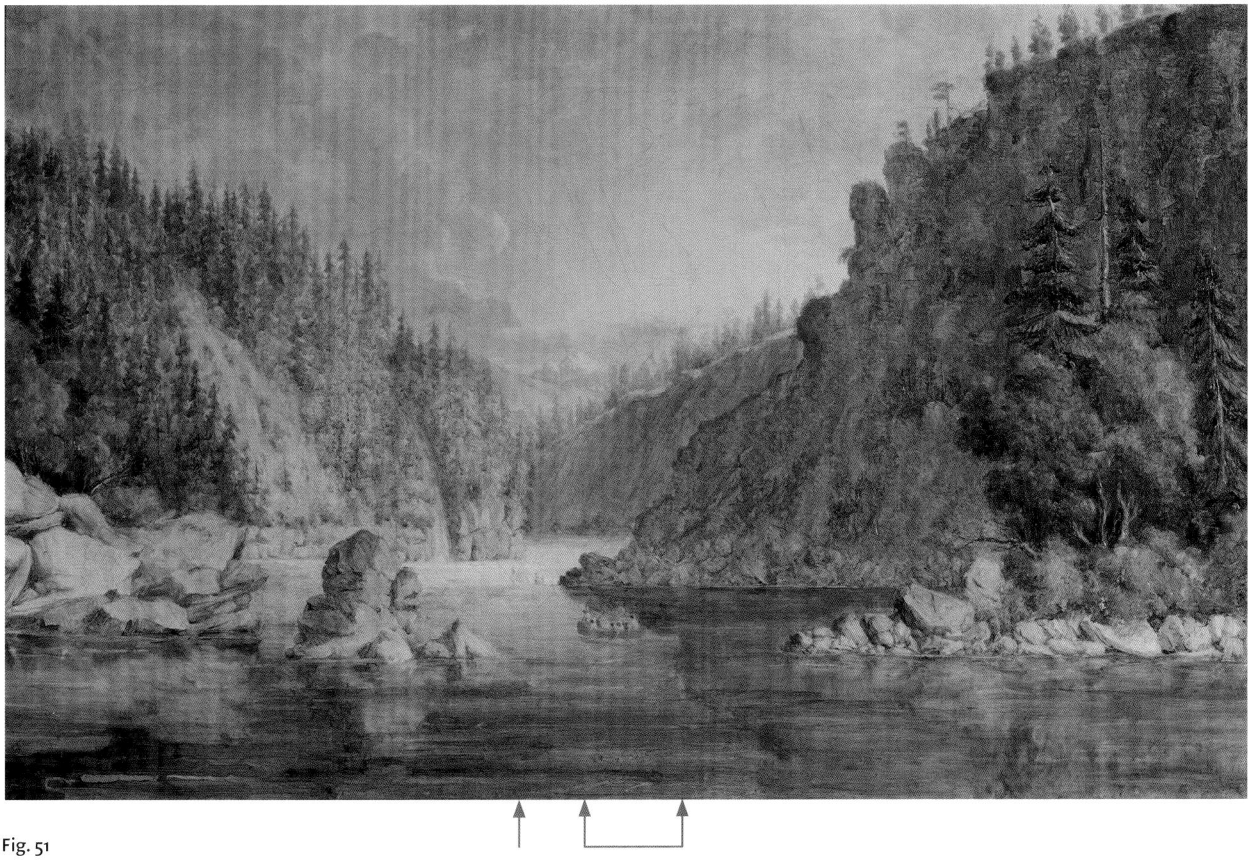

Fig. 51

Why Kane chose to represent canoes in his studio canvas, rather than the bateaux he himself experienced, is a mystery. This is especially curious when in his published narrative he describes the boats he travelled in as "formed canoe fashion, with round bottoms of boards, clinker built" (Kane 1859, 165). Kane has created a conflict between his own narrative and his studio record, and although he writes about travelling in bateaux, it seems that he desired this painting to register the use of canoes.

The NIRR image of *Dalle des Morts, or the Rapid of the Dead* shows that Kane made minimal alterations to the landscape setting. However, close inspection of the two boats deepens the mystery created by the discrepancy between the field sketch and the studio painting.

In the sketch, Kane details the bateaux accurately, showing the raked bow and stern—a design effective for whitewater. In the foreground bateau, with its port side facing the viewer, we see three pairs of boatmen rowing and a sternman with a long oar or paddle negotiating the boat's manoeuvre. Interestingly, the NIRR image reveals that Kane originally painted true to this sketch—and his personal experience—because to the immediate right of the foreground canoe we can see the distinctive shape of a bateau with three sets of rowers and a sternman steering. Similarly, in the distance, to the left of the canoe slipping down the face of the rapids, appears a bateau that matches the image in the sketch (see detail, fig. 13).

Kane's finished studio painting misrepresents Columbia River navigation history. His original version though—subsequently painted over—was true to his own experience that he illustrated in his field sketch. As well, the original image was consistent with his published narrative and commensurate with known Columbia River navigation methods during the nineteenth-century fur trade.

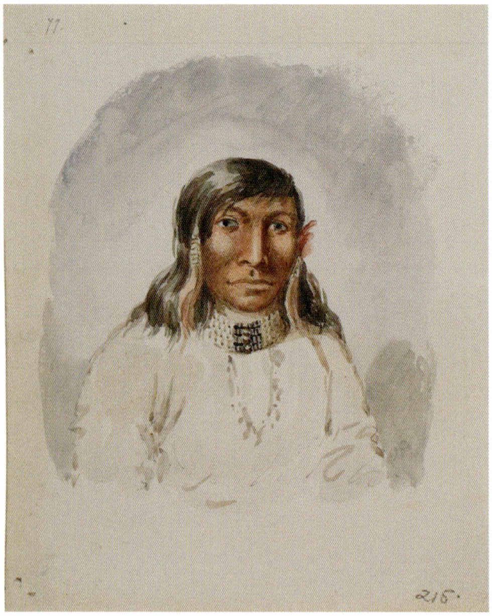

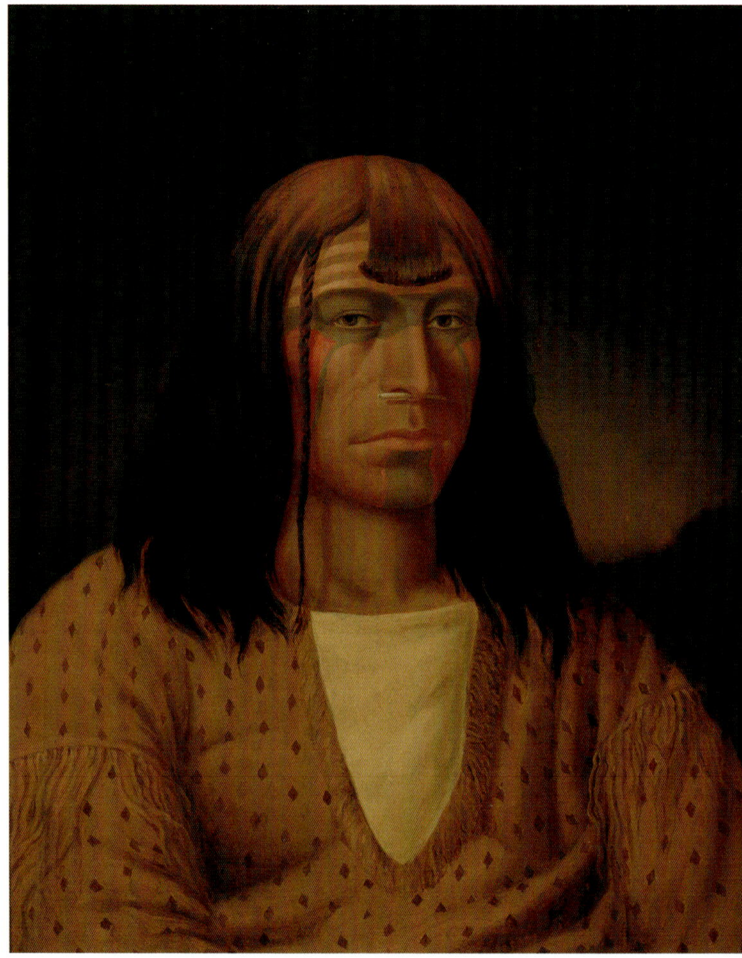

Fig. 52 (Top) *Nach-a-wish, a Nez Percé Indian*
Nez Perce
Columbia and Snake Rivers region, Washington
July 29, 1847
watercolour on paper; 13.3 × 11.4 cm
Stark Museum of Art, Orange, Texas,
31.78.36

Fig. 53 (Right) *A Nesperces Indian*
Nez Perce
Columbia and Snake Rivers region, Washington
1849–1856
oil on canvas; 64.2 × 51.2 cm
912.1.72

> *During the day we passed a large encampment of Nezperees, who were very kind to us, but stole a tin cup (a valuable article in that part of the world) I suppose as a souvenir of my visit. I took a sketch of a man, and might have frightened the chief into getting the cup restored to me by means of this sketch, but I had been so warned of the treachery and villany of these Indians, that I considered it too dangerous an experiment.* (Kane 1859, 290)

Travelling with the western express it took only twenty-three days for Kane to journey down the length of the Columbia River to Fort Vancouver. As such, he did not have the leisure to take sketches and, thus, his records of the Columbia River people were taken on his return journey.

On July 29, 1847, while riding horseback north of the Walla Walla River in the region of the Snake and Columbia Rivers, Kane and a Native companion came across an encampment of Nez Perce. Kane took a sketch of one of the male Indians and the facial features from the sketch are faithfully rendered in his studio oil painting. However, in the oil painting, Kane adds a dentalium shell ornament piercing the subject's nasal septum that is not represented in the sketch. The name Nez Perce translates from the French as "pierced nose" and refers to this custom; however, it was a practice long abandoned by the mid-nineteenth century and would not have been observed by Kane (Walker, Jr. 1998, 437).

The NIRR image of *A Nesperces Indian* shows Kane to have been secure with the composition of the painting's main

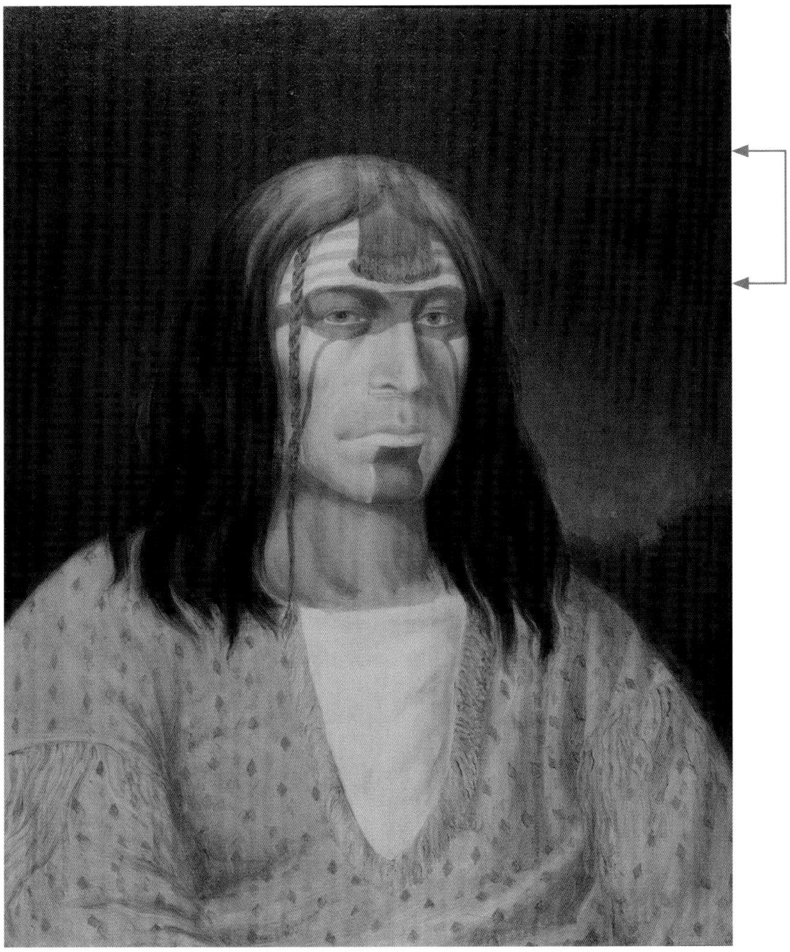

Fig. 54

features, with the exception of the subject's hair. Study of the hair shows that the forelock was added after Kane had painted the hair in a parted fashion, as well as perhaps after laying down the three painted stripes across the forehead.

This addition suggests that Kane was working out the components of the composition as he was developing the canvas. Thus, he was not faithfully following the details of the sketch. This is consistent with the appearance of other elements in the painting, such as the perforated shirt and the face paint.

In *A Nesperces Indian*, Kane incorporates elements from two sketches, the facial characteristics from *Nach-a-wish, a Nez Percé Indian* and the hair style and face paint from a sketch titled *Rocky Mountain Indian* (see Lister 2010, 318 figs. a, b). The latter sketch is a portrait of a Spokane Indian that Kane took over a month after he met the Nez Perce. It shows the subject with hair parted in the middle; forelock curled at the end; and face paint across the forehead, around the eyes, over the cheekbones, and down the chin below the lower lip—all represented in the studio painting. Thus, the studio portrait displays an amalgamation of elements from two different Native groups. If interpretive weight is given to Kane's sketches—with the exception of the dentalium shell nasal piercing that Kane adds to bestow the subject with identity—the hair style, face paint, and clothing suggest a closer representation of a Spokane individual than of a Nez Perce.

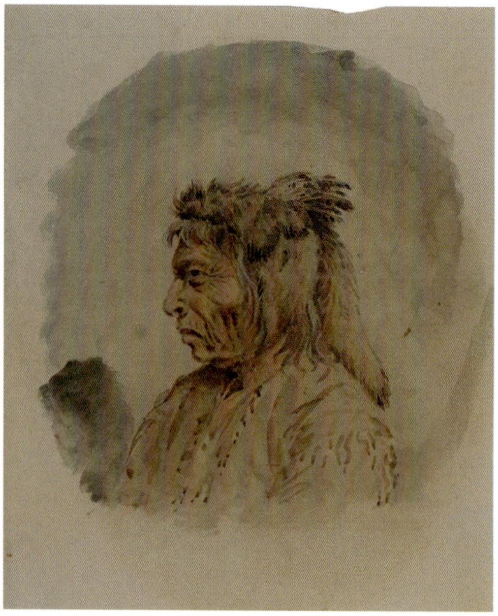

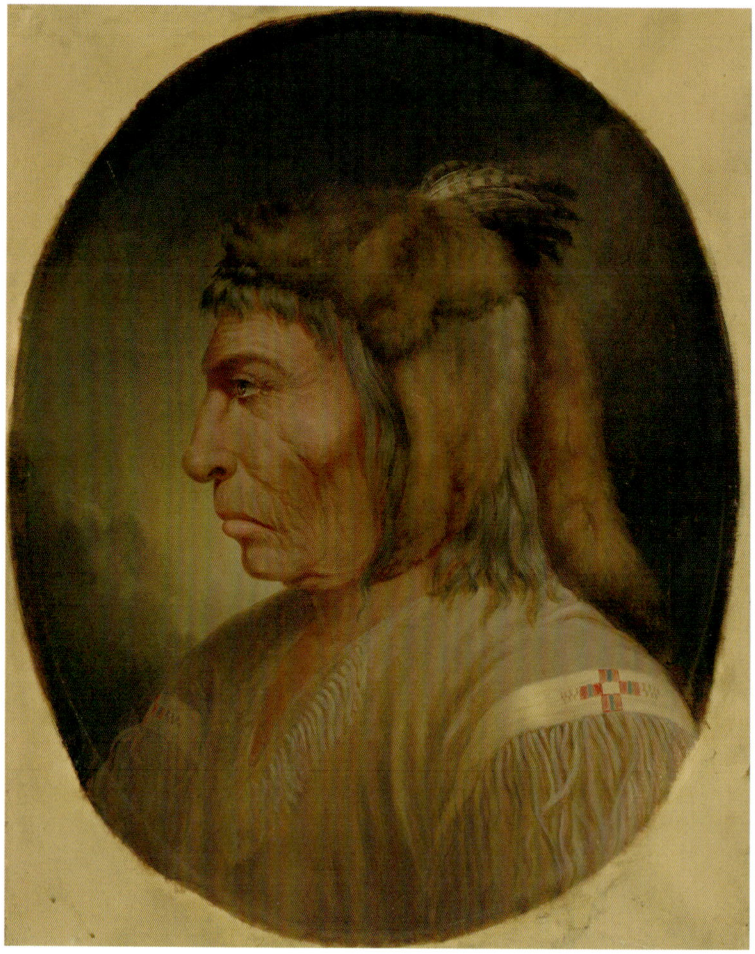

Fig. 55 (Top) *Mancemuckt, Chief of the Skeen*
Western Columbia River Sahaptin
Skin village, Celilo Falls, Columbia River, Washington
July 8, 1847
watercolour on paper; 14.0 × 9.8 cm
Stark Museum of Art, Orange, Texas
31.78.109

Fig. 56 (Right) *An Indian of the Dalles, Columbia River*
Mancemuckt, chief of the Skin village
Western Columbia River Sahaptin
Celilo Falls, Columbia River, Washington
1849–1856
oil on canvas; 63.5 × 50.7 cm
912.1.75

> *The Indians hereabouts catch a few deer and some other game, out of whose skins they make whatever dresses they wear, which are, however, very scanty. I give, in Sketch No. 12, the likeness of Mancemuckt, the chief; he wore a fox skin cap and a leather deerskin shirt at the time.* (Kane 1859, 263–64)

On his return journey up the Columbia River, Kane left Fort Vancouver on July 1, 1847, in a brigade of nine boats. On July 8, the brigade reached Celilo Falls—known as the "Chutes" (Boyd 1996, 31; Kane 1859, 263)—where the Sahaptin of the region were employed to carry the boats and supplies across the portage. Celilo Falls was one of the most productive fisheries on the lower Columbia River. Each year, from April through October, the Sahaptin harvested five species of salmon, in addition to suckers, lamprey, and trout (Boyd 1996, 52–53; Hunn and French 1998, 382; Williams 1980, 60).

As the brigade was being portaged around the falls, Kane had the opportunity to sketch a Sahaptin chief whom he named "Mani-nucht" in his list of portraits (Kane 1846–1848, 91)—a portrait log kept during his travels—and "Mancemuckt" in his published narrative (Kane 1859, 263–64). This chief was from the Skin village situated on the north side of the river, a short distance to the west of the falls.

The Columbia River Sahaptin used dressed deer and elk skins for their clothing, such as dresses, shirts, leggings, and moccasins. Rabbit fur was used for socks, mittens, and blankets while otter and weasel skins were cut into strips for

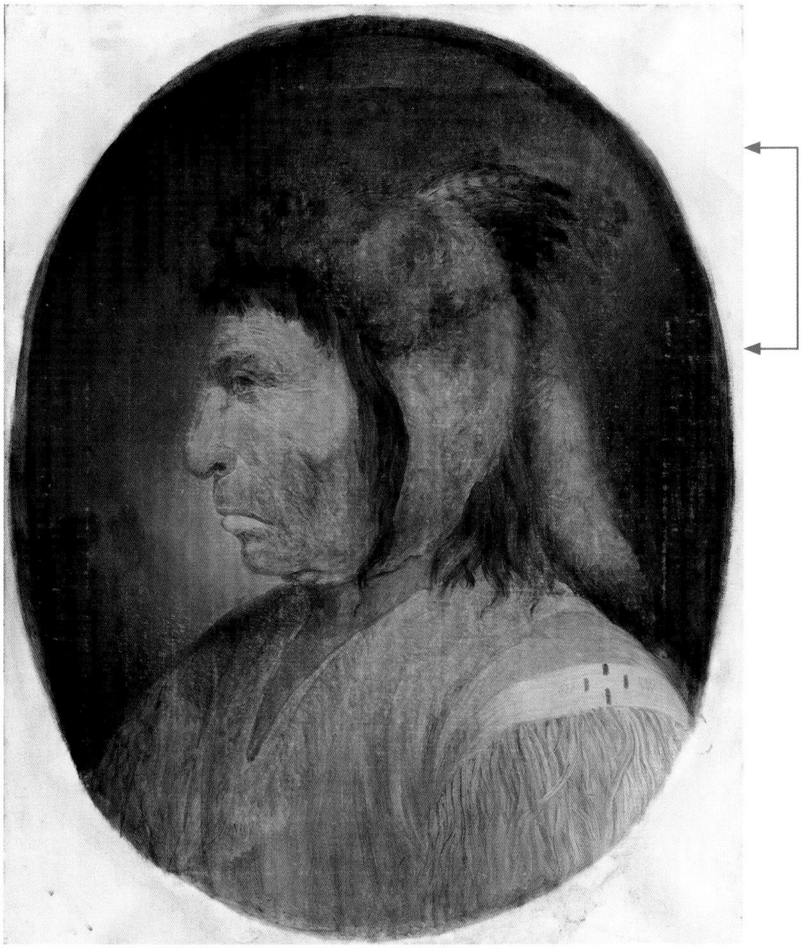

Fig. 57

decorations (Hunn and French 1998, 384). Kane writes that the Sahaptin he met wore clothing of skins and his sketch of Mancemuckt shows the chief wearing, in his words, "a fox-skin cap and a leather deerskin shirt."

The studio painting *An Indian of the Dalles, Columbia River* shows that Kane followed his sketch of Mancemuckt closely. The similarities between sketch and oil painting in the representation of the facial features, the fox-skin cap, and the deerskin or elk-skin shirt show Kane's interest in staying true to his observations. This includes a cluster of feathers protruding from the crown of the cap where the fox tail is attached.

Study of the NIRR image reveals that the feather cluster was initially painted much longer, but Kane subsequently chose to shorten the feathers, transmuting the end section of the cluster into the background sky. The original volume Kane gave to the feather cluster provided it with a more pronounced presence than that represented in the sketch. He may have rethought this detail because he was resisting the urge to depict elements in a grander fashion than observed. Or, he may have felt that the alteration was necessary to balance the edges of the background space and the position of the portrait within its oval setting.

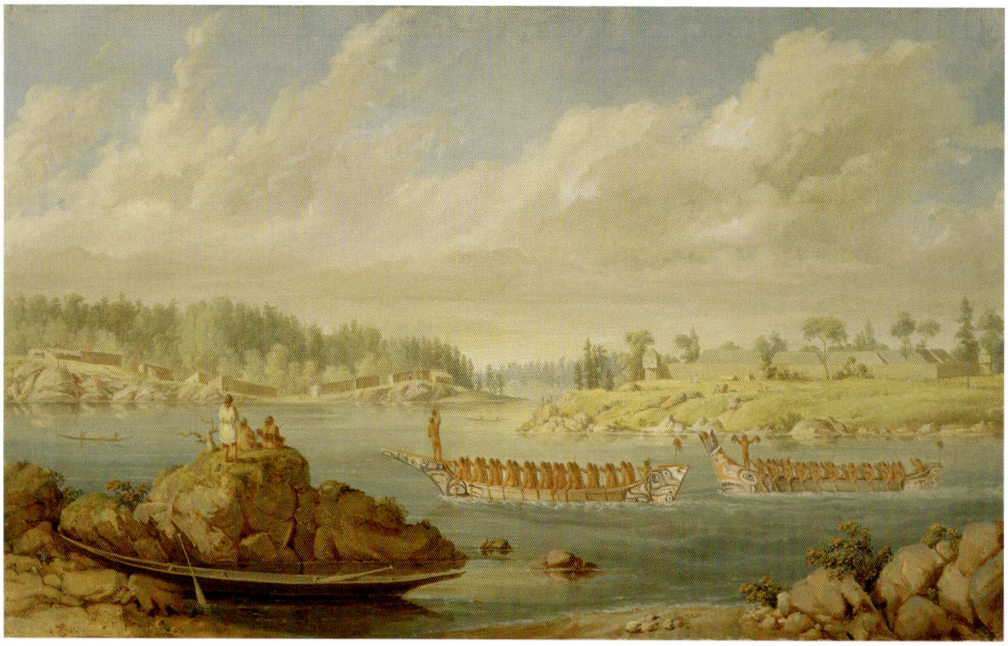

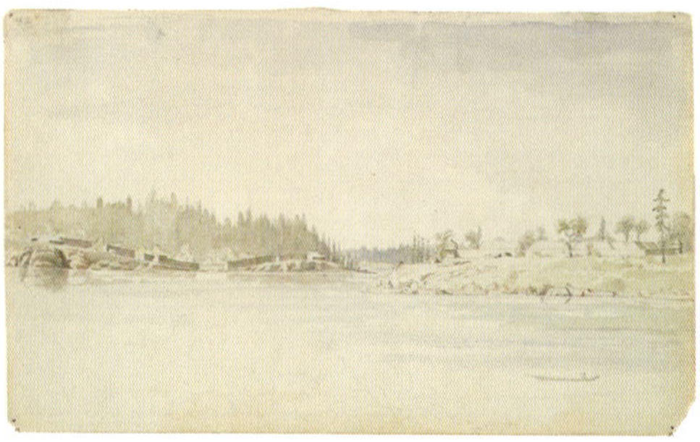

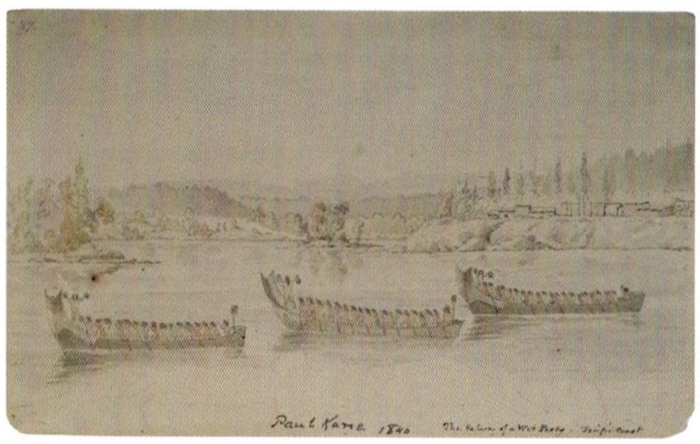

Fig. 58 (Left) *Return of a War Party*
Songhees (Central Coast Salish) and Hudson's Bay Company
Fort Victoria and Songhees village, Victoria Harbour, south Vancouver Island, British Columbia
1849–1856
oil on canvas; 43.0 × 71.0 cm
912.1.91

Fig. 59 (Bottom Left)
Fort Victoria
Songhees (Central Coast Salish) and Hudson's Bay Company
Fort Victoria and Songhees village, Victoria Harbour, south Vancouver Island, British Columbia
April–June 1847
watercolour and graphite on paper; 14.1 × 23.6 cm
946.15.212

Fig. 60 (Bottom Right)
War Party, Juan de Fuca
Makah
Strait of Juan de Fuca
mid–late May 1847
watercolour on paper
14.0 × 22.5 cm
Stark Museum of Art, Orange, Texas
31.78.89

> *Fort Victoria stands upon the banks of an inlet in the island about seven miles long and a quarter of a mile wide, forming a safe and convenient harbour, deep enough for any sized vessel.* (Kane 1859, 208)

On April 8, 1847, Kane arrived at Fort Victoria, established by the Hudson's Bay Company in 1843 on Vancouver Island as its new Pacific centre of operations (Mackie 1997, 259–82). The Songhees established a village on the opposite shore (Suttles 1974, 15) and the trading opportunities provided by the fort attracted Native peoples from Puget Sound to Alaska.

Kane sketched in the region of Vancouver Island for a period of two months and used Fort Victoria as his main base. Kane's watercolour sketch, *Fort Victoria,* taken from across James Bay, shows the fort on the right bank and the Songhees village across the harbour. This scene is accurately rendered in his studio painting, although in the painting he adds two war canoes that seem to be inspired by a sketch of Makah warriors paddling canoes out in the Strait of Juan de Fuca.

The studio painting *Return of a War Party* was inspired by three sketches, and when Kane incorporated their separate details he created a painting of invention. As noted, the background scene of Fort Victoria and the Songhees village is commensurate with Kane's sketch of the scene; the fabrication becomes apparent when we examine the foreground imagery.

Kane shows two war canoes being paddled out of James Bay, an enclosed body of water in Victoria Harbour. The warriors are returning from where? Study of the NIRR image clarifies

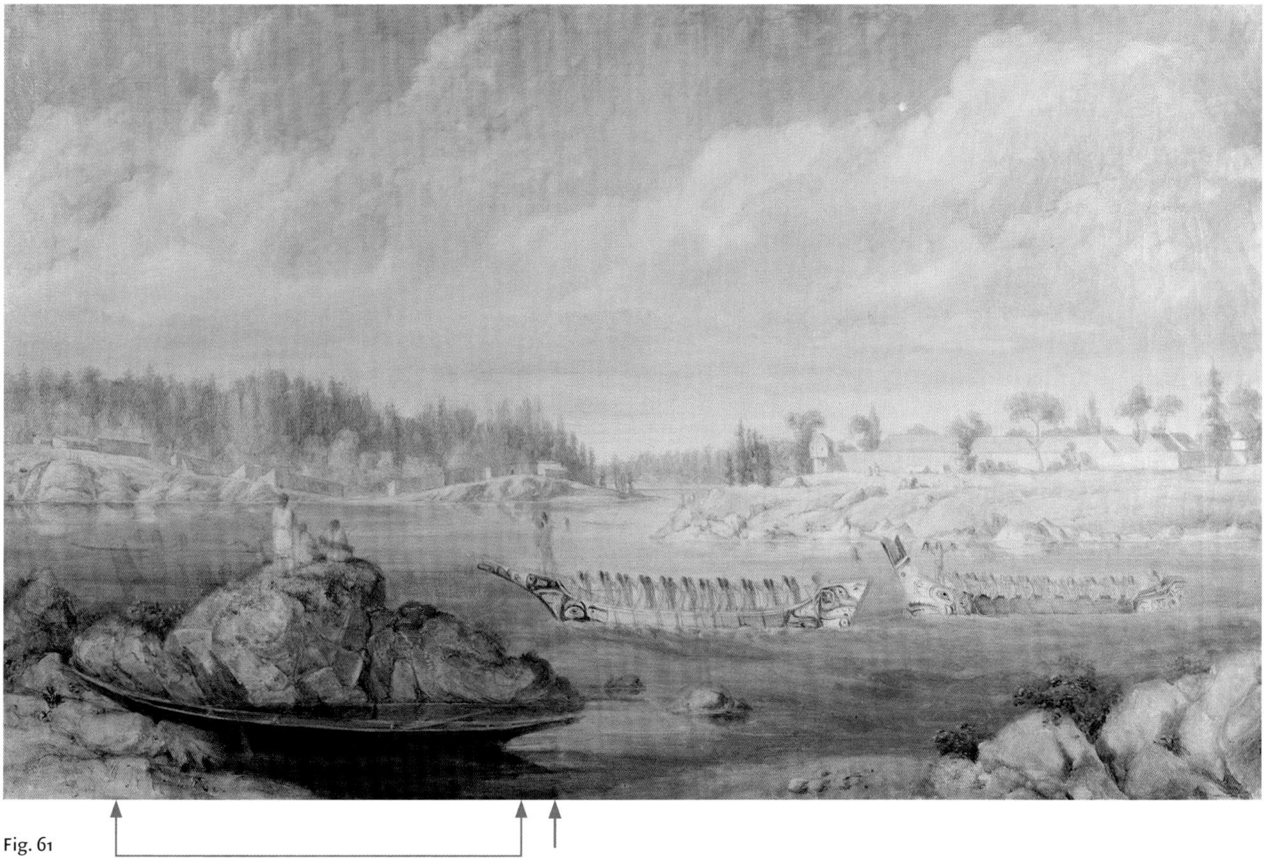

Fig. 61

the artifice, for in the left foreground of the painting we see that Kane originally painted a third leading canoe. This canoe, known as a "Munka" canoe—designed with a high, flared bow to provide the paddlers with protection—and the following two canoes were inspired by a sketch, *War Party, Juan de Fuca.* As in the sketch, all three canoes in the painting show the celebration of warriors holding up scalps of their enemy, and the orientations of the warriors in the sketch and studio painting are identical—the warriors in the lead and rear canoes face the viewer while the central warrior faces the opposite direction.

For the studio painting, Kane changed the central canoe of the sketch from a "Munka" to a "Head" canoe, a style of canoe no longer in use by the time Kane visited the region. It was designed with a near vertical bow effective to ram the canoe of the enemy (see Arima 1999, 56–59; 2002, 112; Brown 2002, 92–93). Kane's inspiration for this canoe was likely taken from a sketched model (Lister 2010, 272 fig. c) and since Kane shows the canoe being paddled backwards this bears evidence that this canoe was not directly observed. The NIRR image shows that the standing warrior in the central canoe was initially painted brandishing scalps in two raised hands as in the sketch, but perhaps in an attempt to modify the terror of the scene, Kane limited the gesture of this warrior to one raised arm.

The NIRR image indicates that the sketch, *War Party, Juan de Fuca,* was Kane's initial inspiration for the foreground of the painting. But perhaps with the realization that his composition was not working, he painted over the lead canoe and in its place created a fictional scene of three admiring onlookers positioned on a rock outcropping, further enhancing the artifice of the overall scene.

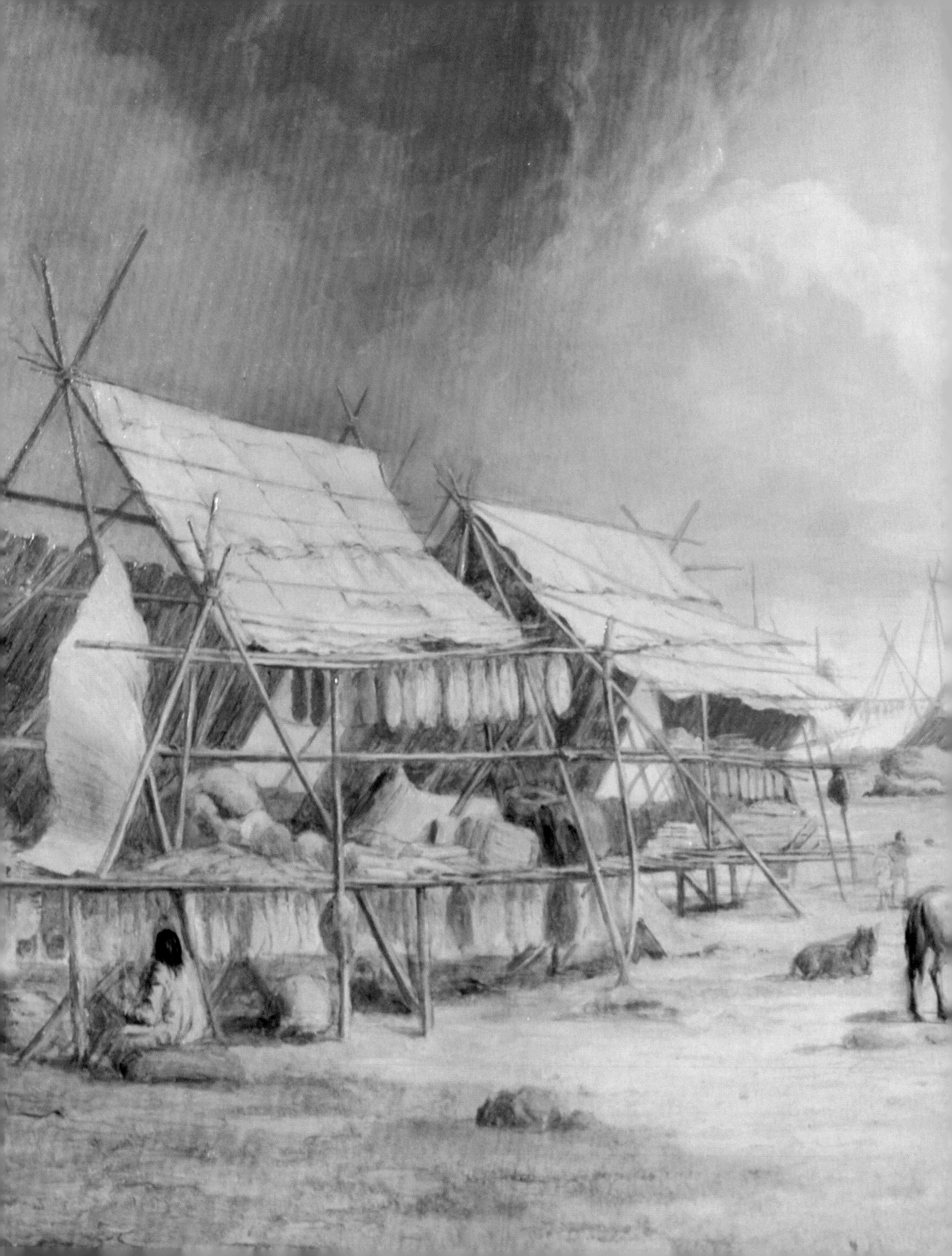

"a most faithful representation"

NIRR reveals that in fifty-seven paintings in the ROM's Paul Kane collection of studio art, Kane made no alterations or modifications from his initial renderings. However, there are a number of examples where NIRR indicates that he struggled with their compositions. In some he adjusted the size of figures or altered their positions. In others he initially included elements, but then later painted over them. These adjustments show Kane working out the compositions, and many relate to his own sense of compositional balance and aesthetics. The reworkings in the paintings in this section, unlike those in the previous two sections, do not affect the paintings' ethnographic significance.

NIRR of the first painting in this section, *Winter Travelling,* indicates no modification from Kane's initial renderings. This is likely because he had worked out the composition earlier in a graphite-on-paper sketch (see Lister 2010, 338 fig. a). In all of the other paintings in this section, however, NIRR shows modifications in details. Kane was secure with the general layout of the scenes, but he removed elements, such as a Red River cart in *Half Breed Encampment* and a group of figures in *Boat Encampment.* He altered the size of a woman and changed the orientation of a horse's head and tail in *Half Breed Encampment*; sketched in a rock in *Indian Camp, Colville,* but then painted over it and added an additional vignette of a woman and horse, perhaps for compositional balance; and with, *Game of Alcholoh,* in addition to revealing numerous modifications, NIRR suggests that he began his painting intending to match the scantily-clad figure details of his sketch, but reconsidered.

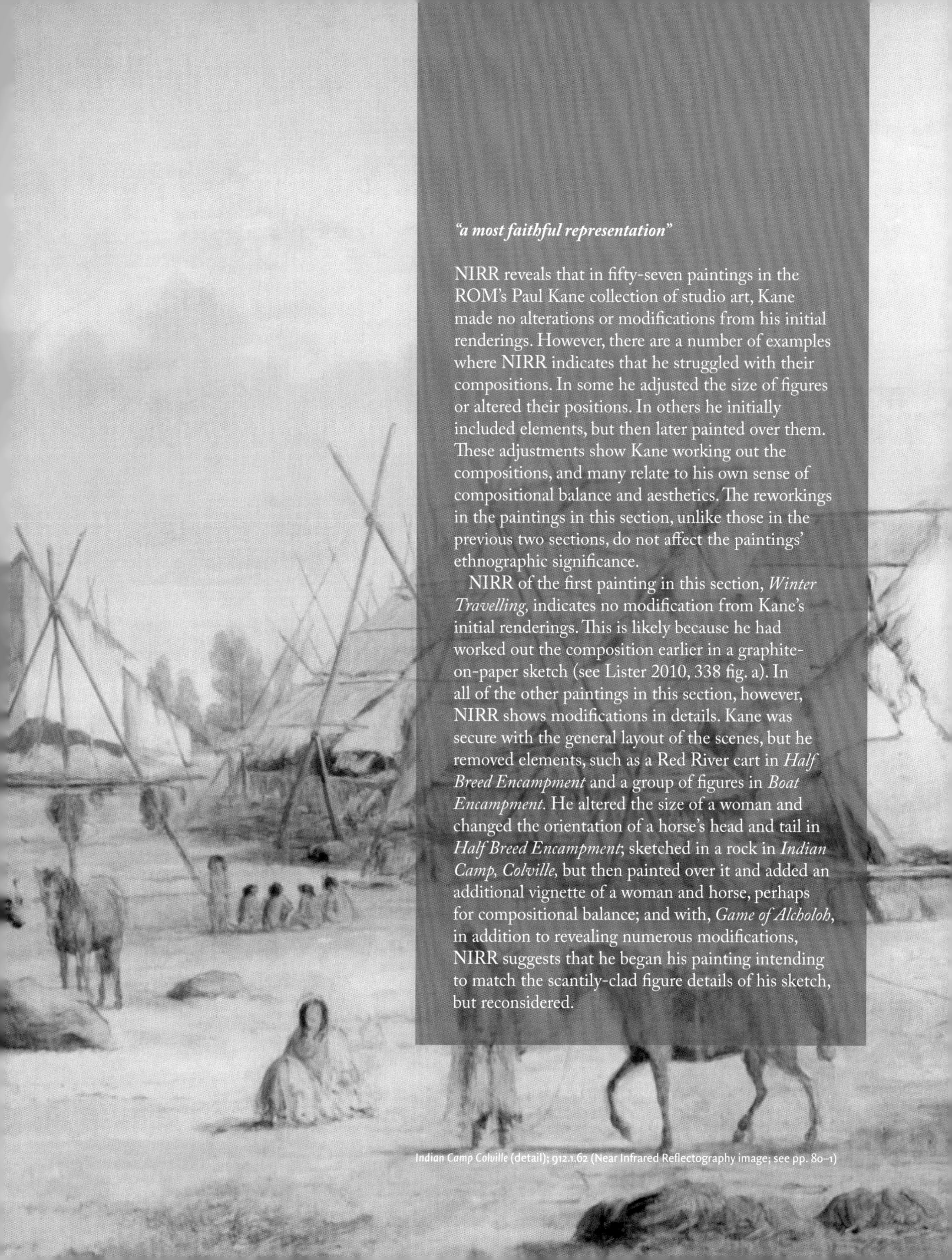

Indian Camp Colville (detail); 912.1.62 (Near Infrared Reflectography image; see pp. 80–1)

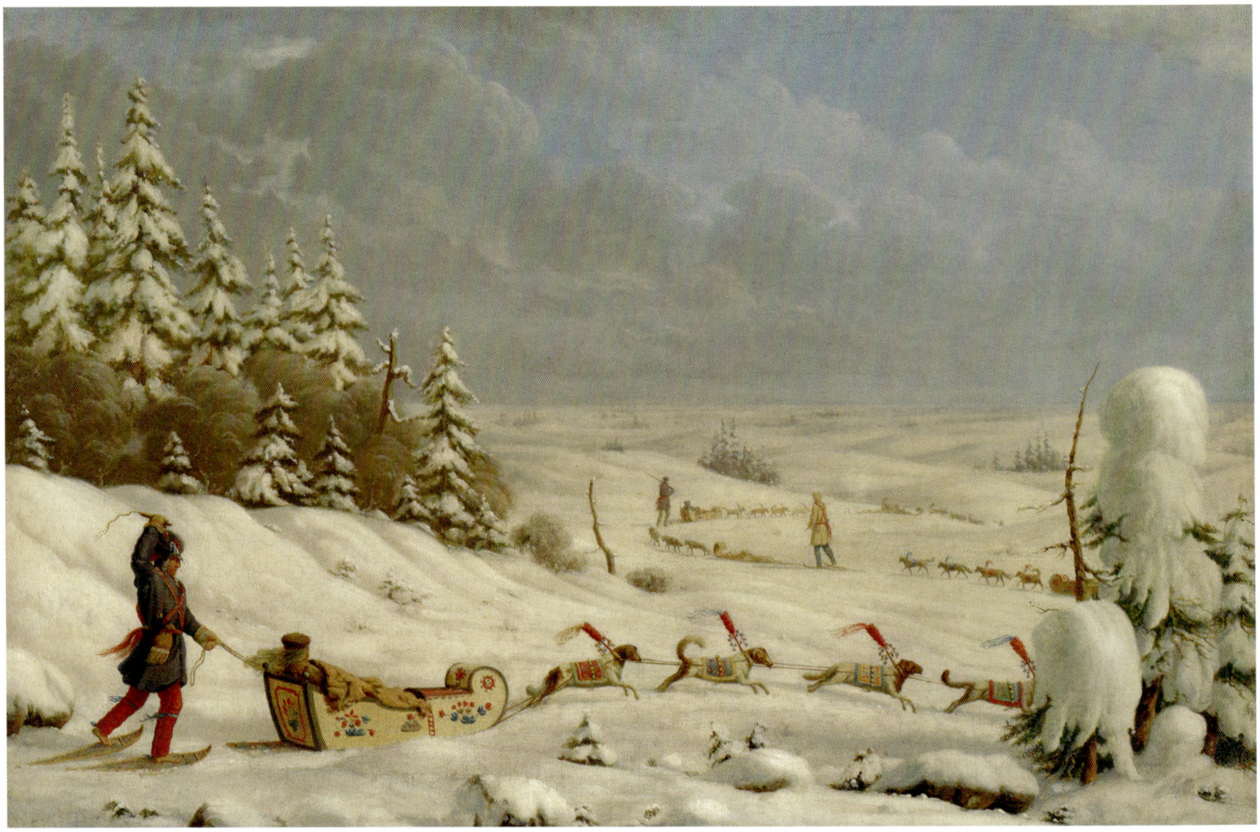

Fig. 62 *Winter Travelling*
Métis and Euro-Canadian
Fort Edmonton to Fort Pitt, North Saskatchewan River, Alberta–Saskatchewan
1849–1856
oil on canvas; 48.8 × 74.8 cm
912.1.48

> *Next morning I was awoke by the yelping of the dogs and the ringing of the bells on the dog-collars, accompanied by the shouts of the men thrashing the brutes into something like discipline, as they harnessed them to the sledges and carioles . . . . We had three carioles and six sledges, with four dogs to each, forming when on route a long and picturesque cavalcade: all the dogs gaudily decorated with saddle-cloths of various colours, fringed and embroidered in the most fantastic manner, with innumerable small bells and feathers, producing altogether a pleasing and enlivening effect.* (Kane 1859, 385–87)

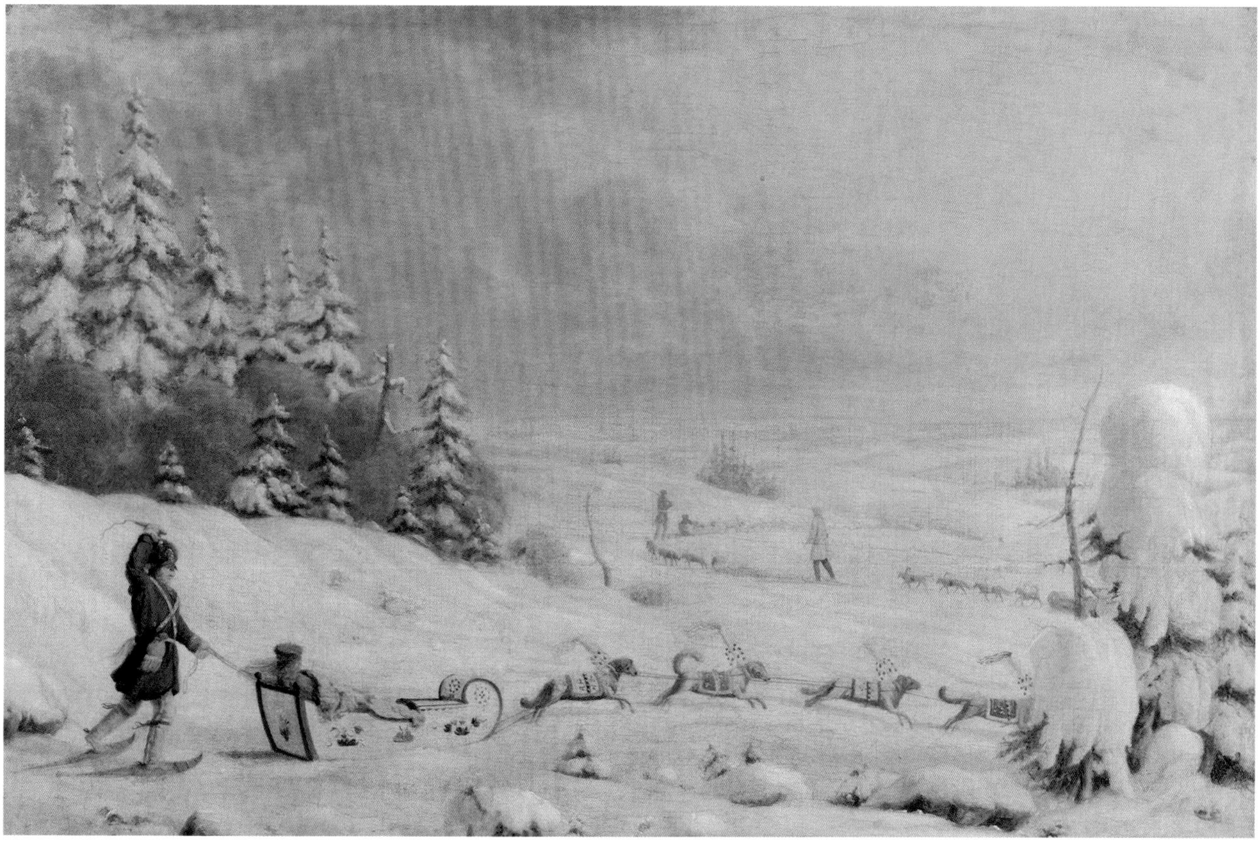

Fig. 63

Kane shows his confidence with this composition as the NIRR image reveals no alterations or modifications.

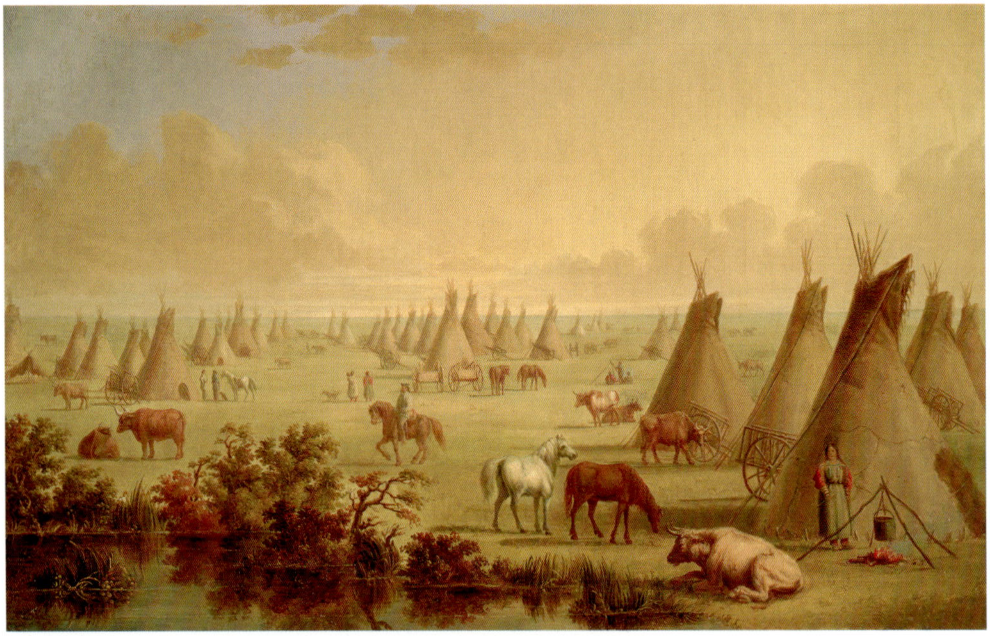

Fig. 64 *Half Breed Encampment*
Plains Métis
Pembina River region, Manitoba–North Dakota
1849–1856
oil on canvas; 45.8 × 74.3 cm
912.1.25

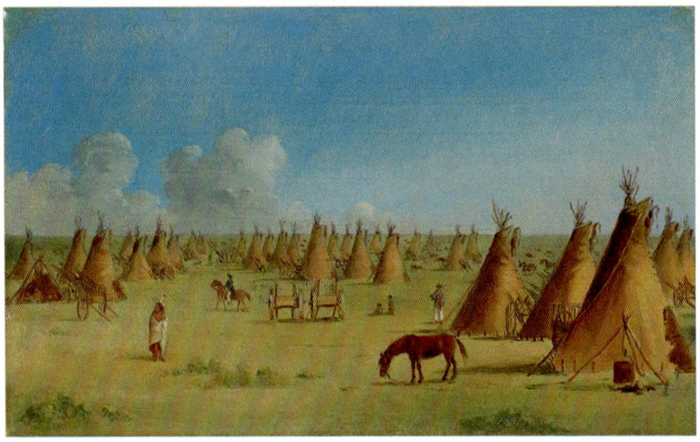

Fig. 65 *A Métis Encampment*
Plains Métis
Pembina River region, Manitoba–North Dakota
1846–1849
oil on paper; 20.9 × 34.6 cm
Art Gallery of Ontario
103726

> *I was received by the band with the greatest cordiality. They numbered about two hundred hunters, besides women and children. They live, during these hunting excursions, in lodges formed of dressed buffalo skins.* (Kane 1859, 78–79)

Paul Kane arrived at Upper Fort Garry and the Red River Settlement on June 15, 1846. Three days later, following the advice of Sir George Simpson to witness the Métis bison hunt (HBCA E.42/1 fol. 43), Kane left Fort Garry for the Pembina River and Turtle Mountain regions of southern Manitoba and North Dakota where the Métis were gathering for the June hunt. Based upon their mixed Native and European ancestry, the Métis developed a distinct lifeway that included employment with the HBC as voyageurs. They also worked as labourers, farmers, trappers, and especially bison hunters. Kane records in his journal that the hunters were divided into two parties of 250. Wives and children accompanied the hunters, and he estimated that there were 1500 Red River carts in use with each cart capable of carrying 454 kilograms (1000 pounds) of dried meat (Kane 1989, 24).

Kane stayed with the Métis hunters for the remaining days of June during which time he participated in the hunt and took sketches of bison, the Métis encampments, details of the Red River carts and their uses, hunters on horseback, and the long line of Red River carts pulled by horses and oxen travelling across the undulating prairie (see Lister 2010, 130 CS-28–31, 131 CS-32, 175 MIS-11–13).

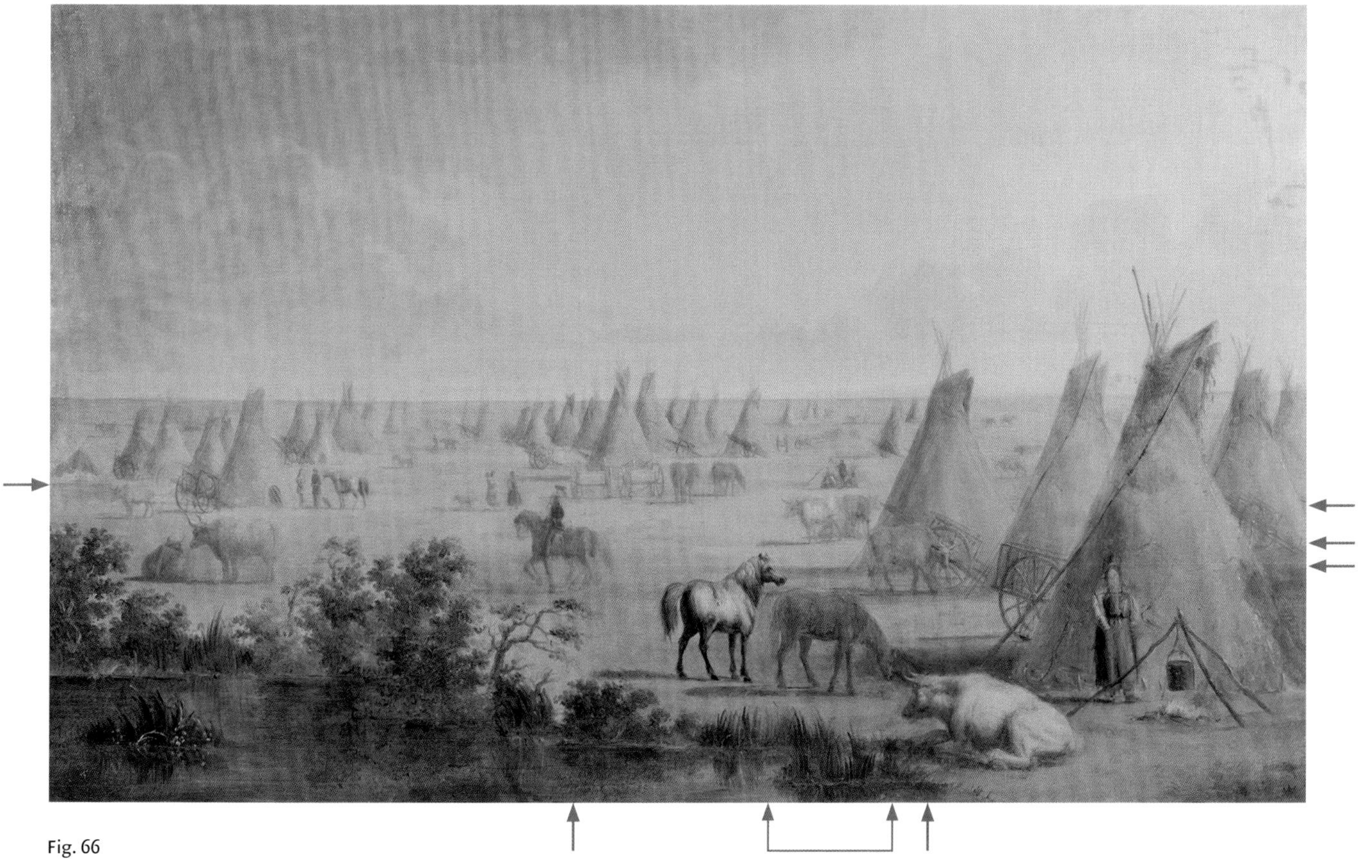

Fig. 66

Kane took a series of sketches that show the hide teepees and the layout of the Métis encampments, but he did not take a field sketch that relates specifically to the composition of *Half Breed Encampment*. However, an oil-on-paper painting that was completed by 1849 for Sir George Simpson (*A Métis Encampment*) shows a version of the composition that Kane would later develop in his studio oil-on-canvas painting. It is interesting to note that the NIRR image of the oil-on-paper painting shows Kane sketched the scene first in graphite and then painted over the composition in oil.

Kane appears to have worked out the general composition for his oil-on-canvas painting of *Half Breed Encampment* in the scene he painted on paper for Simpson. The NIRR image of the oil-on-canvas painting reveals little alteration to the initial composition he laid down and, thus, demonstrates his security with the overall scene. A number of details, however, were altered. The most obvious adjustment was reducing the height of the woman standing behind the cook fire on the right side of the painting. There were adjustments in the dimensions of the ox resting adjacent to the fire. The tail of the horse in front of the ox and the orientation of the horse's neck and head were changed as were the legs of the central horse. Kane initially painted tent poles carried by the cart that is partially hidden by the ox in the right central ground and just beyond, an ox was completely painted out. Similarly, Kane eliminated a cart that was originally positioned between the two carts in the left of the painting, and by painting out the cart he filled in the wall of the hide teepee beyond.

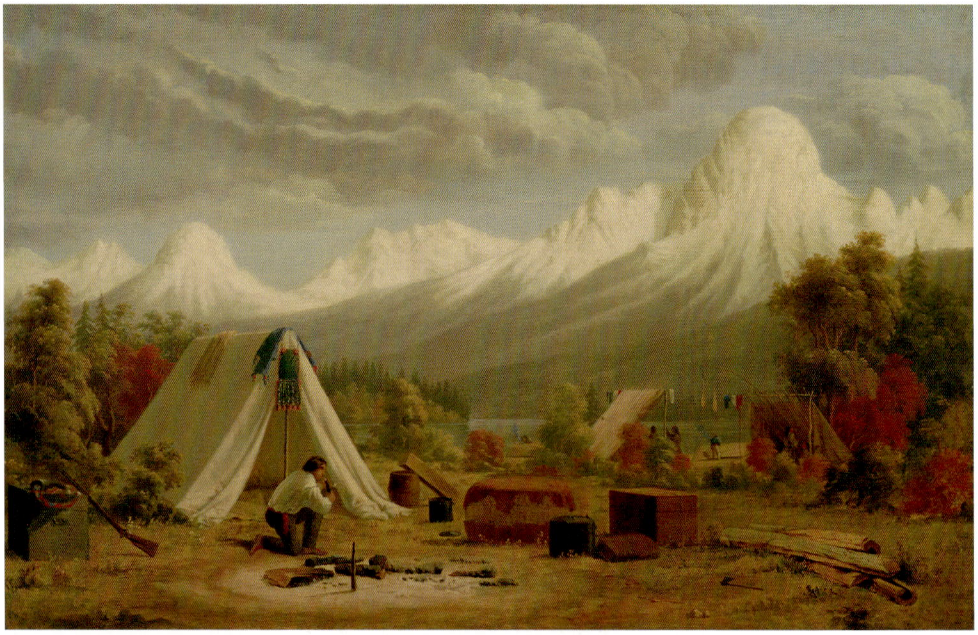

Fig. 67 *Boat Encampment*
Hudson's Bay Company brigade
Confluence of the Columbia, Canoe, and Wood Rivers, British Columbia
1849–1856
oil on canvas; 46.1 × 73.8 cm
912.1.60

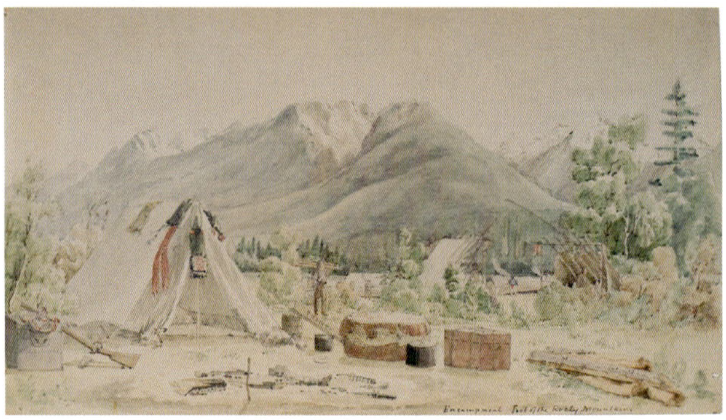

Fig. 68 *Boat Encampment*
Hudson's Bay Company brigade
Confluence of the Columbia, Canoe, and Wood Rivers, British Columbia
mid–late October 1847
watercolour on paper; 13.3 × 22.2 cm
Stark Museum of Art, Orange, Texas
31.78.99

> *Here we made a suitable encampment, and hauled up our boats high and dry on the sand . . . .*
>
> *We now had nothing to do but to try and pass the time pleasantly as we could under the circumstances, until the arrival of the brigade from the east side of the mountains.* (Kane 1859, 336–37)

The location known as "Boat Encampment" at the northern end of the Columbia River was labelled as such in recognition of the experience of North West Company explorer David Thompson, who in 1811 built a boat there to journey down the Columbia River. Birchbark for the construction of a bark canoe was unavailable, so Thompson designed a clinker-style boat built with overlapping cedar boards (Nisbet 1994, 178; 2005, 91–93; Tyrrell 1916, 454–55). Boat Encampment became the rendezvous for the Columbia River fur trade, where the westbound brigade, after crossing over the Athabasca Pass, met the eastbound brigade that had boated up the length of the Columbia River.

Kane travelled through Boat Encampment on both his eastbound and westbound journeys. In November 1846, he spent but a night there since the brigade waiting for him was anxious to leave the snow of the mountains (Kane 1859, 164). On his return east, just short of a year later, from October 10 to 31, 1847, Kane waited at Boat Encampment for the westbound brigade to cross the Athabasca Pass (Kane 1859, 336–39). It was during this lengthy stay that Kane had the opportunity to sketch the distant mountains (see Lister 2010, 119 L-46) and the camp scene.

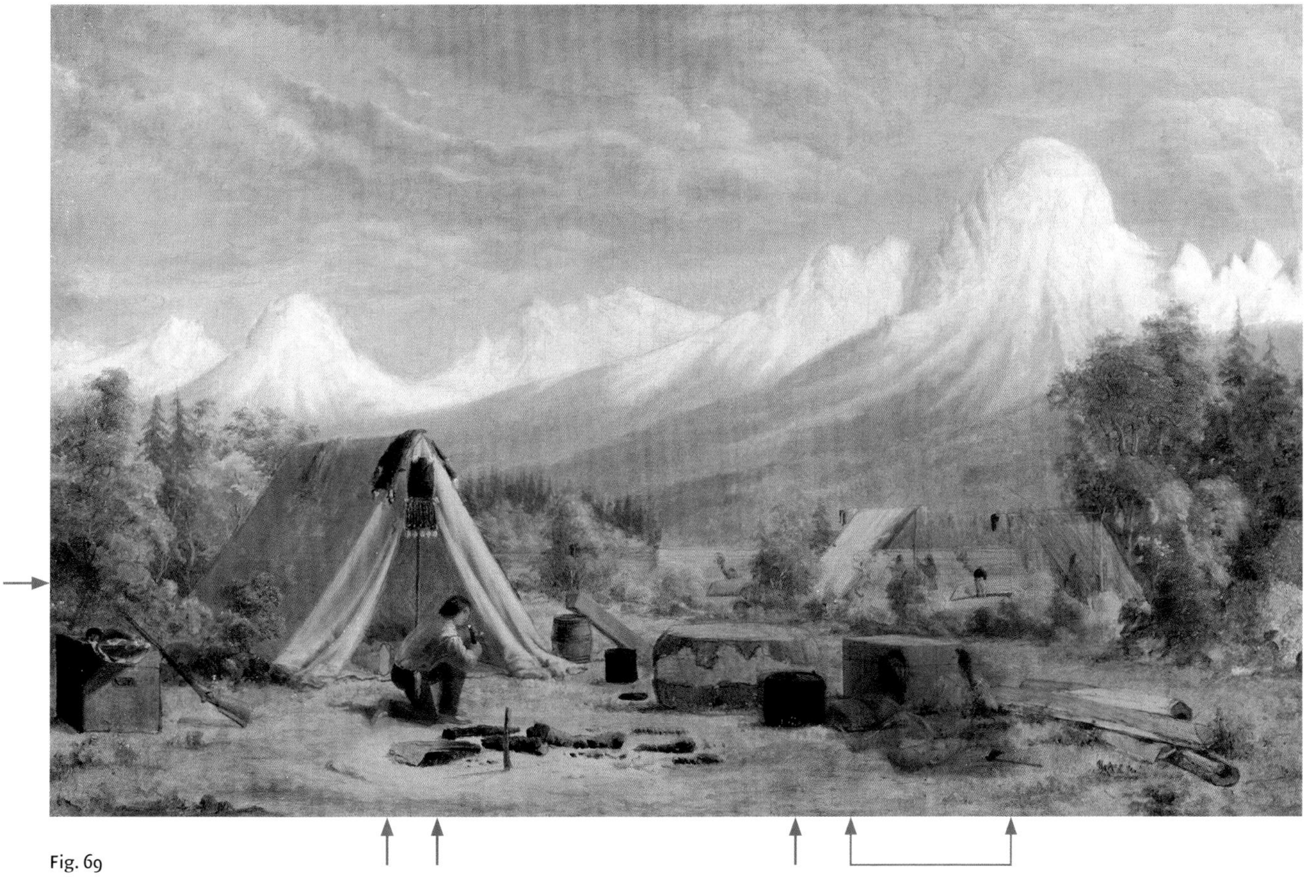

Fig. 69

Comparison of the watercolour sketch and the studio oil painting of Boat Encampment shows that the composition of the sketch was the inspiration for the painting. Many of the foreground details of the sketch's camp scene are incorporated into the painting, although Kane exchanged the background mountain landscape for one he recorded in a different sketch (see Lister 2010, 330–31).

Study of the NIRR image of the painting reveals that Kane was secure with the painting's setting and general scene, but over the course of its development he made a number of alterations in the details. Most noticeably, he initially painted two men spread out in front of the packing box in the right foreground. The front individual was finished in considerable detail as we can see the design of his clothing and its embellishments, including a porcupine-quill embroidered band that runs down the length of his left legging. Kane made a change in the size or position of the black pot to the left of the reclining men and he slightly altered the positioning of the kneeling man's legs and feet.

Behind the packing case in the extreme left of the painting, Kane originally included a tripod that he subsequently painted out to blend into the background vegetation. The stock end of the gun and the trigger guard were initially larger and there is some suggestion that the barrel of the gun was aligned with a tripod leg. Kane may have expunged the tripod to eliminate this potential confusion. Finally, resisting a touch of humour, he painted over the outstretched leg of a man resting in the tent and noticeable by the erect sole of his moccasin.

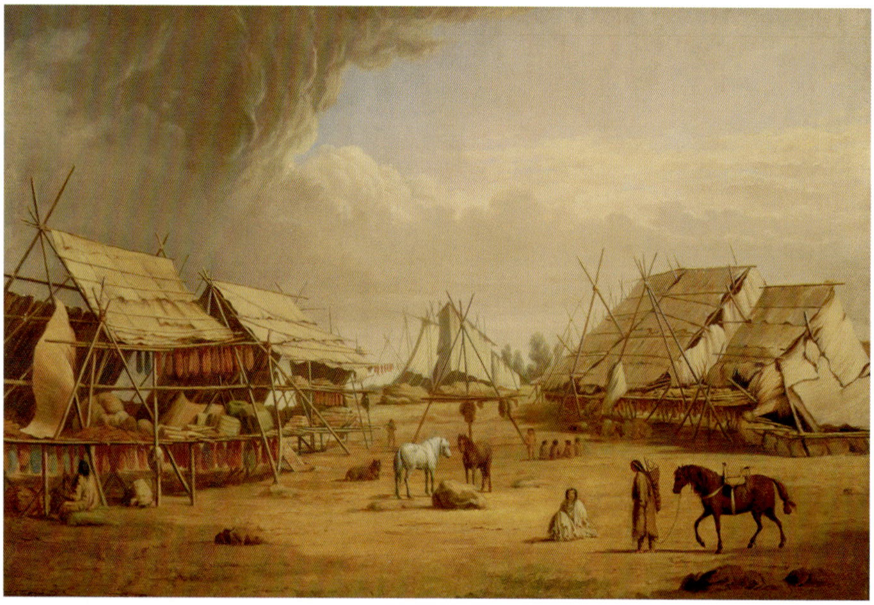

Fig. 70 *Indian Camp, Colville*
Colville (Interior Salish)
Village of Takumakst, Kettle Falls, Columbia River, Washington
1849–1856
oil on canvas; 46.0 × 70.1 cm
912.1.62

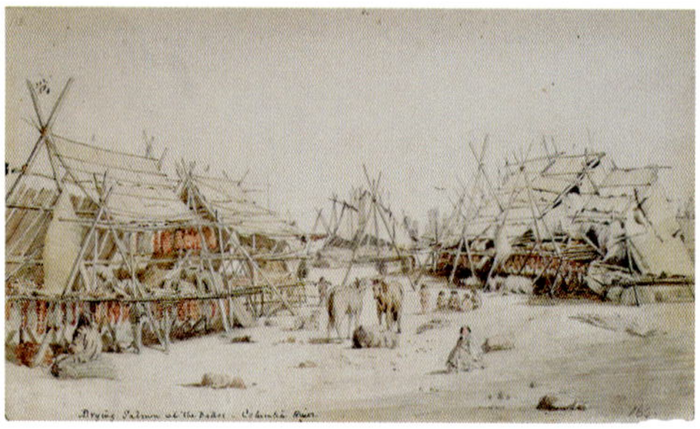

Fig. 71 *Indian Lodges at Colville*
Colville (Interior Salish)
Village of Takumakst, Kettle Falls, Columbia River, Washington
September 16–21, 1847
watercolour on paper; 14.0 × 23.5 cm
Stark Museum of Art, Orange, Texas
31.78.50

> *The village has a population of about five hundred souls, called, in their own language, Chualpays. They differ but little from the Walla-Wallas. The lodges are formed of mats of rushes stretched on poles. A flooring is made of sticks, raised three or four feet from the ground, leaving the space beneath it entirely open, and forming a cool, airy, and shady place, in which to hang their salmon to dry.* (Kane 1859, 309)

The village of Takumakst, translated as "the fishery," was formed each year when the Colville Indians assembled at Kettle Falls for the summer fishing season. Kettle Falls was one of the principal salmon fisheries in the Pacific Northwest (Chance 1985, 1) and it is estimated that throughout the fishing season the falls were visited by as many as five thousand people (Chance 1986, 42). Kane arrived at Kettle Falls at the height of the fishing season on August 6, 1847 and stayed at Fort Colvile. The fort was established in 1825 to be close to the fishery. Fort Colvile became the district headquarters for the HBC, as well as the main boatyard for the construction of the Columbia River bateaux.

Kane took a series of sketches during his stay at the falls and this record has become invaluable for documenting the landscape, people, and cultural practices of the area in the mid-nineteenth century. His sketches of the J-shaped basket trap, its description in his book, *Wanderings of an Artist,* and additional sketches of fishermen wielding spears and their spearing locations provide a rich record (see Lister 2010, 326). In his studio painting, *Falls at Colville* (see Lister 2010, 327), Kane illustrated the river landscape and variety of fishing techniques. With this painting and his sketches, Kane provides the most thorough series of visual ethnographic documentation available for the period.

Kane's sketch of the Takumakst village (*Indian Lodges at Colville*) and the oil painting, *Indian Camp, Colville,* are particularly noteworthy. Here Kane shows lodges raised on poles to provide space beneath for salmon, prepared and hung to dry. The lodges show rush mat roofing in combination with cedar boards positioned to protect the lodges from the strongest winds and the intense sun (Chance 1986, 48–50).

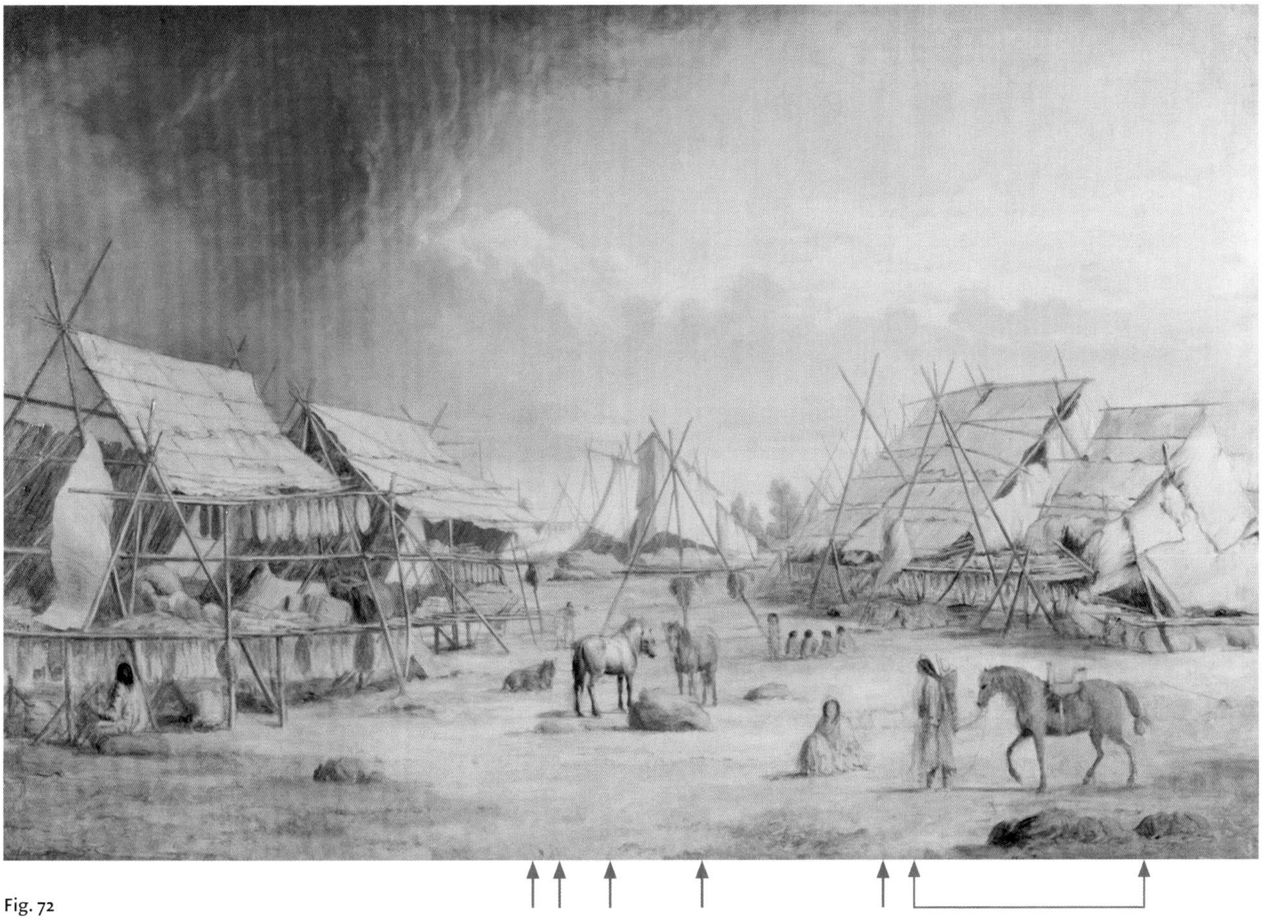

Fig. 72

The watercolour sketch, *Indian Lodges at Colville*, shows Kane's interest in recording both the visual appearance of the scene and its cultural context. The lodge on the right and the two lodges on the left each have a number scribed above their ridge poles and in his Landscape Log Kane uses the numbers to identify ownership: number 1, the head chief's lodge; number 2, the second chief's lodge; and number 3, the salmon chief's lodge (Kane 1846–1848, 136). The composition of the oil painting is a close rendering of the sketch's scene and through it Kane provides a significant visual record to support his published narrative.

Study of the NIRR image shows that Kane made minimal alterations to the background scene of the lodges and their layout. This is the ethnographically significant part of the painting and here he reveals his faithfulness to the field sketch. In similar fashion, an oil-on-paper painting completed for Sir George Simpson illustrates the desire to record a "faithful representation" (see Lister 2010, 320 fig. c).

On the other hand, review of the foreground composition shows Kane to have struggled with arrangements. The position of the head of the white horse in the centre of the painting was reoriented as were the shapes of the two adjacent horses and the tail of the saddled horse on the right. Originally, Kane painted the reins of the saddled horse held taut in the right hand of the leading woman and he slightly altered her positioning. In the centre ground, a figure is shown walking into the open field carrying possibly a large salmon over his right shoulder; this figure is included in the sketch. The NIRR image shows Kane also painted an additional smaller figure that he subsequently painted over. In the sketch, behind the woman seated on the ground, Kane shows a large rectangular-shaped rock. In the oil painting, it appears that Kane originally sketched in the rock, inspired by the composition of the field sketch. However, as the painting was being developed he decided to ignore it, likely because he chose to develop the more complex woman-and-horse vignette—not recorded in the sketch—to add compositional balance.

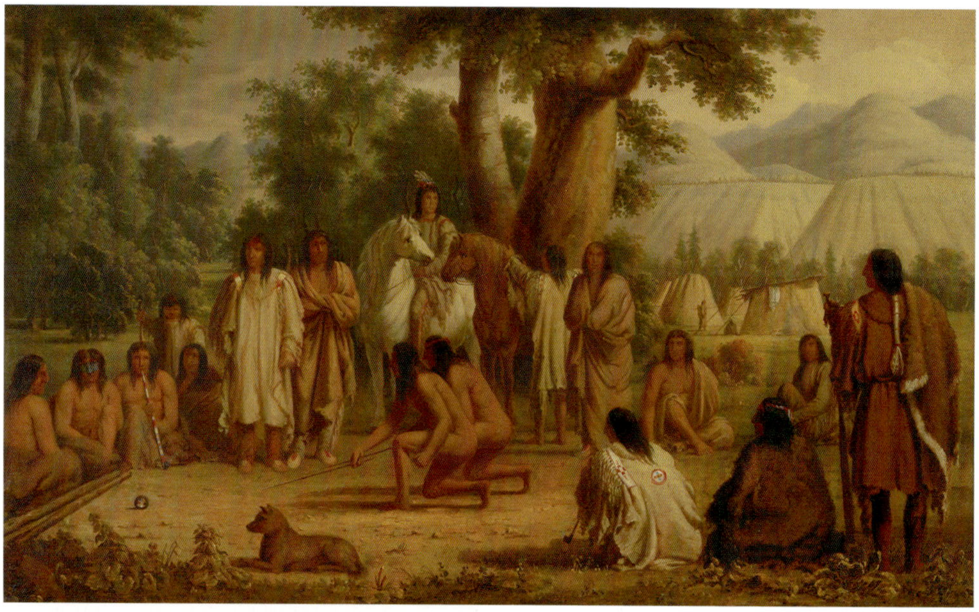

Fig. 73 *Game of Alcholoh*
Colville (Interior Salish)
Kettle Falls, Columbia River, Washington
1849–1856
oil on canvas; 43.0 × 71.3 cm
912.1.65

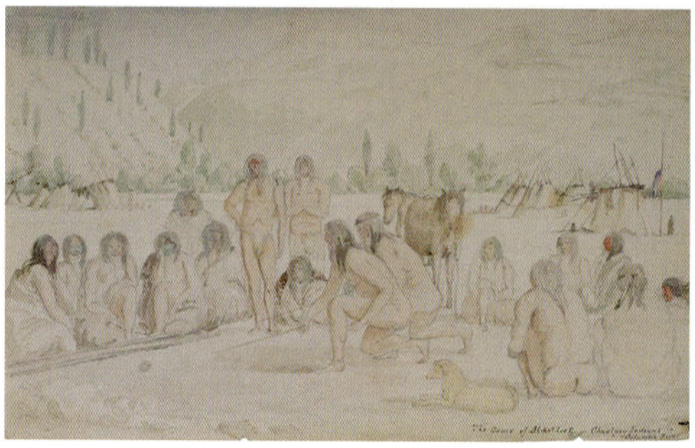

Fig. 74 *The Game of Al-kol-lock, Columbia River*
Colville (Interior Salish)
Kettle Falls, Columbia River, Washington
September 16–22, 1847
watercolour on paper; 14.0 × 22.9 cm
Stark Museum of Art, Orange, Texas
31.78.77

The principal game played here is called Al-kol-lock . . . . A smooth level piece of ground is chosen, and a slight barrier of a couple of sticks placed lengthwise, is laid at each end of the chosen spot . . . . The two players, stripped naked, are armed each with a very slight spear about three feet long . . . ; one of them takes a ring . . . about three inches in diameter, on the inner circumference of which are fastened six beads of different colours at equal distances, to each of which a separate numerical value is attached. The ring is then rolled along the ground to one of the barriers, and is followed at the distance of two or three yards by the players, and as the ring strikes the barrier and is falling on its side, the spears are thrown, so that the ring may fall on them. If only one of the spears should be covered by the ring, the owner of it counts according to the coloured bead over it. But it generally happens, from the dexterity of the players, that the ring covers both spears, and each counts according to the colour of the beads above his spear . . . . (Kane 1859, 310–11)

Gambling among the Colville and other peoples of the Columbia River region was a "cultural theme" and part of the activities encompassed by special events, such as economic gatherings related to salmon fishing, harvesting roots, and gathering berries (Brunton 1998, 573). Games promoted "in-group solidarity and out-group rivalry" and while games accorded prestige they also re-channeled aggression (Desmond in Brunton 1998, 581–82).

The hoop-and-pin game that Kane witnessed while in the Kettle Falls area was recorded initially in a field sketch and subsequently in the studio painting. The game was given an excellent description in his published narrative, *Wanderings of an Artist,* and thus it is printed above at length. In a graphite sketch dedicated to the hoop, Kane recorded the colours of the beads—two black, two green, two blue—that he then illustrated in a watercolour sketch demonstrating his concern for the accuracy of ethnographic details (see Lister 2010, 322 figs. b, c).

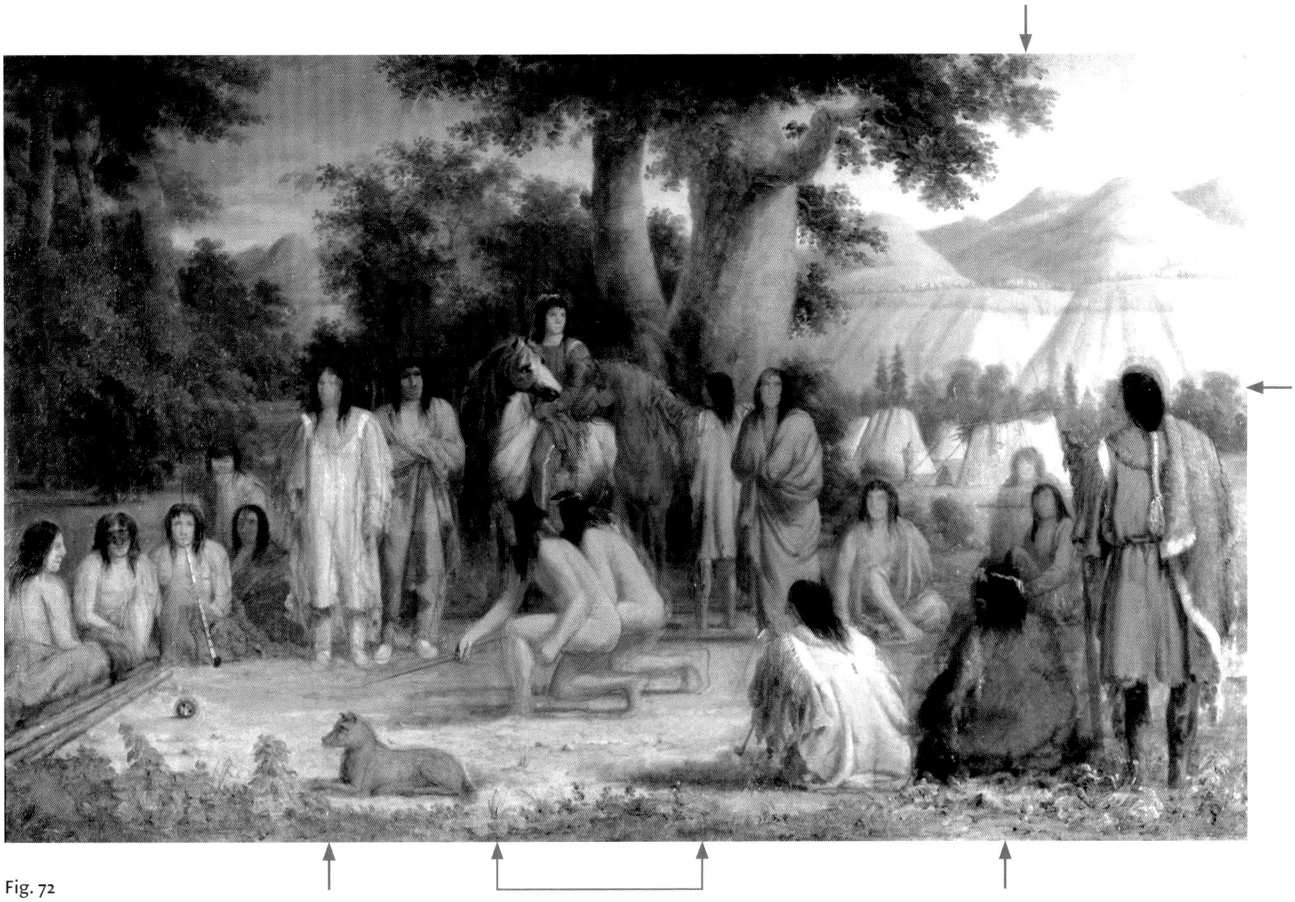

Fig. 72

In his Portrait Log entry for his sketch, *The Game of Al-kol-lock, Columbia River*, Kane writes that the hoop-and-pin game he recorded was played for the win of two horses (Kane 1846–1848, 99). This important detail explains the two standing horses shown behind the players. When Kane developed the oil painting, *Game of Alcholoh,* back in his Toronto studio he stayed true to the elements of the game, including the horses, but he altered considerably details relating to the landscape, clothing, and representations of the witnesses.

In comparing the sketch to the oil painting, we see that Kane maintained the overall scene of the game and the surround of witnesses, but fictionalized the background landscape; gave clothing to those who were more scantily clad; and gave the horses a quality of grandeur, or nobility. In his attempt to give the painting a grand style, Kane created confusion and compromised the integrity of his field sketch. For instance, in the sketch, the two standing men, almost naked, give the appearance that they are waiting their turns to play. This feeling of anticipation—expressed through their assertive stances—is completely lost in the studio painting.

Study of the NIRR image reveals that Kane was fairly secure with the overall composition: the background mountains, lodges, and the trees were painted without further modification; the stances of the horses appear unaltered; and the general configuration of the witnesses seems true to his initial rendering. Kane did struggle though with the size of some individuals and the positioning of limbs. The seated man in the foreground wearing the fur robe was repositioned or made smaller. The height of the standing man on the far right was lessened. A figure standing in the right background was completely expunged. The front leg of the forward game player was moved back and the body of the second player was repositioned, as evidenced by the "ghost" foot.

The forward standing man wearing the white skin shirt deserves careful scrutiny. Dark lines outline the inner shapes of his legs and the creases at the junction of the legs and the groin. Horizontal lines demarcate his chest. Did Kane begin his painting with the notion of following the observations in his sketch and then succumb to propriety?

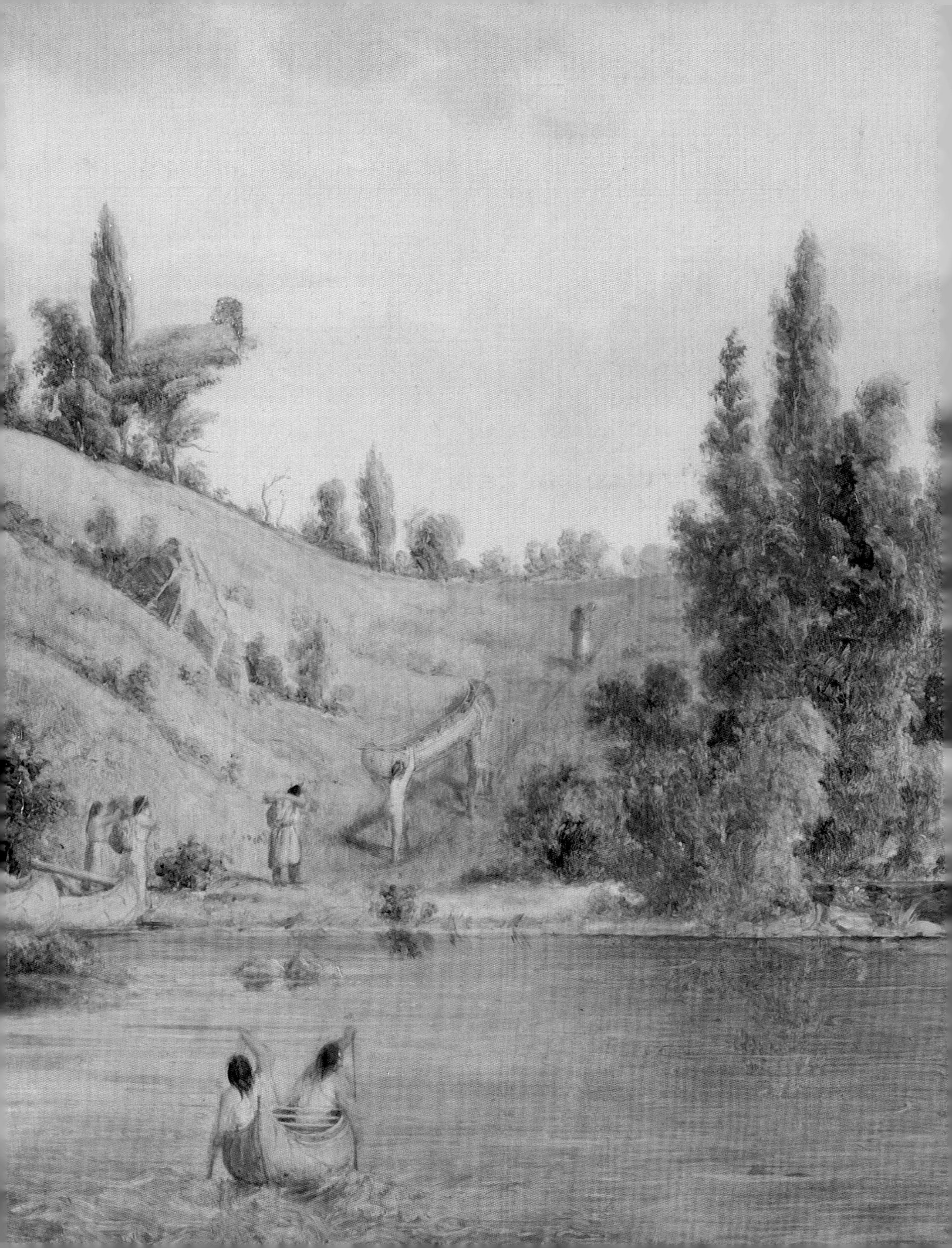

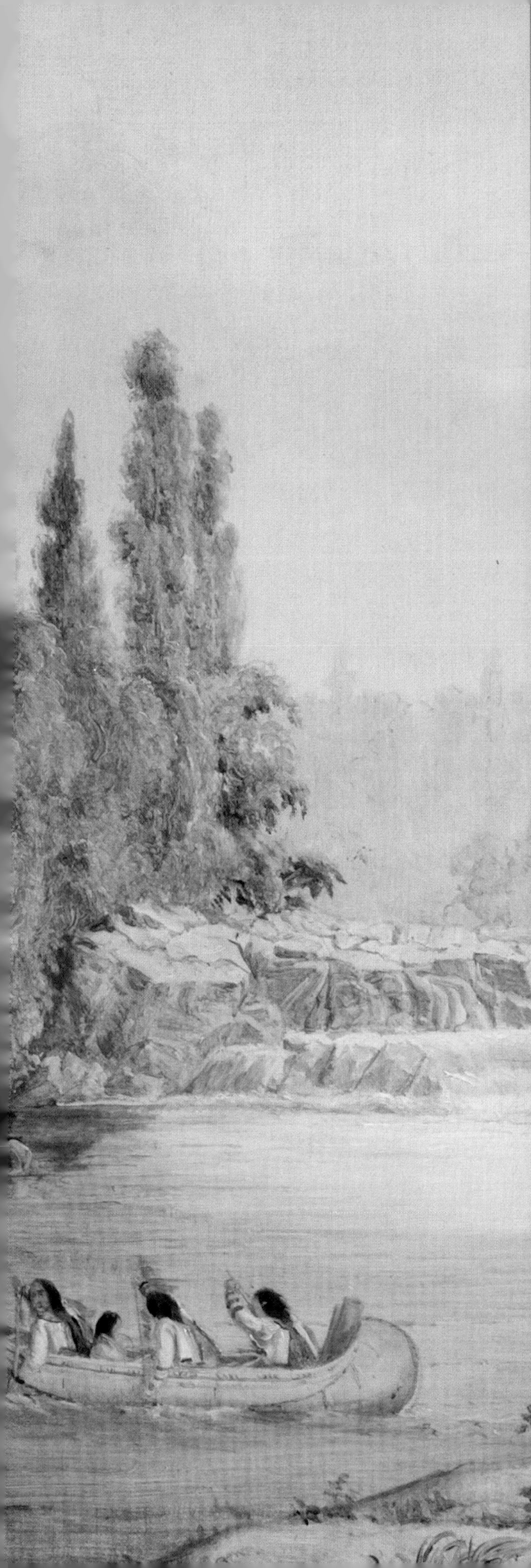

"out of a series of Paintings"

The NIRR technique reveals underdrawings and underpaintings that Kane initially rendered on his canvases. In some paintings, Kane began by following the accuracy of his sketches only to change details later, thereby affecting their ethnographic significance. He also changed elements in an attempt to refine compositional details or satisfy his own aesthetic. The ability of NIRR to record what is below the surface also allows the identification of original paintings versus subsequent versions that Kane painted at a later time. A painting that shows multiple modifications indicates Kane working out the composition. In comparison, a painting of the same scene in which NIRR reveals few modifications indicates confidence, suggesting a later version of the scene previously developed.

The NIRR study of *A Sketch on Lake Huron* in the ROM collection, in comparison to the same scene in the Art Gallery of Ontario (AGO) collection, revealed the surprise that the ROM's painting is a second version. Since the ROM's version is part of the George William Allan commission of paintings, it was assumed to be his initial effort. However, the numerous modifications clearly evident in the AGO version, and missing in the ROM copy, identify it as the one that shows Kane's initial struggle. The comparison of the ROM's *Indian Horse Race* to the same scene in a National Gallery of Canada (NGC) painting shows Kane copied the ROM's version: the elements of toil seen in the NIRR image of the ROM's version are absent in the NGC version. Finally, the NIRR image of the NGC painting *White Mud Portage* reveals areas of heavy outlining that are missing in the ROM's version. This detail suggests that the NGC version may have been traced from the ROM's version—a likely response to the pressure Kane was feeling from the Canadian Parliament to comply with the terms of its commission (see p. 92–7).

White Mud Portage (detail); 912.1.21 (Near Infrared Reflectography image; see pp. 90–1)

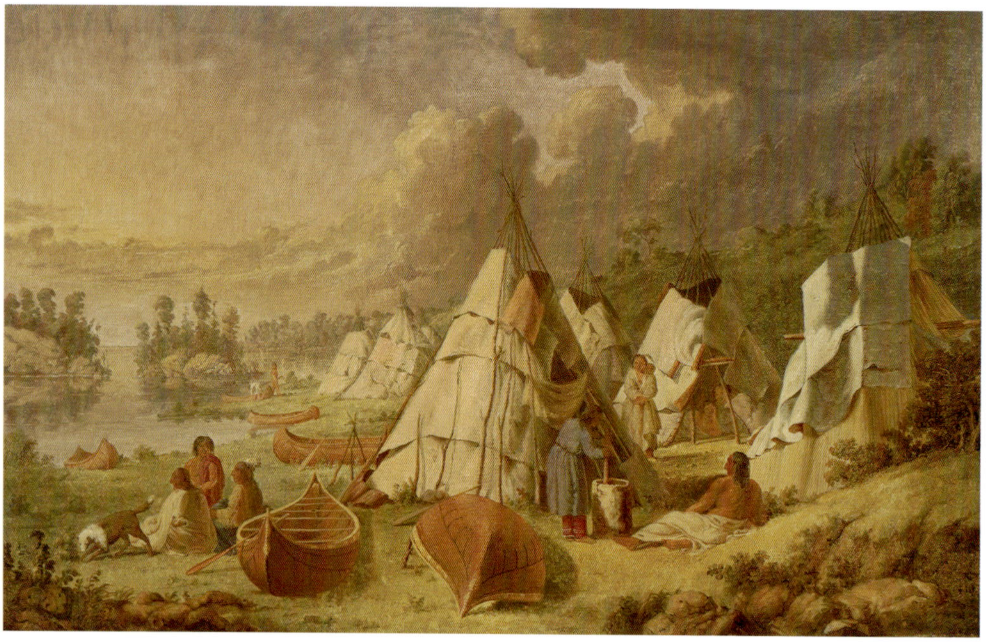

Fig. 76 *A Sketch on Lake Huron*
Southern Algonquian
Thirty Thousand Islands, Georgian Bay, Southern Ontario
1849–1852?
oil on canvas; 46.0 × 74.2 cm
912.1.8

Fig. 77 *Indian Encampment*
Southern Algonquian
Thirty Thousand Islands, Georgian Bay, Southern Ontario
mid-July 1845
graphite on paper; 13.7 × 21.5 cm
946.15.40

> *Sketch No. 1 represents an Indian encampment amongst the islands of Lake Huron; the wigwams are made of birch-bark, stripped from the trees in large pieces and sewed together with long fibrous roots; when the birch tree cannot be conveniently had, they weave rushes into mats, called Apuckway, for covering, which are stretched round in the same manner as the bark, upon eight or ten poles tied together at the top, and stuck in the ground at the required circle of the tent, a hole being left at the top to permit the smoke to go out. The fire is made in the centre of the lodge, and the inmates sleep all round with their feet towards it.* (Kane 1859, 6–7)

Kane paddled through the Thirty Thousand Islands of Georgian Bay during his 1845 journey, when he also visited the Saugeen village at the bottom of the Bruce Peninsula, Manitoulin Island, St. Marys River at Sault Ste. Marie, Mackinac Island, and Fox River, Wisconsin. In his journal he commented upon the "delitefule scenery" (Kane 1845, 106) of the island landscape and in his book, *Wanderings of an Artist*, he expounded upon the islands' "picturesque mazes" and the "beauty of the ever-varying scenery" (Kane 1859, 6).

The composition of the oil painting, *A Sketch on Lake Huron*, is based upon a graphite sketch that shows a shoreline with a village of conical-shaped lodges receding into the distance. Features of lodge design and construction and elements of the encampment were inspired by additional sketches that illustrate details, such as the conical framework of poles for the lodges, the birchbark-sheet covering, bark canoes, and tripods set up over fires for suspending cooking pots (see Lister 2010, 70 figs. CS-1–4; 71 fig. CS-5; 190 figs. a–c).

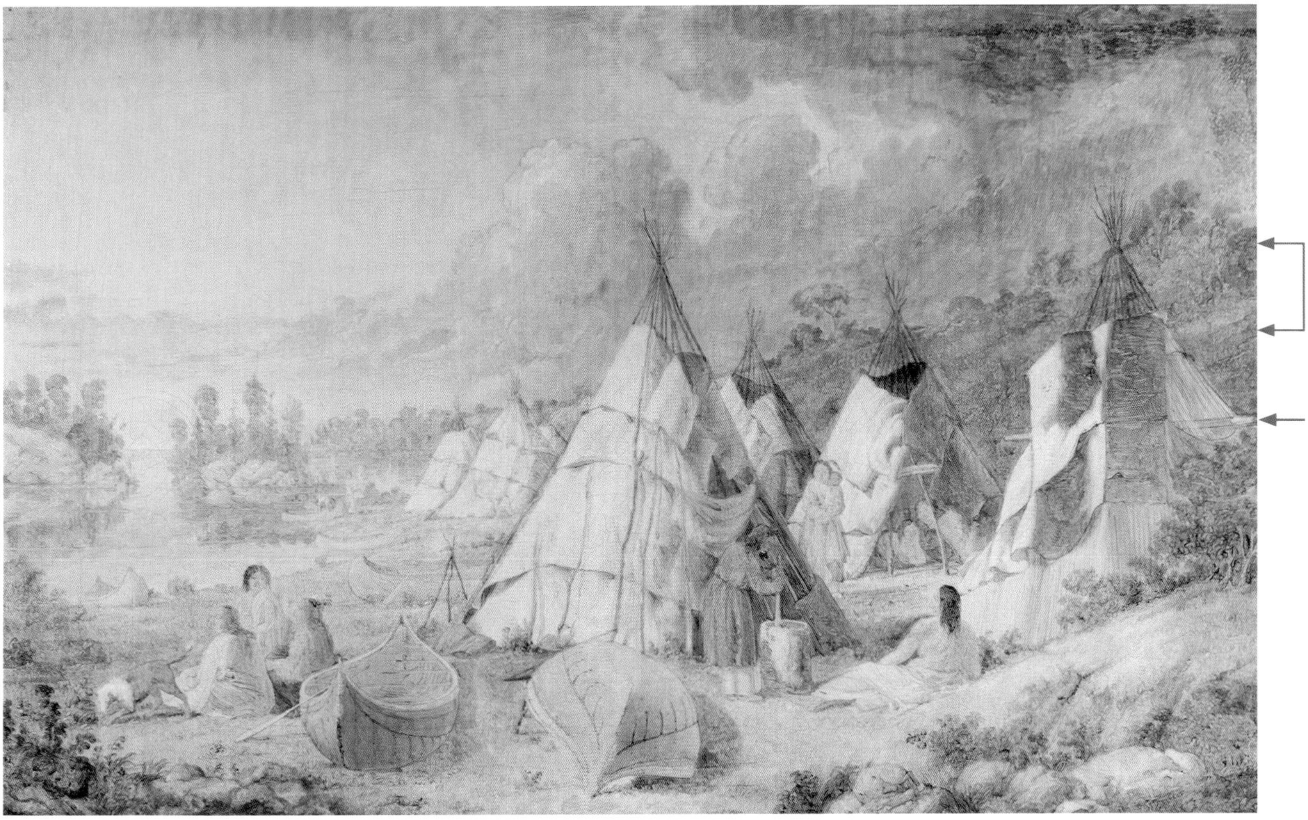

Fig. 78

A Sketch on Lake Huron is a complex composition showing an encampment of lodges receding into the distance, matching the background landscape that withdraws into the centre ground of the painting. The foreground shows cultural activities taking place and Kane provides a number of elements relevant to Southern Algonquian camps, such as a dog, birchbark canoes, lodge construction details, and a tripod for cooking over a fire.

In recognition of the complexity of the composition and with the knowledge that Kane did not have an encampment sketch with this degree of detail to follow, it is intriguing to note that the NIRR image reveals only minimal alterations in the painting's development. For instance, a slight alteration is noticeable to the extended poles at the top of the lodge on the far right. A curious modification that warrants thought and creates further bewilderment is the already enigmatic pole that penetrates through the mid-section of the same lodge.

In the painting, Kane depicts a long pole that extends from the edge of the painting, and thus from the external frame of the lodge, through the central section of the lodge to pierce through the cover on the opposite side. The pole is located over the entrance to the lodge identified by the draped door cover. A possible interpretation, as suggested by Arlene Gehmacher (personal communication, 2013) and illustrated by Kane in a graphite sketch of a lodge (see Lister 2010, 70 fig. CS-1), is that the pole represents the header for the door. However, the extension of the pole through the opposite side of the lodge is puzzling and incongruous for such a purpose. Another possibility is that Kane has used the horizontal pole as a technique to trick the viewer's eye to see a horizontal line in the total composition. The NIRR image adds intrigue for it reveals that Kane initially drew in the pole, but then painted over a section with the representation of the rush mat covering of the lodge. This modification, in combination with the extension of the pole through the opposite side, suggests Kane favoured a compositional role for this element over the accuracy of an architectural feature.

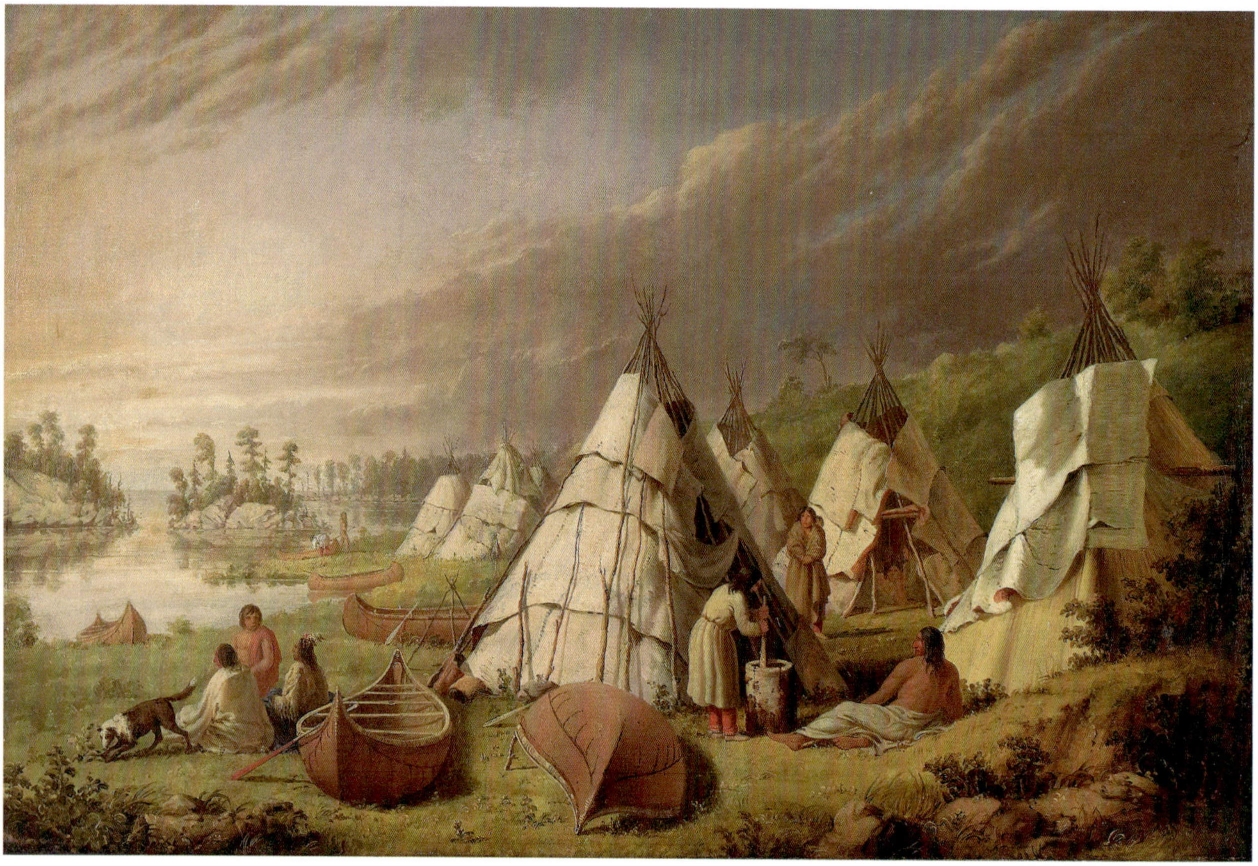

Fig. 79 *Indian Encampment on Lake Huron*
Southern Algonquian
Thirty Thousand Islands, Georgian Bay, southern Ontario
1849–1852?
oil on canvas; 48.3 × 73.7 cm
Art Gallery of Ontario, Purchase, 1932, 2121

In 1852, Kane placed eight of his studio paintings on display in the Fine Arts section of Toronto's Provincial Agricultural Show. A review of the exhibition in the *The Canadian Journal of Industry, Science, and Art* (1852, 60) identified Kane as "foremost" among the exhibited artists showing "eight beautiful paintings of Indian subjects." Susanna Moodie, who visited the fair, concurred, stating, "Eight pictures, illustrative of Indian scenery, character, and customs, by Mr. Paul Kane would have done honour to any exhibition" (Moodie [1853] 1959, 237). She continued by idealizing the paintings' designs, colouring, and faithful representations.

Kane included a version of this encampment scene in the Landscape category of the exhibition, and it was reviewed in the *Anglo-American Magazine* (1852, 373) under the title *Camp of Indians on Lake Huron.* The reviewer commented upon the "Canadian character of the scenery" and admired the way in which the dark clouds in the background emphasized the white bark covers of the conical lodges. The reviewer praised the skill of the lodge builders as evidenced by the layering of birchbark sheets for coverings and noted the "characteristic" woman labouring while the "man lays supine."

The seven other paintings that Kane placed on display in 1852 are in the Royal Ontario Museum collection (see Lister 2010). Up to this time it has been assumed that the ROM's painting, *A Sketch on Lake Huron,* was also part of that exhibition—the one reviewed—and that the version of this painting in the Art Gallery of Ontario (AGO) collection was painted subsequently (Harper 1971, 273, III-19).

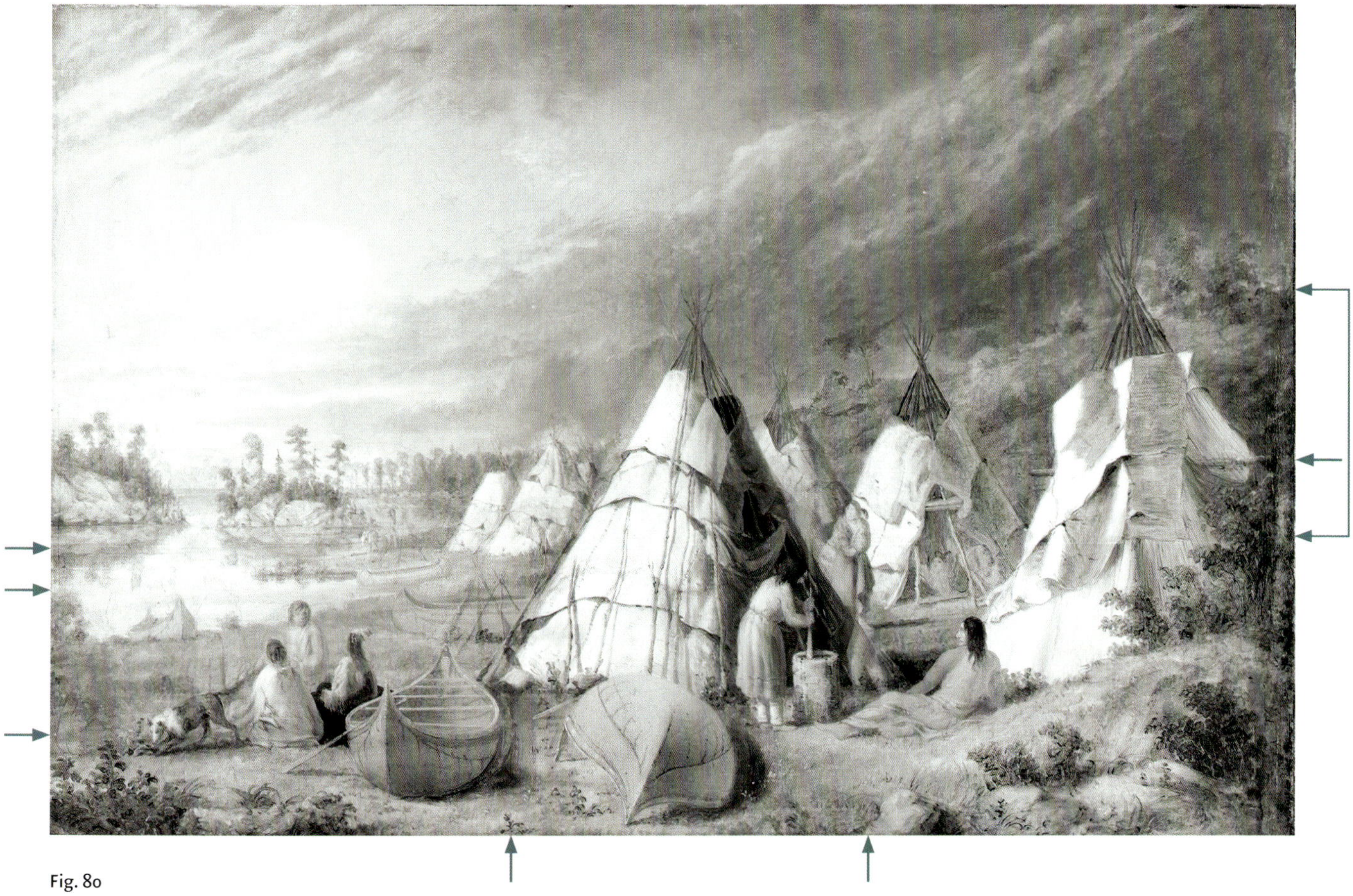

Fig. 80

The two versions of Kane's image of the camp on Lake Huron are very close in composition and details. However, the NIRR image of the AGO painting reveals a variety of alterations that are in stark contrast to the NIRR image of the ROM's version. Where the NIRR image of the ROM's version shows minimal modifications, the NIRR image of the AGO's version exposes the elimination of a tripod between the farthest two canoes; a position adjustment to the tripod in the central ground; the elimination of a seated, naked figure in the left of the painting immediately in front of the dog; and evidence of a standing figure behind the vignette of three seated individuals and the dog. In addition, the breadth of the canoe on the left in the foreground was reduced; the position of the central conical lodge was adjusted; and there appears to be a standing figure between the labouring woman and the supine man. These adjustments tell of the struggle Kane had in developing the composition. The NIRR image of the ROM painting, with its minimal alterations, indicates that Kane was secure with the composition of that version. The ROM painting thus represents a later version of the AGO painting that shows his toil.

Scrutiny of the AGO painting interestingly sheds light on the relevance of the pole extending through the structure of the right-side lodge. Here is where Kane made a significant adjustment in the ROM version and created confusion. In the AGO painting—the original version—Kane was much more precise in his handling of the pole and we can see where the two ends of the draped door covering attach, thus illustrating its purpose as a door header. In the ROM version he confuses this element by painting over a section to represent the rush mat covering; this creates a disconnect between the pole and the door cover, producing the impression that the pole penetrates through the lodge. The position of the pole tip that extends through the lodge wall in the AGO painting was altered, and Kane may have decided to add this feature to satisfy his urge to have the painting give the impression of a horizontal horizon. If this was his intention, his treatment of this element in the ROM's painting seems much clearer, albeit at the expense of showing the architectural integrity of the lodge as he accomplished in the AGO's original version.

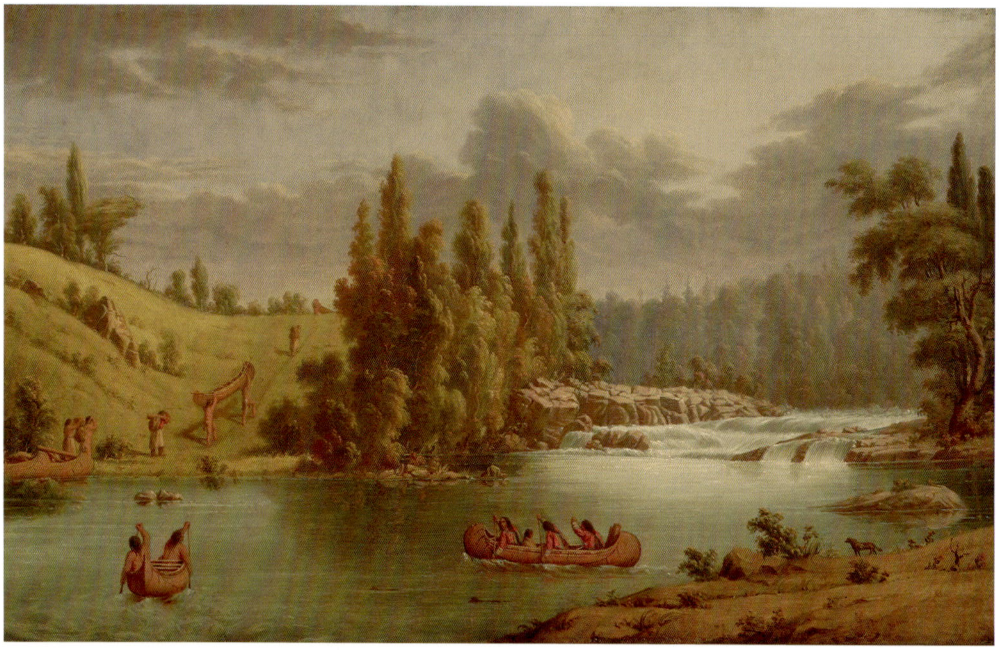

Fig. 81 *White Mud Portage*
Saulteaux
Winnipeg River, Manitoba
1849–1852
oil on canvas; 47.0 × 75.2 cm
912.1.21

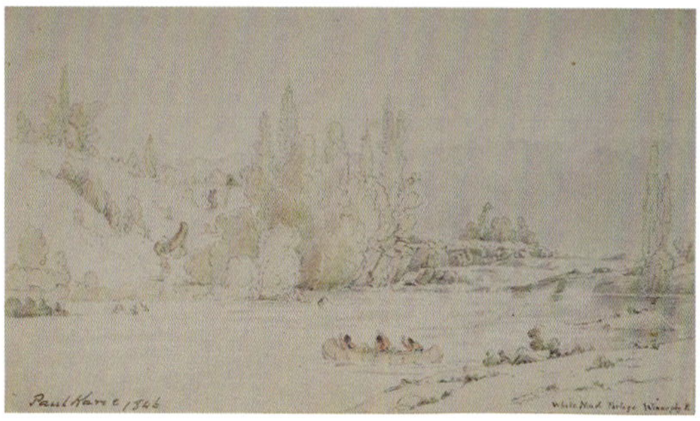

Fig. 82 *White Mud Portage*
Saulteaux
Winnipeg River, Manitoba
August 4, 1848
watercolour on paper; 13.3 × 23.8 cm
Stark Museum of Art, Orange, Texas
31.78.118

> *In the morning, we made the White Mud Portage, which was very picturesque, and of which I took a sketch, No. 20, with the Indians and squaws who were following us, carrying their canoes across.* (Kane 1859, 443)

Kane travelled the length of the Winnipeg River between Lake of the Woods in northern Ontario and Lake Winnipeg in Manitoba during both his westbound and eastbound, or homeward bound, journeys. He was impressed with the splendour of the river, describing it as "broken by numerous beautiful rapids and falls" and being one of the "most picturesque rivers" he had experienced (Kane 1859, 64). Travelling along the river in 1858, Henry Youle Hind was similarly impressed, writing that the "falls and rapids present the wildest and most picturesque scenery" (Hind 1971, 106).

On his journey east, Kane left the HBC's Fort Alexander—located a short distance upstream from the mouth of the Winnipeg River where it enters the eastern side of Lake Winnipeg—on August 3, 1848, in a brigade of four boats and thirty men. The next day they reached the White Mud Portage where Kane had the opportunity to take the watercolour sketch of Saulteaux Indians portaging their small canoes around the rapids. Hind notes that the White Mud Portage had a height of 13.05 feet (4 metres) and that it was the 59th of 62 portages that needed to be taken on the water route headed west between Fort William on Lake Superior and Fort Alexander (Hind 1971, 402).

Comparison of the sketch to the painting shows that Kane used the sketch as his studio model. The background and foreground landscapes in the painting are quite similar to those of the sketch. His main alterations for the painting were adding a second canoe being paddled across the river, a dog standing on the right bank, two dogs swimming, and two figures in front of the canoes at left preparing their loads for the portage.

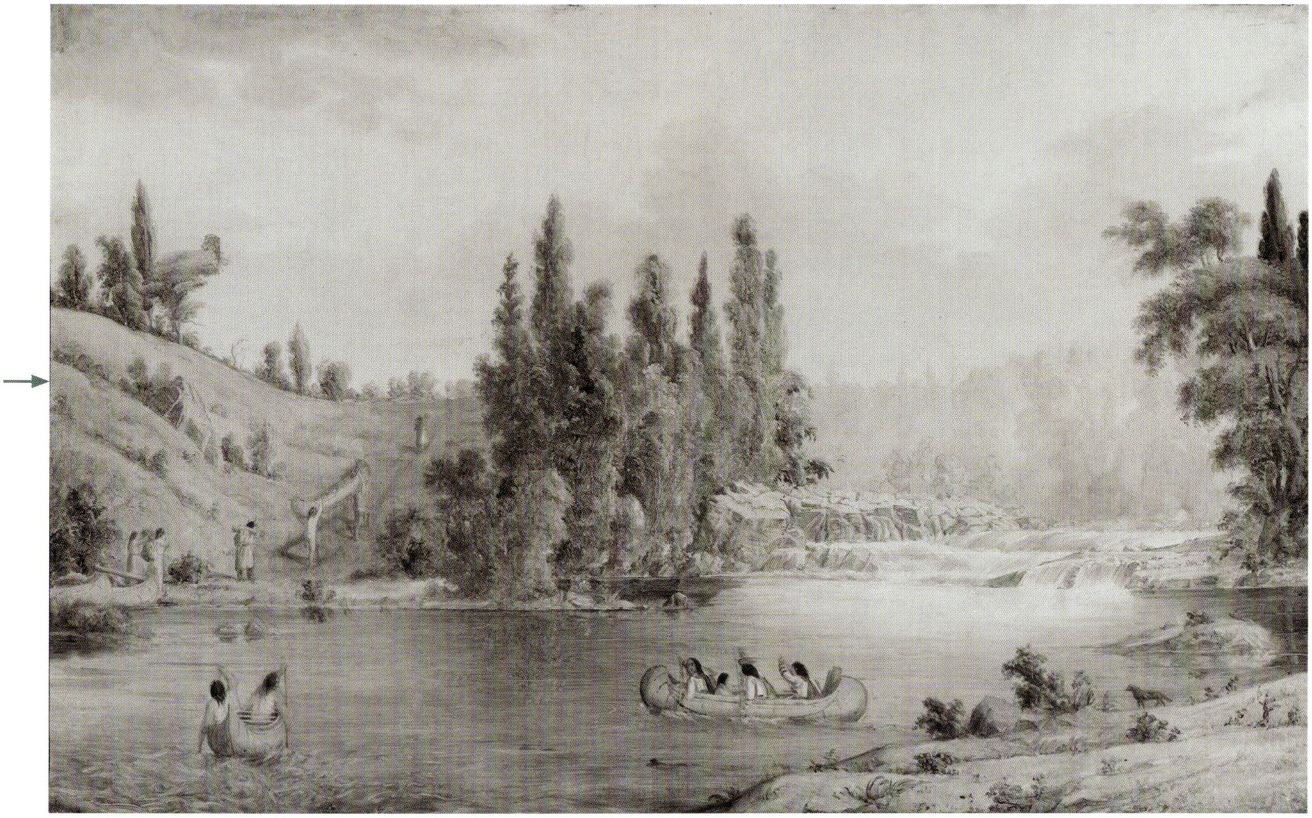

Fig. 83

Study of the NIRR image of *White Mud Portage* reveals that Kane was very secure in laying down his composition. There are no noticeable alterations in the background and foreground landscapes and the renderings of the human figures and their activities are confident.

One notable exception is the large, dark, round shape that appears at the top of the portage. This shape has the general contour of a bark canoe end and may represent Kane's initial attempt at rendering the end of the canoe as it was carried over the hill. Realizing that he had painted it too large and out of scale he then altered the size. Notice that in the sketch, Kane paints just the end of the canoe and the man carrying it, similar to the reworked—albeit oversized—shape in the oil painting. The finished image, however, shows more of the canoe as it heads over the hill and could be the result of Kane's effort to mask, or paint over, his initial attempt.

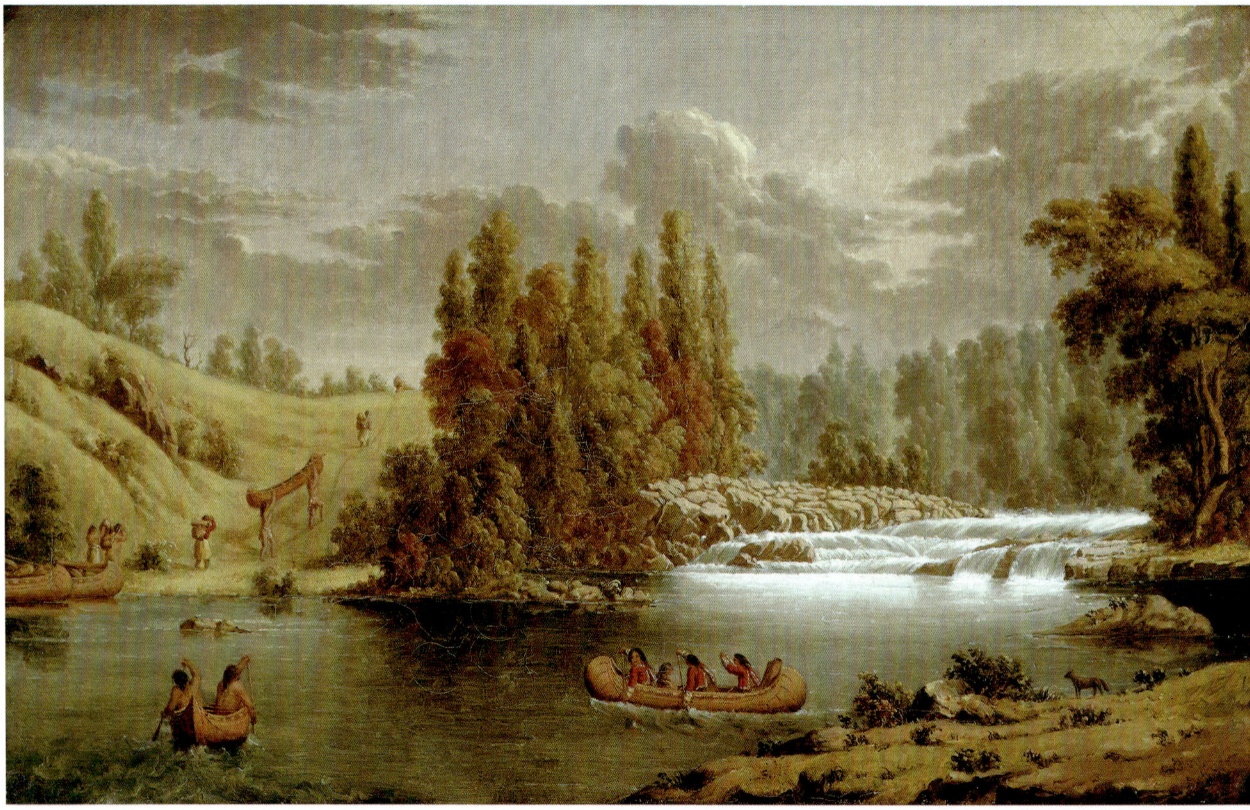

Fig. 84 *White Mud Portage*
Saulteaux
Winnipeg River, Manitoba
1851–1856
oil on canvas; 46 × 74 cm
National Gallery of Canada, 138
Transfer from the Parliament of Canada, 1888
Photo © NGC

Similar to Kane's image of the encampment on Lake Huron discussed previously, *White Mud Portage* was one of eight paintings exhibited by Kane at the 1852 Provincial Agricultural Show. The reviewer for the *Anglo-American Magazine* (1852, 373) praised the "truthfulness of the colouring" and the correctness of "the distant wall of wood" that would be apparent to all those familiar with the American forest in autumn.

This version of *White Mud Portage* was one of twelve paintings commissioned by the Parliament of Canada in 1851 for display in the Library of the Legislature. The commission was in response to a petition forwarded by Kane requesting financial support to allow him to concentrate upon his studio project, to "devote the necessary time to the completion of the sketches in question, in a style and of a size best suited to the subject" (Canada 1851, 310). Kane was paid £500 pounds for the twelve paintings, but by early 1856 he had yet to honour his commitment. In May of that year, the Clerk of the Legislative Assembly sent a letter to Kane requesting that the paintings be delivered, or, the letter stated, "legal proceedings will be instituted against you and your surety" for noncompliance (Canada 1856, 533).

Kane responded to the letter, explaining his tardiness as resulting from concern for the potential loss of his "intellectual control" over the paintings if displayed in such a public place as the Library of the Legislature. His argument was that he needed to maintain control of his paintings prior to their publication in his forthcoming narrative. Nevertheless, in his response he committed to delivering the paintings before the opening of the next session of Parliament and this resulted in the withdrawal of legal action against him (Canada 1856, 556–57, 635, see Lister 2010, 41 note 67 for a discussion of this issue).

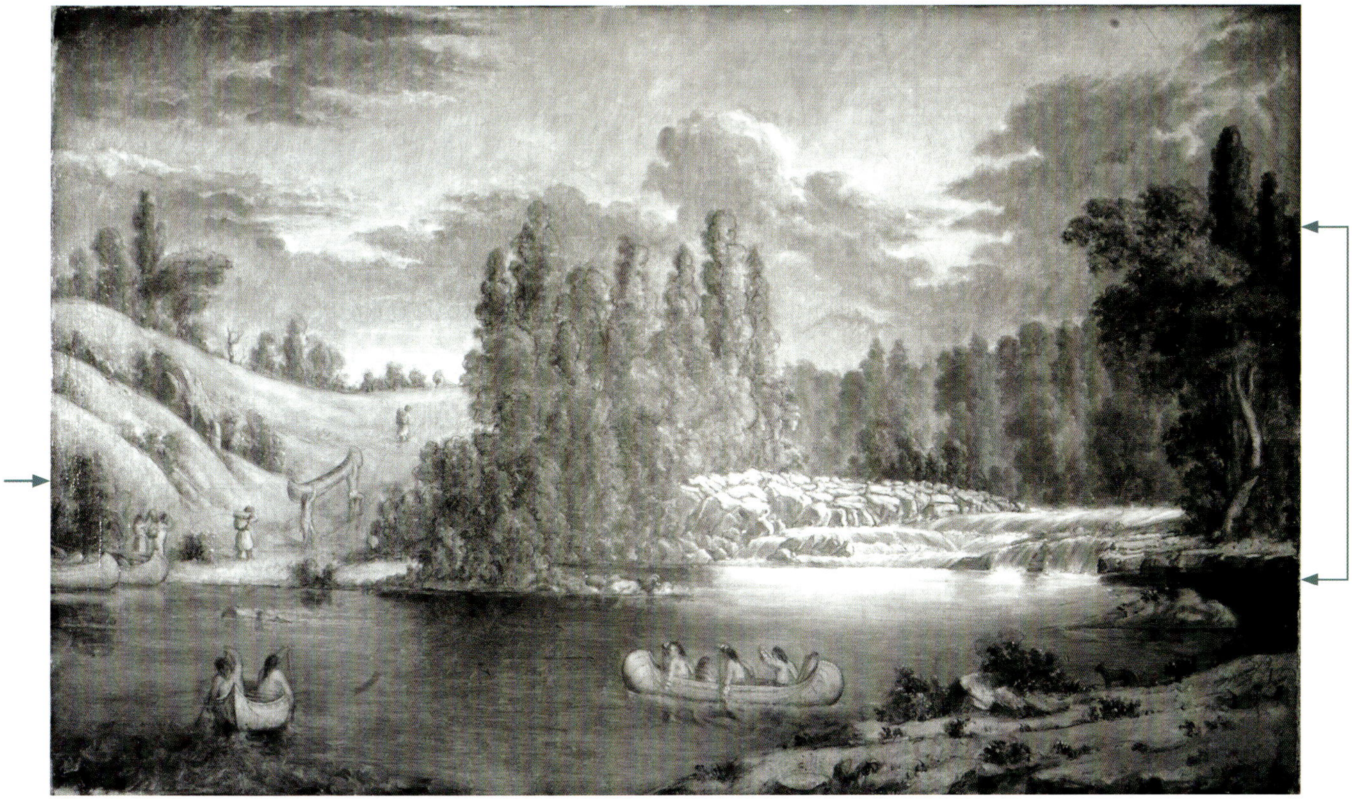

Fig. 85
Photo © NGC

With a few exceptions, such as the swimming dogs and the paddles in the bow and stern of the portaged canoe that are missing in the National Gallery of Canada painting, the two versions of this painting are remarkably similar in composition. However, study of the NIRR image of the National Gallery of Canada painting in comparison to the ROM's version is revealing and provides an explanation for these discrepancies.

In particular, compare the rocky shore defining the far side of the rapids in both NIRR images. In the ROM version, the rocks are lightly drawn or painted, whereas in the National Gallery of Canada version, the rocks are heavily outlined with unambiguous delineations. The ROM version shows a feathery characterization in the central clump of trees and bushes while, in comparison, the National Gallery of Canada version displays edges with bold outlines and limbs with poor definition. In the ROM version, the canoe being portaged shows an attentive rendering of the hull shape and the careful placement of the thwarts. Conversely, the National Gallery of Canada version illustrates the hull darkly outlined and the thwarts roughly positioned.

The comparison of the two versions using the NIRR images suggests that the National Gallery of Canada painting was less carefully painted. In fact, the bold outlines indicate that its main elements may have been initially traced from the ROM version possibly using a device such as a camera obscura—an optical apparatus that projects an image onto a surface, such as a canvas, that can then be traced. This characteristic along with the swimming dogs that are missing, the paddles that are not included, and the less careful rendering of details throughout the composition suggests a quick or rushed painting process, likely a result of Kane's correspondence with the Clerk of the Legislative Assembly.

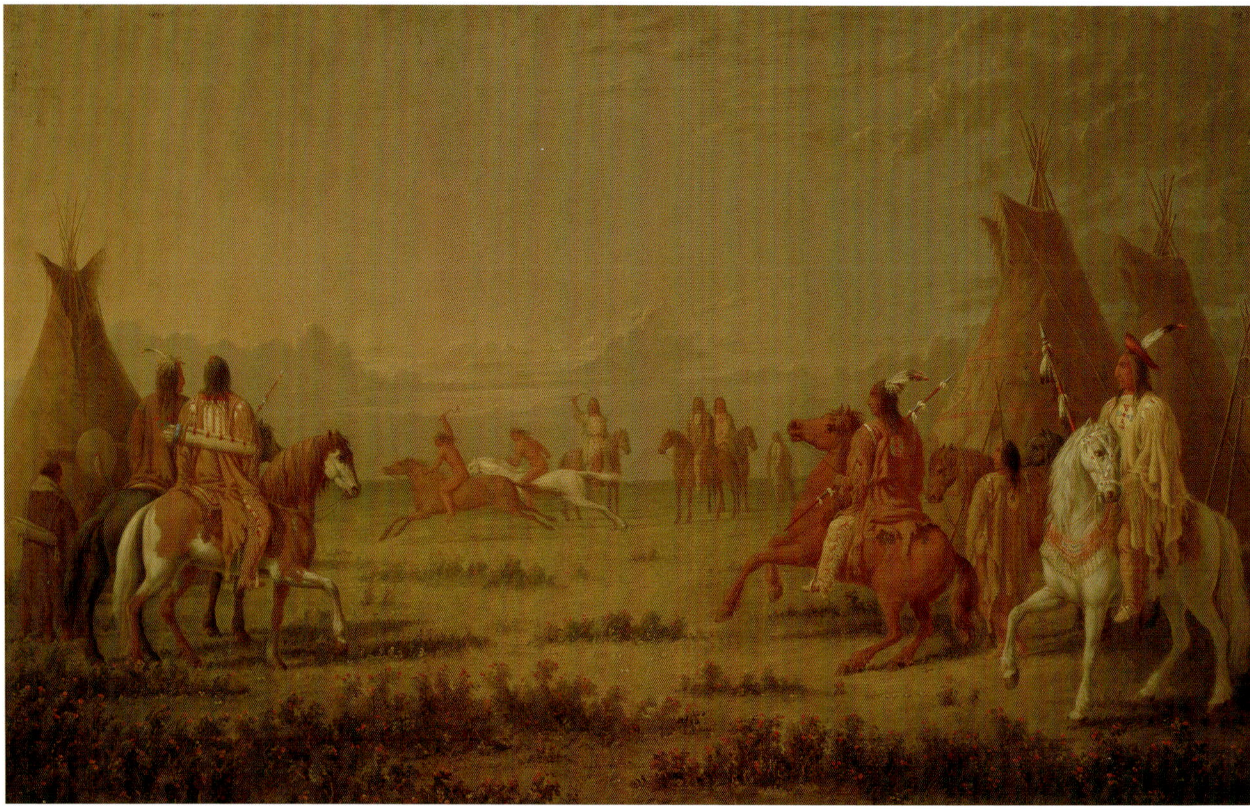

Fig. 86 *Indian Horse Race*
Blackfoot
Fort Pitt region, North Saskatchewan River, Saskatchewan
1849–1852
oil on canvas; 46.2 × 74.0 cm
912.1.51

> *After our smoke several of the young Braves engaged in a horse race, to which sport they are very partial, and at which they bet heavily; they generally ride on those occasions stark naked, without a saddle, and with only a lasso fastened to the lower jaw of the horse as represented in Sketch No. 16.* (Kane 1859, 419–29)

Kane did not mention in his field journal that he witnessed a horse race and there does not seem to be a field sketch of a horse race scene. However, in *Wanderings of an Artist*, in his entry for June 1, 1848, he writes that the boat brigade he had joined, that was then east of Fort Pitt voyaging down the North Saskatchewan River, was approached by a large party of Blackfoot warriors. They defined their numbers, Kane writes, to be 1500 warriors and 1200 lodges (Kane 1859, 419). They were heading toward the Fort Edmonton region farther west up the North Saskatchewan River, for the purpose of warring against the Plains Cree and the Assiniboin. Kane was impressed and wrote, "They were the best mounted, the best looking, the most warlike in appearance, and the best accoutred of any tribe I had ever seen on the continent during my route" (Kane 1859, 419). The HBC officer of the boat brigade was anxious to "cultivate" their "friendship" and accepted their invitation to join their camp for the night. It was at this time, after sharing a pipe, that a number of warriors engaged in a horse race as recorded in Kane's oil painting.

Study of the NIRR image shows that Kane was fairly confident in the initial rendering of *Indian Horse Race*. The overall composition of the foreground horses and the race action in the middle ground, along with the teepees, were

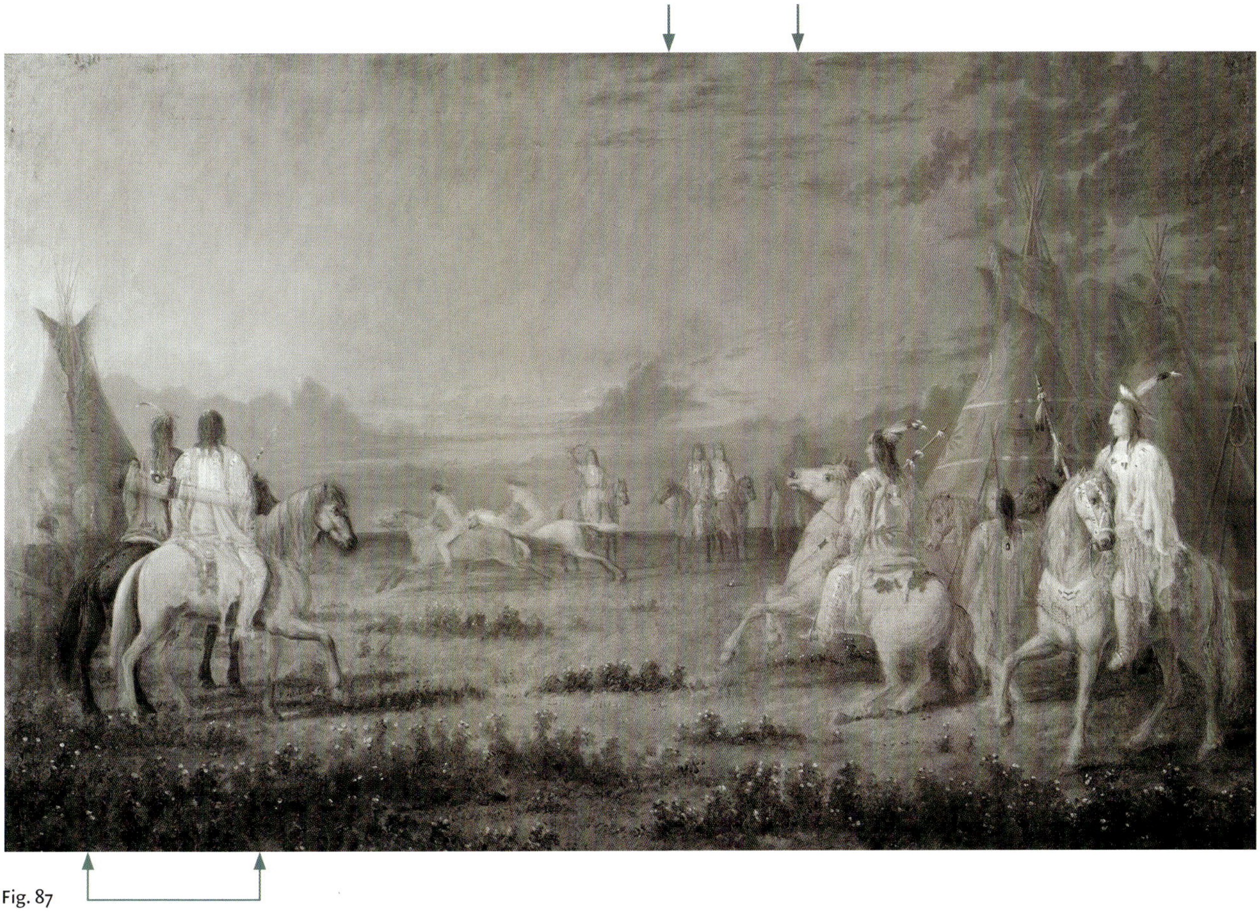

Fig. 87

securely rendered. In the background though, on the right half of the painting, he made a significant alteration by expunging a horse and rider. Kane likely realized that this vignette was too large in scale and perhaps presented a confusing backdrop to the rearing horse in the foreground. In the background he also made a slight modification to the position of the head of the horse that is directed to the race action.

An interesting modification relates to the alteration of the quiver of arrows slung over the back of the warrior in the immediate left foreground. Initially, Kane painted the second mounted warrior wearing the quiver. He changed the bearer of the quiver to be the foremost rider possibly because he felt that it was important to show the complete object. In the initial rendering the end of the quiver was blocked from view by the body of the adjacent rider and here Kane eliminates any confusion as to what is being shown.

The original rendering of the quiver reveals that it held both a set of arrows and a bow. In the final version, painted on the foremost rider, the bow was eliminated—again perhaps to limit confusion or the complexity of the vignette. Part of the repainting of this element is his rendering of the rosette embroidered on the back of the second rider's shirt that is clearly shown overlapping the quiver.

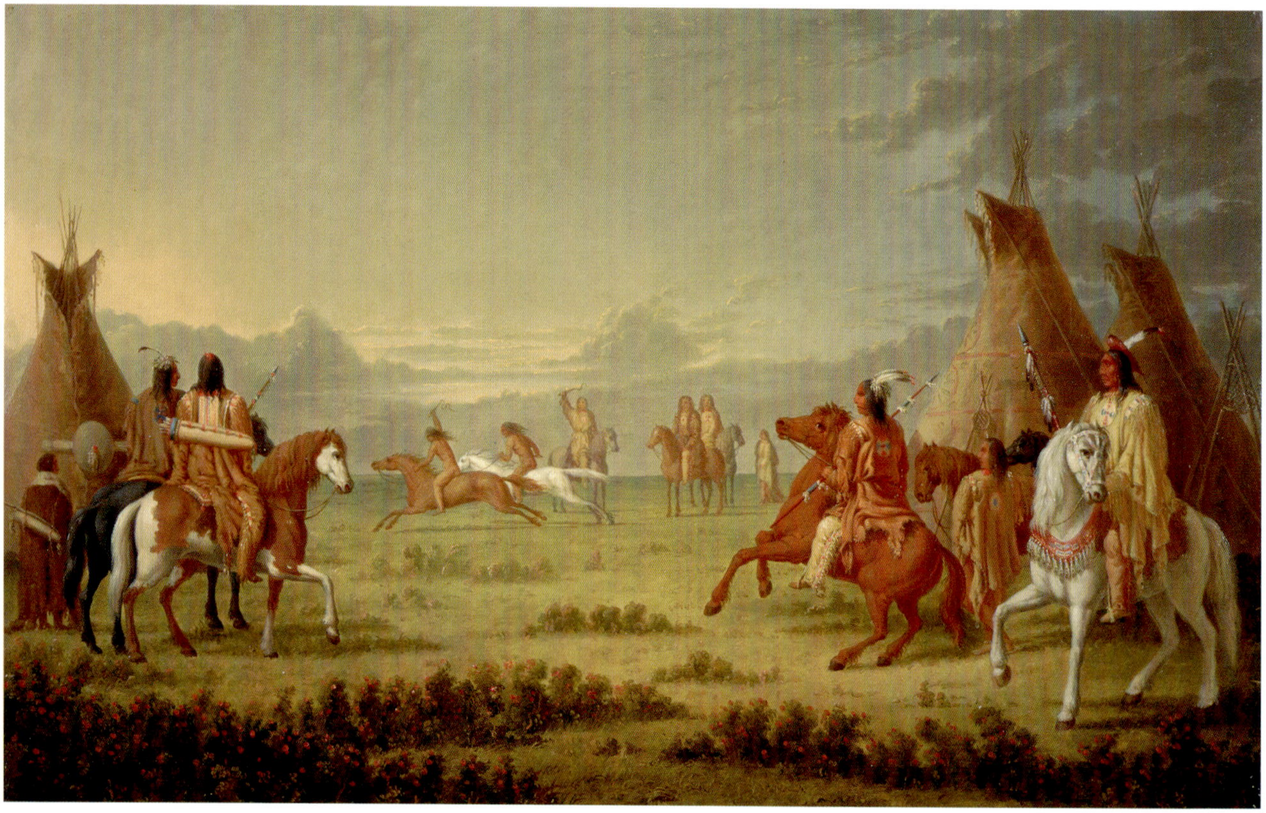

Fig. 88 *Horse Race Among the Blackfoot Indians*
Blackfoot
Fort Pitt region, North Saskatchewan River, Saskatchewan
1851–1856
oil on canvas; 45.8 × 73.8 cm
National Gallery of Canada, 6921
Transfer from the Parliament of Canada, 1955
Photo © NGC

Indian Horse Race was also one of the eight paintings exhibited by Kane at the Provincial Agricultural Show. In its review of this painting, the *Anglo-American Magazine* (1852, 372) was particularly enthusiastic about Kane's rendering of the right group of horses and riders, stating that it in itself, "is remarkable for composition, colour, and drawing." Here, similar to comments relating to the other Kane paintings reviewed, emphasis is placed on the "truthfulness" of Kane's art with the interesting observation that, "There is not a fold of the robe, or plait of the dress, which has not been sketched from nature."

This version of the painting in the National Gallery of Canada collection, along with that of *White Mud Portage*, was one of the twelve canvases commissioned by the Canadian Parliament in 1851. Since by 1856 Kane had not delivered the paintings for which he had already received £500 we might expect that this painting was also completed under the threat of legal action. The commission Kane received from George William Allan, although it came after he had received the support of the Canadian Parliament, was much more significant than the former commission and thus Kane clearly felt that his first priority was the completion of the cycle of paintings for Allan.

The NIRR image of this version of the scene shows Kane to be extremely confident with his initial rendering of the painting. There do not seem to be any noticeable modifications in composition or in details. Significantly, the alterations that Kane made with the ROM version were accepted for the

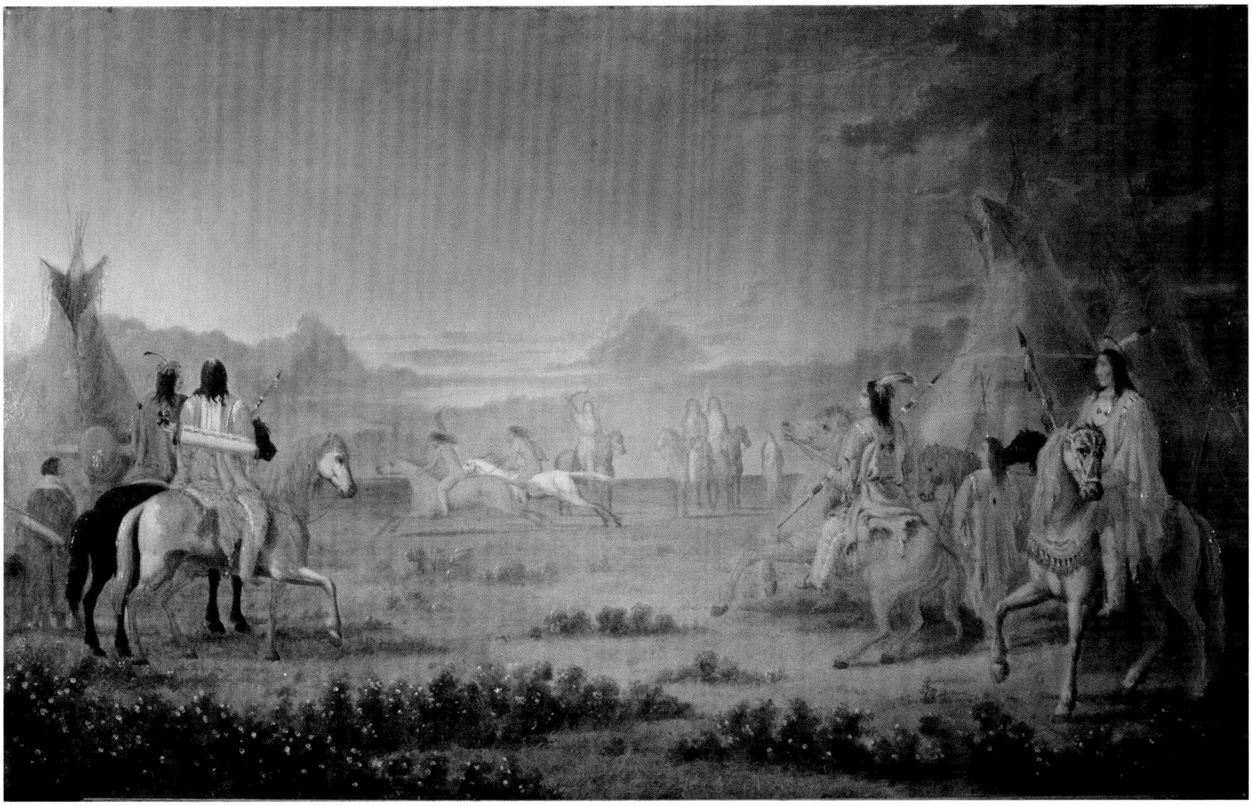

Fig. 89
Photo © NGC

National Gallery of Canada version. For instance, there is no evidence that he initially attempted to include a horse and rider in the background as he did with the ROM's version. The quiver was only painted on the foremost rider on the left of the canvas and it is painted without the insertion of the bow as Kane indeed finalized in the ROM's painting.

The National Gallery of Canada's version does not show the same characteristics of being traced as seen with the Gallery's version of *White Mud Portage*. However, as the ROM's painting of *A Sketch on Lake Huron* appears to be a subsequent version of the AGO's painting of the same scene, the National Gallery of Canada's version of *Indian Horse Race* appears to be a later version, as it reveals none of the markings of Kane's earlier toil over composition and detail. This is consistent with the expected relationship between the paintings for the Canadian Parliament commission that are now in the National Gallery of Canada and those commissioned by George William Allan, now part of the Royal Ontario Museum collection. In this respect, and with the knowledge that Kane was under great pressure to comply with the terms of his 1851 commission, it is significant to note that all of the scenes Kane finally delivered to the Canadian Parliament were representations of scenes he also completed for Allan.

REFERENCES

Aborigines' Committee. 1839. *Facts Relative to the Canadian Indians, Published by Direction of The Aborigine's Committee, of The Meeting for Sufferings*. London: Harvey and Darton.

Ainsworth, Maryan W. 2005. "From Connoisseurship to Technical History: The Evolution of the Interdisciplinary Study of Art." *Conservation, Getty Conservation Institute Newsletter* 20:4–10.

Anglo-American Magazine. 1852. "The Provincial Exhibition." *Anglo-American Magazine* 1(4):371–76.

Arima, Eugene. 1999. "Barkless Barques." In *The Canoe in Canadian Cultures*, edited by John Jennings, Bruce W. Hodgins, and Doreen Small, 43–61. Toronto: Natural Heritage Books.

———. 2002. "Building Dugouts." In *The Canoe: A Living Tradition,* edited by John Jennings, 97–118. Toronto: Firefly Books.

Assmus, Alexi. 1995. "Early History of X-rays." *Beam Line* 25(2):10–24.

Baronti, S., A. Casini, F. Lotti, and S. Porcinae. 1998. "Multispectral imaging system for the mapping of pigments in works of art by use of principal-component analysis." *Applied Optics* 37(8):1299–1309.

Beck, David R. M. 2002. *Siege and Survival: History of the Menominee Indians, 1634–1856*. Lincoln, NE: University of Nebraska Press.

Bertani, D. and L. Consolandi. 2006. "High Resolution in the Near Infrared." In *Digital Heritage–Applying Digital Imaging to Cultural Heritage*, edited by Lindsay MacDonald. Amsterdam: Elsevier.

Boyd, Robert. 1996. *People of the Dalles, The Indians of Wascopam Mission: A Historical Ethnography Based on the Papers of the Methodist Missionaries*. Lincoln, NE: University of Nebraska Press.

Brown, Steven C. 2002. "Vessels of Life: Northwest Coast Dugouts." In *The Canoe: A Living Tradition,* edited by John Jennings, 74–95. Toronto: Firefly Books.

Brunton, Bill B. 1998. "The Stick Game." In *Handbook of North American Indians, Vol. 12, Plateau*, edited by Deward E. Walker, Jr., 573–83. Washington, DC: Smithsonian Institution.

Bulow-Jacobson, A. 2008. "Infra-Red Photography of Ostraca and Papyri." *Zeitschrift für Papyrologie und Epigraphik* 165:175–85.

Burmester, Andreas, and Florian Bayerer. 1993. "Towards improved infrared reflectograms." *Studies in Conservation* 38(3):145–54.

Burpee, Lawrence J. 1968. Introduction to *Wanderings of an Artist among the Indians of North America*, by Paul Kane, xxi–xlvii. Edmonton: Hurtig Publishers.

Canada. 1851. *Journals of the Legislative Assembly of the Province of Canada*. August 22.

Canada. 1856. *Journals of the Legislative Assembly of the Province of Canada.* June 2 and June 16.

Canadian Journal of Industry, Science, and Art. 1852. "The Provincial Agricultural Show." *The Canadian Journal of Industry, Science, and Art* (October), 51–67.

Cassels, Maude. 2010. "Paul Kane: 'Dedicated to Us All.'" In *Paul Kane /the Artist/: Wilderness to Studio*, by Kenneth R. Lister, 28–43. Toronto: Royal Ontario Museum Press.

Census of Canada, 1871. Entries for Fannie Kane, Florence Kane, Frederick W. Kane, Paul Kane, Paul Kane II, and Robert Arthur Donaldson. Database Ancestry.com. http://www.ancestry.com.

Chance, David H. 1985. "Kettle Falls 1978: Further Archaeological Excavations in Lake Roosevelt." *University of Idaho Anthropological Reports*, No. 84.

———. 1986. *People of the Falls*. Colville, WA: Kettle Falls Historical Center, Inc.

Daffara, Claudia, and Raffaella Fontana. 2011. "Multispectral infrared reflectography to differentiate features in paintings." *Microscopy and Microanalysis* 17:691–95.

Davin, Nicholas Flood. 1877. *Irishman in Canada*. London: Sampson Low, Marston & Co.

Davis, Ann. 1982. *A Distant Harmony: Comparisons in the Painting of Canada and the United States of America*. Winnipeg: Winnipeg Art Gallery.

Desneux, Jules. 1958. "Underdrawings and pentimenti in the pictures of Jan Van Eyck." *The Art Bulletin* 40:13–21.

Dieke, G. H. 1956. "Robert Williams Wood 1868–1955." *Biographical Memoirs of Fellows of the Royal Society* 2:327–45.

Dippie, Brian W. 1982. *The Vanishing American: White Attitudes and U.S. Indian Policy*. Middletown, CT: Wesleyan University Press.

———. 2007. "In the Enemy's Country: Western Art's Uneasy Status." In *Redrawing Boundaries: Perspectives on Western American Art*, Denver Art Museum, 14–27. Denver, CO: The Institute of Western American Art, Denver Art Museum.

Eastman Kodak Company. 1963. "Infrared and Ultraviolet Photography." *Kodak Adv. Data Book M3.*

———. 2008. "Kodak Professional High-Speed Infrared Film." Technical Data. Publication No. F-13. Last modified Feburary 2008. http://www.kodak.com/global/en/professional/support/techPubs/f13/f13.pdf.

Falco, Charles M. 2010. "High-Resolution Infrared Imaging." In *SPIE Optical Engineering and Applications, 7782, The Nature of Light: Light in Nature III.* Paper presented at the SPIE Optics + Photonics Conference, San Diego, California, August 2, 2010. http://fp.optics.arizona.edu/SSD/art-optics/papers/IR_SPIE2010.pdf. Accessed September 29, 2013.

Faries, Molly. 2005. "Analytical Capabilities of Infrared Reflectography: An Art Historian's Perspective." In *Scientific Examination of Art: Modern Techniques in Conservation and Analysis*, 87–104. Washington, DC: The National Academies Press.

Farnsworth, Marie. 1938. "Infra-red absorption of paint materials." *Technical Studies in the Field of the Fine Arts* 7:88–97.

Fay, George E. 1970. "Treaties Between the Menominee Indians and The United States of America, 1817–1856." *University of Northern Colorado Greeley Museum of Anthropology Miscellaneous Series* 12 (April).

Fischer, Christian, and Ioanna Kakoulli. 2006. "Multispectral and hyperspectral imaging technologies in conservation: current research and potential applications." *Studies in Conservation* 51:3–16.

Fredrickson, N. Jaye, and Sandra Gibb. 1980. *The Covenant Chain: Indian Ceremonial and Trade Silver*. Ottawa: National Museums of Canada.

Fuller Ossoli, Margaret. (1844) 1970. *Summer on the Lakes*. New York: Haskell House Publishers Ltd.

Gargano, M., N. Ludwig, and G. Poldi. 2007. "A new methodology for comparing IR reflectographic systems." *Infrared Physics and Technology* 49:249–53.

Gayer, John R. 1996. "The Analysis and Treatment of Two Portraits Attributed to Paul Kane (1810–1871)." *Journal of the International Institute for Conservation-Canadian Group* 21:16–27.

Harper, J. Russell. 1971. *Paul Kane's Frontier*. Toronto: University of Toronto Press.

Hind, Henry Youle. 1971. *Narrative of The Canadian Red River Exploring Expedition of 1857 and of the Assinniboine and Saskatchewan Exploring Expedition of 1858*. Edmonton: M.G. Hurtig Ltd.

Hoffman, Walter J. 1896. "The Menomini Indians." United States Bureau of American Ethnology, *Fourteenth Annual Report, 1892–93*. Washington, DC: Government Printing Office.

Holden, Edward Singleton. 1881. S*ir William Herschel, His Life and Works*. New York: Charles Scribner's Sons.

Horan, James D. 1972. *The McKenney–Hall Portrait Gallery of American Indians*. New York: Crown Publishers, Inc.

Hunn, Eugene S., and David H. French. 1998. "Western Columbia River Sahaptins." In *Handbook of North American Indians, Vol. 12, Plateau*, edited by Deward E. Walker, Jr., 378–94. Washington, DC: Smithsonian Institution.

Ibarra-Castanedo, Clemente, Stefano Sfarra, Dario Ambrosini, Domenica Paoletti, Abdelhakim Bendada, and Xavier Maldague. 2010. "Infrared vision for the nondestructive assessment of panel paintings." *CINDE Journal* 31(5):5–9.

Johnston, Darlene. 2004. Transcripts of the evidentiary hearings, July 14, 2004, 219–221, 232. *The Ipperwash Inquiry*, comp. Sidney B. Linden, 2007. Online transcript. http://www.attorneygeneral.jus.gov.on.ca/inquiries/ipperwash/transcripts/index.html.

Kane, Paul. 1848. *Catalogue of Sketches of Indians, and Indian Chiefs, Landscapes, Dances, Costumes, &c. &c.* Toronto: Scobie and Balfour.

———. 1859. *Wanderings of an Artist among the Indians of North America*. London: Longman, Brown, Green, Longmans & Roberts.

———. 1989. "Journal of Paul Kane's Western Travels." Transcribed by I. S. MacLaren. *The American Art Journal* XXI(2):23–62.

Kane, Paul James. 2010. "The Paul Kane Family." In *Paul Kane/ the Artist/: Wilderness to Studio*, by Kenneth R. Lister, 44–57. Toronto: Royal Ontario Museum Press.

Keesing, Felix M. 1987. *The Menomini Indians of Wisconsin: A Study of Three Centuries of Cultural Contact and Change*. Madison, WI: University of Wisconsin Press.

King, Duane H. 2004. "Cherokee in the West: History Since 1776." In *Handbook of North American Indians, Vol. 14, Southeast*, edited by Raymond D. Fogelson, 354–72. Washington, DC: Smithsonian Institution.

Laing, G. Blair.1982. *Memoirs of an Art Dealer 2*. Toronto: McClelland and Stewart.

Liang, Haida. 2012. "Advances in multispectral and hyperspectral imaging for archaeology and art conservation." *Applied Physics A* 106 (2):309–23.

Lie, Henry. 2003. "Digital Imaging for the Study of Paintings: Experiences at the Straus Center for Conservation." In *Recent Developments in the Technical Examination of Early Netherlandish Painting: Methodology, Limitations and Perspectives*, edited by M. Faries and R. Spronk, 117–34. Cambridge, MA: Harvard University Art Museums; Turnhout, Belgium: Brepols Publishers.

Lister, Kenneth R. 2010. *Paul Kane /the Artist/: Wilderness to Studio*. Toronto: Royal Ontario Museum Press.

Lyon, R. Arcadius. 1934. "Infra-red radiations aid examination of paintings." *Technical Studies in the Field of the Fine Arts* 2:203–12.

Mackie, Richard Somerset. 1997. *Trading Beyond the Mountains: The British Fur Trade on the Pacific, 1793–1843*. Vancouver: University of British Columbia Press.

MacLaren, I. S. 1997. "Paul Kane Goes South: The Sale of the Family's Collection of Field Sketches." *Journal of Canadian Studies* 32(2):22–47.

Mandelbaum, David G. 1940. *The Plains Cree*. Anthropological Papers of the American Museum of Natural History 37, Part 2. New York: The American Museum of Natural History.

Moffatt, E. and J. Poulin. 2010. "Analysis of Samples from the Portrait of Eliza Clench." Unpublished report No. CSD 4797, CCI 121821, Canadian Conservation Institute.

Moodie, Susanna. (1853) 1959. *Life in the Clearings*. Toronto: Macmillan of Canada.

Nisbet, Jack. 1994. *Sources of the River: Tracking David Thompson across Western North America*. Seattle, WA: Sasquatch Books.

———. 2005. *The Mapmaker's Eye: David Thompson on the Columbia Plateau*. Pullman, WA: Washington University Press.

Nitske, Robert W. 1971. *The Life of W. C. Röntgen, Discoverer of the X-Ray*. Tucson, AZ: University of Arizona Press.

Osler, E. B. 1904. *Catalogue: Pictures of Indians and Indian Life by Paul Kane*. Toronto: E. B. Osler.

Ourada, Patricia K. 1979. *The Menominee Indians: A History*. Norman, OK: University of Oklahoma Press.

Pearsall, T. P., and R. W. Hopson Jr. 1977. "Growth and characterization of lattice-matched epitaxial films of $Ga_xIn_{1-x}As/InP$ by liquid-phase epitaxy." *Journal of Applied Physics* 48(10):4407–9.

Rigden, John S. 2005. *Einstein 1905: The Standard of Greatness*. Cambridge, MA: Harvard University Press.

Robson, Albert H. 1938. *Paul Kane*. Toronto: The Ryerson Press.

Seabrook, William. 1941. *Doctor Wood, Modern Wizard of the Laboratory: The Story of an American Small Boy who Became the Most Daring and Original Experimental Physicist of Our Day—but Never Grew Up*. New York: Harcourt, Brace.

Sirois, Jane. 1997. "Delving Into the Paintboxes of Paul Kane and David Milne." *CCI Newsletter* No. 19 (March):6.

Skinner, Alanson. 1921. *Material Culture of the Menomini*. New York: Museum of the American Indian.

Suttles, Wayne P. 1974. *Coast Salish and Western Indians I: The Economic Life of the Coast Salish of Haro and Rosario Straits*. New York: Garland Publishing Inc.

Taché, J. C. 1856. *Canada at the Universal Exhibition of 1855*. Toronto: Printed by J. Lovell.

Torres, J., A. Posse, J. M. Menéndez, A. Gabaldón, C. Vega, T. Antelo, M. Del Egido, and M. Bueso. 2008. "VARIM: A computer vision system for the automatic creation of high resolution reflectographic mosaics." In *ELMAR, 2008. 50th International Symposium* 2:487–90.

Truettner, William H. 1979. *The Natural Man Observed: A Study of Catlin's Indian Gallery*. Washington, DC: Smithsonian Institution Press.

Tyrrell, Joseph Burr, ed. 1916. *David Thompson's Narrative of His Explorations in Western America, 1784–1812*. Toronto: The Champlain Society.

Van Asperen de Boer, J. R. J. 1968. "Infrared reflectography: a method for the examination of paintings." *Applied Optics* 7(9):1711–14.

———. 1969. "Reflectography of paintings using an infrared vidicon television system." *Studies in Conservation* 14(3):96–118.

———. 1974. "A Note on the Use of an Improved Infrared Vidicon for Reflectography of Paintings." *Studies in Conservation* 19(2):97–99.

———. 2003. "Slowly Towards Improved Infrared Reflectography Equipment." In *Recent Developments in the Technical Examination of Early Netherlandish Painting: Methodology, Limitations and Perspectives*, edited by Molly Faries and R. Spronk, 57–64. Cambridge, MA: Harvard University Art Museums; Turnhout, Belgium: Brepols Publishers.

Verhoeven, Geert. 2008. "Imaging the invisible using modified digital still cameras for straightforward and low-cost archaeological near-infrared photography." *Journal of Archaeological Science* 35(12):3087–100.

Viola, Herman J. 1976. *The Indian Legacy of Charles Bird King*. Washington, DC: Smithsonian Institution Press; New York: Doubleday & Company, Inc.

Walker, Jr., Deward E. 1998. "Nez Perce." In *Handbook of North American Indians, Vol. 12, Plateau*, edited by Deward E. Walker, Jr., 420–38. Washington, DC: Smithsonian Institution.

Walmsley, Elizabeth, Catherine Metzger, John K. Delaney, and Colin Fletcher. 1994. "Improved visualization of underdrawings with solid-state detectors operating in the infrared." *Studies in Conservation* 39(4):217–31.

Wandell, Brian A. 1995. *Foundations of Vision*. Sunderland, MA: Sinauer Associates.

White, Jack R. 2012. "Herschel and the Puzzle of Infrared: An astronomer took a mental leap to first connect light and heat." *American Scientist* 100(3):218–25.

Williams, Chuck. 1980. *Bridge of the Gods, Mountains of Fire: A Return to the Columbia Gorge*. New York: Friends of the Earth; White Salmon, WA: Elephant Mountain Arts.

Wilson, Daniel. 1859. "Review of *Wanderings of an Artist Among the Indians of North America* by Paul Kane." *The Canadian Journal of Industry, Science, and Art*. No. 21:186–93.

———. 1862. *Prehistoric Man: Researches in the Origin of Civilisation in the Old and the New World*. London: MacMillan and Company.

Wilson, Garrett. 2007. *Frontier Farewell: The 1870s and the End of the Old World*. Regina: Canadian Plains Research Centre, University of Regina.

Wood, R. W. 1910a. "A New Departure in Photography." *The Century Magazine* 79:565–72.

———. 1910b. "Photography by invisible rays." *The Photographic Journal* 50:329–38.

———. 1916. "Monochromatic photography of Jupiter and Saturn." *Proceedings of the National Academy of Sciences of the United States of America* 2(2):109–12.

Manuscripts and Archives

Canadian Museum of Civilization, Hull, Quebec MCC/CMC Archives, Ethnology Archives

Waugh, F. W. "Ojibwa Fieldwork: various notes." B218, F 23.

Hudson's Bay Company Archives (HBCA), Provincial Archives of Manitoba, Winnipeg

E.42/1. Letters and Documents pertaining to Paul Kane.

fol. 16d. Paul Kane to John Johnston, secretary of the Toronto Society of Arts, March 6, 1849.

fol. 43. Letter from Sir George Simpson to Paul Kane, May 31, 1846

fol. 44. Circular letter from Sir George Simpson to "The Gentlemen of the Hon. Hudsons Bay Co's Service," May 31, 1846.

fol. 52. Letter by James Douglas, June 30, 1847.

fol. 54. Letter by William McBean, July 30, 1847.

B.45/a/1. Fort Colvile (Columbia River) Post Journal, 1830–1831.

MG 14 C23/2/42. *Catalogue of Sketches and Paintings* by Paul Kane, March 20, 1922.

Royal Ontario Museum, Toronto, Ontario

Allan, George William. 1871. "Notes to Daniel Wilson." Paul Kane collection, Royal Ontario Museum. Gift of Raymond A. Willis.

"Inventory" of Paul Kane's Estate, Surrogate Court, County York, Number 1336, 1872 (copy). Paul Kane collection, Royal Ontario Museum.

Stark Museum of Art, Orange, Texas

Kane, Paul. 1845. Journal, 1845. 11.85/4, 105–108.

———. 1846–1848. Portrait and Landscape Logs. 11.85/4.

INDEX

Page numbers in bold refer to illustrations.